The European Demographic System, 1500–1820

**The Johns Hopkins Symposia
in Comparative History**

The Johns Hopkins Symposia in Comparative History are occasional volumes sponsored by the Department of History at The Johns Hopkins University and The Johns Hopkins University Press comprising original essays by leading scholars in the United States and other countries. Each volume considers, from a comparative perspective, an important topic of current historical interest. The present volume is the twelfth. Its preparation has been assisted by the James S. Schouler Lecture Fund.

Michael W. Flinn is Professor Emeritus of Social History in the Department of Economic History at the University of Edinburgh.

Also by the author:

An Economic and Social History of Britain, 1066-1939
Men of Iron: The Crowleys in the Early Iron Industry
An Economic and Social History of Britain since 1700
Origins of the Industrial Revolution
Public Health Reform in Britain
British Population Growth, 1750-1850
Scottish Population History from the Seventeenth Century to the 1930s
  (editor and co-author)

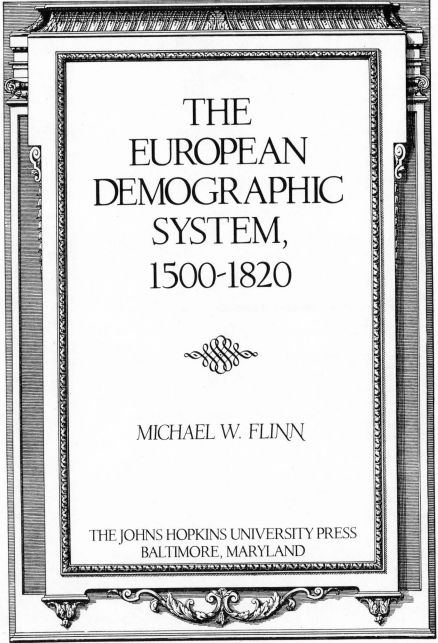

THE
EUROPEAN
DEMOGRAPHIC
SYSTEM,
1500-1820

MICHAEL W. FLINN

THE JOHNS HOPKINS UNIVERSITY PRESS
BALTIMORE, MARYLAND

The Johns Hopkins University Press, Baltimore, Maryland 21218

ISBN 0-8018-2426-5

Library of Congress Cataloging in Publication Data
Flinn, Michael Walter.
   The European demographic system, 1500–1820.

   (The Johns Hopkins symposia in comparative history; 12)
   Based on the 1979 Schouler lectures.
   Bibliography: p. 138.
   Includes index.
   1. Europe – Population – History. I. Title.
II. Series: Johns Hopkins symposia in comparative history; 12.
HB3581.F54   304.6'094   80–19574
ISBN O-8018-2426-5

Contents

List of Tables

Acknowledgments

I would like to thank the many colleagues in every country referred to in this book who assisted me by sending offprints or xeroxes of publications not otherwise easily obtainable. All who were present at The Johns Hopkins University in September 1979, where most of the contents of this book were presented as the Schouler Lectures, contributed enormously by their enthusiasm and critical discussion of issues, interpretations, and methods. Some of my errors and misconceptions were tactfully corrected by them as well as by other colleagues in the universities of Geneva, Michigan (Ann Arbor), Emory (Atlanta), and California (Berkeley), where some parts of this book were also presented at seminars. The errors that remain are my responsibility alone. Above all, I would like to thank my wife for her encouragement and assistance in meeting deadlines for lectures and book and for tolerating a major intrusion into what has been miscalled "retirement."

Gloucestershire

Note on References

Throughout the text, references to sources are given within square brackets. The italicized numbers refer to the corresponding numbered items in the bibliography at the end of the book, for example, [*246*]; and where page references are necessary they are shown in roman characters after a comma: [*246*, 192-94]. In multiple references the italicized numbers are separated by semicolons: [*156; 209; 486-87*]. After some general sections, the arrangement of the bibliography is alphabetical, by country (in alphabetical order), and sources are numbered consecutively.

The European Demographic System, 1500–1820

1   The Revolution in Historical Demography

THE UNDERSTANDING OF EARLY MODERN European demography as it was propounded in the mid-1950s must be the starting point of this book. There are two good reasons for this plan. First, it was in 1955 that Karl Helleiner contributed to volume 4 of the *Cambridge Economic History of Europe* a survey of the field that, for its time, was comprehensive and definitive. Second, and more important, in 1956 there appeared in France a small technical manual, seemingly of interest only to specialists, the *Manuel de dépouillement et d'exploitation de l'état civil ancien,* by Michel Fleury and Louis Henry [*11*]. The book has probably been read only by specialists, but it nonetheless heralded a revolution in the discipline of historical demography of far-reaching importance. Briefly, it expounded a method of deriving meaningful modern measures of demographic change from ancient, often defective parish registers. Hitherto, demographic history had proceeded on the basis of very sparse aggregate data derived from censuses, taxation returns, and very occasional counts of births and deaths. For periods before the nineteenth century these were seldom very reliable, and they only very rarely permitted the calculation of accurate measures of population dynamics. What was lacking in the data had to be, and was, made good by hypothesizing on an heroic scale.

But demographic history, like demography itself, aims to inform and explain through the medium of precise measures. It is not too much to say that without this statistical base there is no historical demography. The hope of Fleury and Henry's new method was to provide, virtually for the first time in the whole field of historical demography, a firm basis of statistical measurement of demographic behavior and change in the past.

The new method was taken up speedily and vigorously, above all in France, and the length of the bibliography at the end of this book is testimony to the marvelous flowering of historical demography as soon as the feasibility of the new methods was established. This book's intention is to base generalizations solely on the demographic facts as they have been established by the new processes of measurement.

It is true that before Fleury and Henry announced their revolution there had been one or two harbingers. Jean Meuvret [442] had opened a door in 1946 to what was then the new world of demographic crises, while a Swedish demographer, Hyrenius, as far back as 1942, had employed methods that, though not developed systematically, were strikingly similar to those of Fleury and Henry [17; 140]. And while Henry, a demographer, was at work, unknown to him a French historian, Pierre Goubert, was simultaneously evolving the same technique in the course of a now-famous study of the Beauvaisis [372]. Henry, however, quickly followed up his exposition of method with two classic exemplars—his study of the Genevan bourgeoisie of the seventeenth century [683] and, with Etienne Gautier, his statistical examination of that now-famous Normandy parish, Crulai [364].

The core of the methodological revolution was the technique known as "family reconstitution." This involved following in exact detail from the baptismal, marriage, and burial registers in a single parish or group of parishes the vital histories of individuals. Following a birth, the subsequent marriage, progeny, and burial of an individual could be extracted from the registers, thus permitting the precise establishment of that individual's demographic behavior—his or her age at marriage and perhaps at remarriages, age at the birth of children and therefore the intervals between these births, age at birth of the last child, and age at death and, therefore, the length of life itself. There are, of course, so many possible variations within the broad parameters set by human biology that no two individuals could share identical experiences; but by aggregating the data from individual families and deriving means from them, generalizations about the average behavior of the whole parish community at a given period of time could be constructed. It was, of course, the sum of individual patterns rather than the eccentricities of individual behavior that determined the overall demographic trend of a community or a society.

Not all families in a parish can be recaptured and fed into the averages. Migration, or problems of linking names recorded for each of the three events of baptism, marriage, and burial oblige the discarding of incompletely or uncertainly reconstituted families; and since for certain purposes it is necessary to break the populations down into small age or occupational groups and therefore subdivide what might already be fairly small groups, it has mostly been found necessary to aggregate the data from cohorts born (or married) in fairly long periods in order to produce numbers judged to be sufficiently large to yield reliable averages. Clearly, the shorter the cohort, the more exactly may the smaller changes over time in demographic behavior be measured. When a cohort extends over the whole of, say, the eighteenth century, during which some significant changes might be expected, this kind of analysis may conceal more than it reveals. Ideally, shorter cohorts of not more than fifty years are desirable, but where the proportion of families that can be completely and certainly reconstituted is small, longer cohorts may be unavoidable.

Of the three main determinants of demographic change — fertility, nuptiality, and mortality — the family reconstitutors have, on the whole, concentrated their attention rather heavily on fertility. Above all, in almost all studies, they have calculated several variants of the measure of age-specific marital fertility — the number of births per 1,000 married woman-years to women in specific five-year age groups. This is an excellent, though not on its own wholly satisfactory, measure that makes possible intercommunity comparison and, when used for successive cohorts, permits reasonably reliable generalization about trends over time. Calculations have also been made of the mean intervals between the births of successive children in a family, as well as of the mean age of mothers at the birth of their last child. The latter is invaluable for determining, with the mean age of women at their first marriage, the mean length of the reproductive period of married women in different societies at different periods. The importance of this variable in the determination of demographic change in Europe will emerge later.

The reconstitutions have been less successful in measuring marriage and mortality rates in the past. While mean or median ages of women at their first marriage, and often remarriage rates, have commonly been assessed, it has rarely been possible to calculate the important measure of the proportion of women in various age groups ever married, since the total female population "at risk" mostly cannot be known. This is a great pity, because it is a valuable qualifier of the measure of age-specific marital fertility. Mortality, unfortunately, has been least consistently measured. Many reconstitutions have measured infant mortality, and this is important, since, given the generally very high level of infant mortality in early modern times, variations over time could be important contributors to changes in the rate of growth of population. But mortality in higher age groups has been less frequently measured, and, while we are very well informed about short-run fluctuations in mortality, it remains difficult to generalize about secular mortality trends.

From the foregoing it will be obvious that there must be certainty that a family "reconstituted" by the abstraction from the registers of its history of baptisms, marriages, and burials has been *completely* reconstituted. The loss of some data will falsify the reconstitution and distort the emerging picture of the community pattern of demographic behavior. And vital events may very easily be lost, particularly through migration or nonregistration. The temporary migration of a married woman may conceal the birth of a child; a subsequent burial may, however, reveal its existence. A family migrating before the completion of the mother's reproductive period must raise doubt as to the total number of births to the mother and her completed family size. Not all forms of incompleteness will invalidate all measures that may be derived from the reconstitution process, but for some measures, very clearly, certainty about the completeness is a first essential. The French demographic historians have devised a classification for the varying degrees of completeness of the data.

By making available a range of standard demographic measures, the new technique of family reconstitution has made possible for the first time the analysis of demographic change in all parts of Europe where parochial registration of the vital events was practiced. Information gleaned by the reconstitution process has been supplemented by the extensive aggregation of entries in the three series of parish registers into monthly, quarterly, and annual series. These aggregations have made valuable contributions to our understanding of short-run fluctuations of the main demographic variables. Time series of burials reveal the pattern of short-run fluctuations. Given the extreme lack of stability of mortality in early modern Europe, these fluctuations played an important part in determining the overall progress of population. Observation of the pattern of short-run fluctuations, and in particular of the changes over time of this pattern, has contributed materially to our understanding of early demographic development. Similar study of the short-run movements of marriages and baptisms has also revealed the complex interaction of all three variables in the process of reaction and adjustment to the mortality fluctuations. Aggregations from baptismal, marriage, and burial registers are less valuable for the study of secular demographic change: the long run is more likely to be affected by underregistration arising from the schisms in hitherto monolithic churches, as well as by variations in the quality of registration arising from changes in incumbency.

Broadly, then, the aggregations have instructed us about the character of short-run demographic change, while the reconstitutions have illuminated the nature of secular development. Once the French scholars had shown the way, historians and demographers in many European countries followed; but even with the aid of computerization, a development that has occurred alongside them, the new techniques remain slow, tedious, and laborious, and the fruits of the methodological revolution have matured only slowly. Until the mid- or later 1960s the number of reconstitutions, each related to either a single parish or a small group of parishes, remained extremely small. But the trickle of the fifties and sixties has become a flood in the seventies. Reconstitution studies have been undertaken, and their results published, in almost all western and northern European countries and even in one or two eastern European countries. It goes without saying that these reconstitutions cover only a tiny fraction of the European population at any one point in time — a few hundred parishes out of the several hundred thousand in early modern Europe. Nor are they evenly distributed by country, geographically within countries, or by type of society — urban, rural, industrial, agricultural, peasant, estate, servile, or free.

The methodological revolution was, and is, predominantly a French revolution. Not less than half of the reconstitutions and aggregations available in print by 1979 relate to France, the others being distributed widely over the rest of western Europe. For a long time, for example, the registers of only one English parish — Colyton, as well known now to aficionados as Crulai — had to stand proxy for the other twelve thousand parishes of England. Now, however, we have results from upwards of a dozen English parishes — still, admittedly, far, far too small a proportion of the total but, because we are still at the stage of increasing returns, more than twelve times better than reliance on a single parish. Excellent work of this kind has now come also from Germany, Italy, Switzerland, Spain, Hungary, the Low Countries, and all the Scandinavian countries. In Scotland and Ireland the poor quality of the old parish registers has so far discouraged the use of the reconstitution technique, and the same reason no doubt explains the absence of all but isolated forays in eastern Europe. For its statistical foundation, therefore, this survey will be obliged to depend almost exclusively on data from western Europe. Though unavoidable, this is a pity, since comparisons between east and west could be very instructive.

If work by the new techniques has not yet achieved a satisfactory geographical distribution, neither has it achieved a satisfactory chronological one. The earliest, rare parish registers become available in Mediterranean Europe in the fifteenth century, but only in the sixteenth century does parochial registration become at all widespread. Even then, however, continuous runs of well-kept registers are few, and it is not until the seventeenth century, even the later seventeenth century, that registers of adequate quality are more widely available. In the event, much of the reconstitution work, particularly in France, relates only to the eighteenth century. In France only a handful of the reconstitutions reach back to the first half of the seventeenth century, and work touching the sixteenth century is exceptional. There is a better chronological balance in England, where much of the work takes us back to the mid-sixteenth century. Elsewhere — in Germany, Italy, Spain, and Scandinavia, for example—there is little to show before the mid-seventeenth century, while much of the work on Switzerland and Hungary takes us back only as far as the later eighteenth century. Some of the work—most of the French work, for example—by dint of the long cohorts employed, can give us no more than static pictures. A typical French study will give great detail with many important demographic variables accurately measured in respect of, say, women married between 1740 and 1789. Some of the English and German reconstitutions, on the other hand, with longer runs of registers to work on, can give us cameos of successive fifty-year cohorts running from the late sixteenth to the early nineteenth century. Fortunately, there are already enough French single-cohort studies to permit us to group their single cohorts into broad periods in a way that allows some analysis of secular change to be undertaken.

For obvious administrative reasons, the majority of the French reconstitution studies terminate in 1789 or 1792. Some, however, have been carried through to the early nineteenth century. In other countries it has been more common to continue the analysis to the mid-nineteenth century. Because the civil registration of births, marriages, and deaths was initiated in most western European countries at some point during the nineteenth century, the need for the use of the highly labor-intensive technique of family reconstitution becomes much diminished at this point. It remains the fact, however, and a pity, that the measures that may be derived from civil registration or from civil registration in conjunction with censuses are not identical to those derived from reconstitution, and the termination of the reconstitution studies in the late eighteenth and early nineteenth centuries leaves us with a rather serious discontinuity in the broader analysis of long-run change at what is often a key period in that change.

In one important respect, however, the reconstitution and aggregation studies possess a supreme virtue. They register facts, not hypotheses; and their facts relate to whole populations, not just to selected social groups within them. In this area of history, as in almost no other, we can penetrate the opacity of history and the inarticulateness of the peasant to discern how the common man behaved as accurately and comprehensively as we are able to discern how a ruling class behaved. It is true that for certain periods and in certain places there are additional or more comprehensive data relating to particular social classes, and some valuable studies—of the British peerage [208-9], the Genevan bourgeoisie [683], or the Florentine [552] and Milanese [563] patriciates—have been made using these data. For its main framework, however, this survey will restrict itself very largely to conclusions derived from the parish registers and will exclude measures relating exclusively to particular social groups except in situations where social and occupational differentials enter into the analysis.

When it is said that the reconstitutions register demographic facts, a mild warning should perhaps be added. These "facts" are statistical abstractions, and though there is every ground for accepting most of them for the accurate measures they purport to offer, the skeptic can frequently find technical reasons for questioning their absolute accuracy. The key variables in demographic change interact so closely that the significance of the levels or movement of any one variable measured by reconstitutions is often dependent upon the level of another. Where this second, "explanatory" measure is not available, as is sometimes the case, extreme caution is called for in the interpretation of the first measure. Plausibility must therefore be the first requirement of data in historical demography.

Reconstitution studies draw their raw data heavily, though not exclusively, from the parish registers. The uneven coverage and varying quality of these registers explains why relatively few reconstitutions have been possible for the early part of the modern period and why each researcher has been obliged to select particular rather than standardized cohorts for study. As early as the fifteenth century in dioceses in France, Spain, and Italy (there are even one or two fourteenth-century registers in Italy) bishops ordered that registers of baptisms, marriages, and burials be kept by parish priests, but it was the sixteenth century before the regular maintenance of registers was ordered on a nationwide scale. In the 580 parishes of the ancient French province of Anjou, for example, the registers of no less than 111 parishes date back to before 1580; of 25, to before 1539; and of 3, to before 1527 (the last three all belong to the city of Angers and begin between 1489 and 1497 [421]). In England the assumption by the crown of the supremacy of the church enabled it to order the universal keeping of registers from 1538, and, although we are far from having a complete set of registers from that date, sets of registers from that year are fairly numerous. In Scotland the more hesitant progress of the Reformation delayed the systematic keeping of registers, and there are now few extant from the sixteenth century. On the other hand, the early start of the Reformation in Switzerland led to the initiation of parochial registration in some dioceses from the 1520s. In other countries, in spite of sporadic endeavors by the episcopacy to inaugurate the ecclesiastical registration of the vital events and the possible execution here and there of these orders, the earliest extant registers date no further back than the seventeenth or even eighteenth century. Registers are very scarce in Holland before 1650, in Estonia before the 1660s, while in Poland survivals of registers are very few indeed before the eighteenth century.

Family reconstitution depends for its success on the availability of all three registers—of baptisms, marriages, and burials. The three series, however, are rarely concurrently extant for some decades after the initiation of the first. Baptismal registers were normally the first to appear, while in some dioceses burial registers made relatively late appearances. Madrid, for example, is favorably placed for the availability of registers. Out of thirteen original parishes of the early modern city, complete sets of registers have survived for seven parishes, and incomplete sets for another three. In San Sebastian parish the baptismal register opens in 1541, the marriage register in 1572, and the burial register in 1578 [650, 170]. In Anjou, of the 111 pre-1580 registers, only 21 include burials, and these relate to adult burials only.

In countries with a more diverse religious history than those that experienced the Counter Reformation the existence of disparate church allegiances complicates the problem of registration. In Holland, for example, while a few Reformed Church registers exist before the mid-seventeenth century, Catholic registers rarely begin before about 1700, and Mennonite registers rarely before about 1750. The problems arising from increasing underregistration in Church of England registers following the growth of nonconformity in the eighteenth century have been discussed frequently [194]. Ireland suffers most of all from this difficulty: while the Protestant (Anglican) Church of Ireland registers were instituted in the seventeenth century (the earliest dates back to 1619), their entries relate only to a minority of the population; registration of the Catholic majority scarcely began before the nineteenth century, and the same is true for the substantial Presbyterian minority in Ulster [533, 294–5].

All registers, early or late, Catholic or Protestant, are exposed to certain weaknesses that inhibit the task of reconstitution. Few are free from gaps, which represent the loss of some data essential to the reconstitution process. All involve the problems of "nominal linkage"—the linking of information about an individual from the different registers [18]. It was common for the range of both first and family names to be very restricted in an area as limited as that of a single parish, and many sons were named after their father, making distinctions between generations, so essential to the procedure, extremely difficult. The naming system in Estonia, which is quite different from that of western European countries, makes nominal linkage even more hazardous [151, 143–4], while in Holland another kind of difficulty arises from the practice, common among lower-class Dutch before the nineteenth century, of not using family names.

These and many other practical problems have limited but not deterred researchers. Where the survival rate and quality of registers are high, as in France, Spain, and Italy, the possibilities of employing the reconstitution method are greatest, and progress has depended on the orientation of historical studies in the countries concerned. In other countries, like Ireland and some eastern European countries, the weaknesses and scarcity of the extant registers are probably absolute barriers to the employment of the technique. The problem, as is clear, however, is not solely one of availability of all three series of registers: their quality — principally in respect of freedom from gaps and of the extent of under-registration arising from the existence of dissenting or schismatic congregations, as well as from infant deaths or from extra-parochial baptism — is of much greater importance, since undetected omissions of vital events must distort the means and rates that are the end products of the family reconstitution process. It is incumbent, therefore, on all researchers not only to satisfy themselves by all available tests and checks of the completeness of registration but also to reassure their readers that they have scrutinized their sources critically in this way before embarking on tabulation and calculation. This is not always done nowadays, and some reconstitution results inevitably carry less credibility on account of the omission of these essential precautions and reassurances.

Two countries — Sweden (with Finland) and Germany — developed important variants of, or additions to, the usual procedures of ecclesiastical registration, and these offer special advantages to the work of reconstitution. Starting in 1628, but becoming more general from 1686, the Swedish church superimposed on the system of parochial registration the annual (or periodic) listing of inhabitants, house-by-house, with notes of migrations and the precise recording of reading ability and state of religious knowledge of individuals. These *husförhörslängder* were kept, and have survived, a little erratically [*588*], but from 1749 they were put on a nationally aggregated footing by the state, thus providing Sweden and Finland with probably the most valuable demographic statistics of any European country for the eighteenth and early nineteenth centuries. Rather belatedly, Swedish demographic historians are beginning to make effective use of these remarkable sources.

In Germany, the Nazi government in the 1930s, with a view to establishing the racially pure origins of each family, initiated the creation by the parochial clergy from the data in the parish registers of the *Ortssippenbücher*, or family trees of the families in the parish. These are, effectively, ready-made family reconstitutions, which enormously facilitate the labor of data processing. Though the original aim of making these books has disappeared, in many places they have been kept up-to-date after the end of the Nazi era [*501*].

The civil registration of births, marriages, and deaths has superseded, for the purposes of demographic history, ecclesiastical registration at dates during the nineteenth century varying from country to country. But this generally more comprehensive and accurate form of recording, like the official censuses, began too late to provide sources for the period covered by this book. Because of their absence during the early modern period, historical demographers have drawn on a very wide range of other records — tax returns or surveys for tax purposes, private local or national censuses, listings of inhabitants for ecclesiastical or military purposes, burgess rolls, and many others. Some of these are valuable for helping to determine absolute levels of population at specific points in time, while the listings, in particular, have recently found an invaluable new use in the burgeoning studies of household size and family structure. Within the narrower confines of strictly demographic history, however, the parish registers remain overwhelmingly the prime source.

In consequence of the steady build-up of reconstitution and aggregation studies, there is now available a considerable corpus of information about demographic behavior in early modern Europe. At the present time it leaves, as has been suggested, something to be desired in terms of geographical and chronological distribution, but, thanks to the general adoption, with only a few minor departures, of the new methods, the results made available are comparable on a European scale. It is not possible to claim that the analysis that forms the core of this book is based on a complete study of all the European reconstitutions and aggregations. There has, in truth, been a veritable explosion of work in this field in the last decade and a half, and the results of the local studies and the accompanying comment and interpretations are not necessarily all at the first level of accessibility. The appendix tables and bibliography of this book, however, indicate the range of work surveyed. The limits have been set by the ordinary constraints on travel and library availability.

Reduced to essentials, the results of the recent work by the new methods are conveyed through the medium of a limited number of basic demographic variables. These measures aim to assess mortality, nuptiality, and fertility or the principal factors influencing them. Ten of these measures have been selected to form the core of the analysis of this book. These are the principal measures generally made available by the family reconstitution technique, though not all reconstitutions have necessarily produced them all; they are available in directly comparable form for all or most countries in which reconstitutions have been undertaken; and they are the best, or the only, measures available for the assessment of what are really the very elusive concepts of fertility and mortality. Seven of the measures made available by reconstitutions and utilized in this book relate to fertility, one to marriage, and two to mortality. This is a poor balance, but fertility was formerly extraordinarily difficult to measure, and much ingenuity and probably a disproportionate amount of energy have been devoted to its measurement in the reconstitutions, producing a wider range of measures. The measurement of mortality, too, is not without its difficulties, and the two measurements employed here are not really adequate; they are, however, the best and most widely available.

All the data used in the tables in chapters 2, 3, and 6 are set out in the appendix tables. They are drawn from a very wide range of studies, and their sources are indicated in the right-hand column of each appendix table by numbers that correspond to entries in the bibliography. Each appendix table also indicates the cohort selected by the reconstitutor. The choice of years for each cohort is determined, of course, principally by the availability and quality of the parish register from which the raw data are drawn, and for this reason almost every cohort in the many hundreds of reconstitutions now completed relates to a different period. This bewildering disparity makes the task of generalizing about trends extremely difficult. The solution adopted here has been to group the cohorts into three broad periods. To ease the task of fitting the disparate cohorts into these periods, they have been overlapped slightly, and the periods chosen — pre-1750, 1740–90, and 1780–1820 — are designed to focus attention on changes during the eighteenth and early nineteenth centuries, when, it is believed, the developments that were most significant for the long-run demographic history of Europe probably occurred. Needless to say, not all the cohorts reconstituted by the researchers fit comfortably into a small number of broad periods chosen arbitrarily in this way, though most do. Where the cohorts manifestly did not relate largely to one of the periods, they have been reluctantly discarded. The first period chosen — pre-1750 — embraces all reconstituted cohorts ending before 1750, regardless of their start. A glance at the appendix tables will show that very few reconstituted cohorts indeed extend back into the sixteenth century: more start in the first half of the seventeenth century, but the majority start in the second half of the seventeenth century or even in the early eighteenth century. The disadvantage of grouping all reconstituted cohorts before 1750 into a single period is the clear risk of concealing important movements over time within it. Attention, for example, has been drawn in the first English reconstitution [274] to what could have been a very significant fall in fertility in the late seventeenth century with a subsequent recovery in the early eighteenth century. Too few of the reconstitutions, however, offer a sufficient number of multiple cohorts before 1750 to permit the subdivision of the early modern period.

Means have been calculated of the data for each of the ten basic variables for each country within each of the three periods. Sometimes the means, which are shown at the foot of each division of the appendix tables and are the figures that appear in the summary tables in chapters 2, 3, and 6, are means of means, for example, in cases where the reconstitutions have been made for a series of short cohorts. Most reconstitutions are of single parishes, but some have embraced groups of parishes. The number of parishes embraced by a reconstitution is shown in the second column of the appendix tables, and the means have been weighted on the assumption that each parish is an approximately equal unit of measurement. A parish is not, of course, a standard unit of a given number of inhabitants. It would rarely have been possible, however, to weight the data according to the populations of the parishes concerned: indeed, in one or two instances it has been a difficult enough task to determine how many parishes were involved in a reconstitution. Entries have mostly not been made where only a single reconstitution is available for one country or period. Needless to say, only data that are strictly comparable are entered: disappointingly, this requirement has led to the discarding of a very considerable proportion of the calculations available in print. The possibilities for varying methods and units of measurement in this field are almost infinite.

The figures in these tables are necessarily approximations that indicate, at best, orders of magnitude. The possibilities of error arising both from the original reconstitution method, which is not flawless, and from the crude averaging employed in the summary tables in this book are manifold. Small variations therefore probably have very little significance, though larger shifts, particularly where based on a larger number of reconstitutions, must surely reflect real changes. In particular, we should be cautious about means derived from a very small number of reconstitutions. No one parish in any country can claim to be "representative," and in this kind of area safety must be sought in numbers.

2

The Demographic
System of the
Ancien Régime

THE METHODOLOGICAL REVOLUTION described in chapter 1 is an ongoing one. A great deal of work is currently in progress; many resources are committed to the work of family reconstitution in many countries; advances are being made in the techniques of analysis and computerization that will reduce the labor intensiveness of the task and therefore encourage the initiation of even more work; and there is an enthusiasm abroad that will clearly sustain the momentum of research for many years to come. Even in France, where enough work has already been done to establish beyond dispute certain main parameters, there are some unanswered or inadequately answered questions that will maintain unremitting attention to the *fiches de famille*. The survey attempted in this book can therefore be no more than an interim one that must become out-of-date very quickly. It could, however, scarcely have been possible earlier. Though based almost entirely on work published during the last twenty-five years, the generalizations in this book rely heavily, as a glance at the bibliography will show, on work that has appeared only very recently. With only a few exceptions, for example, it is the last few years that have witnessed the extention of the work beyond the borders of France.

In many important respects this recent work does not radically alter the picture presented by Helleiner in his classic survey of 1955 [*34*]. Using largely estimates of total populations derived in their turn principally from counts for tax purposes of households rather than of individuals, he traced the recovery of European population in the sixteenth century after its stagnation in the late Middle Ages. He saw the seventeenth century as one of "reverses," in which the principal features were the Thirty

Years' War, the decline of Spain abetted by the expulsion of the Moriscos, and famine and plague in Italy. He warned against regarding the beginning of the eighteenth century as a key turning point. "There was little, if anything," he wrote, "to herald the impending changes" [*34, 58*]. The Malthusian positive checks of wars, disease, and famine, he argued, remained potent in much of Europe. Helleiner's remit, presumably, to deal only with the sixteenth and seventeenth centuries exonerated him from pursuing too closely the dynamics of the eighteenth century, and he was content to sketch in "the eve of the Vital Revolution" in terms very little different from those of the preceding centuries. But his use of the phrase "Vital Revolution" in the context of the later eighteenth century was sufficient recognition of the crucial importance of the developments at that time. Whatever constraints had formerly discouraged secular growth were finally shaken off then. Growth in the late eighteenth century may not have been faster than it had been in the late sixteenth century, but this time it did not come to a halt as in the seventeenth century: it continued with gathering momentum into the nineteenth century to produce a multiplication of European populations on a scale far beyond anything of medieval or early modern times.

But the revolution in methods of historical demography has added a lot of detail, which has inevitably blurred the edges of Helleiner's outlines, and it has complicated the chronology by pointing to national and regional departures from the broad European pattern. Its greatest value has been in uncovering the mechanisms by which populations passed from one generation to another: it has given us a new understanding of the system of checks, balances, pressures, resistances, and constraints by which populations grew, stagnated, or declined. What has emerged very clearly is a picture of a system of a *population d'ancien régime* — what Chaunu has described as the *schéma mécaniste de la démographie ancienne* [*24, 189*], which may be differentiated from the less constrained dynamic that emerged in the late eighteenth and early nineteenth centuries.

In general, European population grew at only the most moderate rates during the whole of the early modern period. In the later fifteenth century there was a lot of lost ground — population destroyed in the Black Death and in epidemics of the following century — to recover. The demographic lost ground of the late Middle Ages also meant lost ground in reality, so that in the sixteenth century there was still room for more people in terms of land and potential food supplies. But such growth as occurred in the sixteenth and seventeenth centuries was halting and irregular. In a European society in which it was necessary to allocate generally three quarters of the population to food production, the availability of cultivable land and the going levels of agricultural productivity necessarily set upper limits to the rates of population growth, which societies would ignore at their peril. Insofar as it was in their power, the onus was on them to restrain their own rates of natural increase—the annual excess of births over deaths—to the very low levels of what could possibly be accommodated as a result of the intake of new land for cultivation, the improvement of poor land, or the advance of agricultural technology. None of these processes could be speedy. Some determinants of rates of growth of population—disease and weather—were beyond human control; but others—marriage and fertility—even allowing for human nature, what Malthus called the constancy of "the passion between the sexes," were not. The problem of the necessary equilibrium between the secular growth rates permitted by economic and political progress and demographic growth rates was posed by man's ecological circumstances; its solution could lie only in human demographic behavior. The study of historical demography during the last two or three decades has gone some way towards uncovering the nature and scale of these constraints and responses.

It was some of the work that immediately preceded the methodological revolution of the mid-fifties, above all that of Jean Meuvret [*442*], that opened up the study of the positive checks to growth of war, famine, and disease that has been so fruitful to our understanding of the mortality side of the early modern European demographic system. We now have a clear picture of the demographic crisis—the *crise démographique de type ancien*—that was one of the dominant features, one of the determining elements, of the European demographic system of the early modern period. In the twentieth century an epidemic in Europe, even a major war, raises normal national mortality rates by no more than a few percent. In the sixteenth and seventeenth centuries, on the other hand, war, famine, or epidemic, or more commonly a combination of them, could double national mortality rates or multiply the mortality rate of a region, town, or parish many times. "Normal" mortality—that is, mortality in the absence of a mortality crisis occasioned by war, famine, or epidemic—might carry off roughly 3 percent of a population each year. (Today in Europe the figure is little more than 1 percent.) In a crisis year, over a wide area this figure might rise to 6 percent or even 10 percent, and in more restricted areas it was known on occasions to rise to 30 percent or 40 percent. Since fertility rates were normally such that there was rarely a surplus of births over deaths to the extent of more than 1 percent per year and mostly less, losses of population on this scale might take anything from two or three to twenty or thirty years to recoup. Of course, it is important to keep the scale of these losses in perspective. While one locality might be experiencing losses of the order of 30 percent or 40 percent of its starting population, another, even quite close, might escape serious mortality altogether. For this reason crisis mortality was commonly in in-

Table 2.1. Infant Mortality, pre-1750
(Deaths under age one per 1,000 live births; both sexes; weighted means)

Country	Number of Reconstitutions	Deaths per 1,000 Live Births
England	18	187
France	33	252
Germany	8	154
Scandinavia	2	224
Spain	2	281
Switzerland	2	283

Sources: See appendix table 10.

verse relation to the size of the area studied. But it is easy to understand why repeated crises of these kinds could prevent population growth in all but the very short run and even produce some secular decline.

This general short-run instability of mortality created by the mortality crises makes the measurement of mortality in the medium or long run extremely difficult. The general level of non-crisis mortality becomes a meaningless measure, since in anything beyond the short run of two or three years the crises become the effective determinants of levels of mortality. Furthermore, the measurement of mortality either by average age at death or by expectation of life is rendered hazardous by the high levels of infant and child mortality prevailing throughout Europe in the early modern period. The measurement of infant mortality itself, in spite of the frequency with which it has now been attempted, is not entirely free from difficulties. There was a widespread tendency, varying in degree substantially from parish to parish and country to country, not to register the burial of an unbaptized infant. Where baptism followed birth within a day or two, as for example in late-seventeenth-century Geneva [695, 393–94], the loss to the count of total burials through this omission might not be too severe; but where the birth-baptism interval stretched to weeks, the loss could be substantial. The study of birth-baptism intervals [258] is one of the several esoteric subcultures that flourish within the general field of historical demography, and there are clearly good reasons why it should.

Where we can be reasonably confident that most or all infant burials and births have been registered, the returns from all parts of Europe for which data are available during all or most of the three centuries of the early modern period show infant mortality running at around 150–250 per 1,000 live births: in some countries around one quarter of infants born failed to survive the first year of life.

There were, of course, wide variations: on the one hand, rates of

Table 2.2.   *Survival Rates, pre-1750*
(Survivors per 1,000 live births to various ages; both sexes; weighted means)

Country	Number of Reconstitutions	Number of Survivors at Age:			
		1	5	10	15
England	6	799	668	624	—
France	10	729	569	516	502
Switzerland	1	766	597	533	506

Sources: See appendix table 9.

350–450 per 1,000 were reached in southern Germany in the late eighteenth century, while in the few instances where reliable measurement has been possible the larger cities tended to show very high rates; at the other extreme, rates of under 100 have been derived from parish registers. While the high rates can hardly be queried, the low rates can be explained by some degree of underregistration. More skepticism should probably be exercised therefore about the lower than about the higher rates. There is no clear pattern in the local or regional variations in the level of infant mortality; high and low rates were fairly randomly distributed and seem not to be characteristic of any particular type of region or economy. Clearly we shall not go far wrong if we accept that a widespread, if not universal, characteristic of the early modern European demographic system was a very high rate of infant mortality in which one out of every four or five children born failed to survive the first year of life.

From the point of view of mortality the first birthday is no more than a demographer's convenience: death itself did not recognize it as a barrier. Mortality between ages one and five — commonly called child mortality to distinguish it from infant mortality — remained high, and, as an age-specific rate, appreciably higher than that for most higher age groups. Unfortunately, this rate has not been very widely measured. Most of the available calculations relate to England, France, and Switzerland, but in these countries there was some degree of conformity in the pattern of child mortality, though less than for infant mortality. Even less work has been done on rates of survival to higher ages.

These limited sources (reproduced in table 2.2), however, agree broadly that mortality after the first year of life continued to be severe: not many more than half of children born survived to their tenth birthday. What evidence there is from other countries suggests that these levels of mortality were very likely to have ruled there too. A common feature, then, of the European system was the failure of almost one child in two to survive to the age of ten.

Within this broad spectrum there were, however, substantial variations, first, between urban and rural environments, and, second, among
occupations. In England, for example, four London parishes averaged
only 556 survivors to age ten out of every 1,000 babies born between 1570
and 1653 [*192*], whereas the parish of Shepshed in Leicestershire achieved
782 survivors to the same age during the seventeenth century [*224*, 68]. In
one of the few available studies of occupational mortality differentials of
the seventeenth century, Perrenoud has shown how, in Geneva, infant
mortality for the *grande* and *moyenne* bourgeoisie was 208 per 1,000
births, while for the working class the corresponding figure was 358 —
more than one third of all infants born failing to live to their first birthday. By age ten, 380 out of 1,000 children born to parents in the upper
bourgeoisie had died, but 628 of those born to working-class parents
[*689*, 233]. In seventeenth-century Geneva fewer than half of all children
born survived to age ten. There were similar, though smaller, differentials in eighteenth-century Ingouville, a suburb of Le Havre. There, 526
of every 1,000 children born to artisan parents survived to age ten, while
only 482 of 1,000 born to laboring parents did so [*482*].

Mortality in early modern Europe was, one might say, in God's sector; man was virtually powerless to control either its general levels or its
short-run fluctuations. Fertility, on the other hand, was, within certain
physiological parameters, entirely in man's sector. All societies at all
times have been faced, consciously or unconsciously, with the problem
of adjusting their fertility to the pace determined autonomously for them
by mortality. Too low a level of fertility would allow populations to
decline, and most societies have hoped to avoid that for economic or military reasons. Too high a level of fertility, however, would lead to population growth, and here the constraints were even more compelling. The
first and most demanding limitation, of course, was agricultural technology. Throughout the early modern period most of the easily cultivable,
fertile land of western Europe was already carrying as many inhabitants
as its agriculture, at the going levels of productivity, could support after
allowing for the small surplus necessary to maintain the relatively small
urban and industrial populations. Greater populations than these could
be supported only by migration to hitherto uncultivated or under-utilized
areas (there were still some of these in the east and southeast); by taking
into cultivation inferior, often hill land (Ladurie [*418*] has given us a
striking example of this being done in seventeenth-century Languedoc);
or by improvements to agricultural techniques that would raise yields per
acre. Most communities in wide areas of western Europe had, for most
of the early modern period, extremely limited access to these alternatives,
so that the penalties for fertility levels that permitted anything beyond
minimal growth were obvious and immediate. Given the parameter of

high, fluctuating mortality, how did European society of the early modern period regulate its fertility in such a way as to preserve the fine balance between unwanted demographic decline and unmanageable demographic growth?

The first determinant of overall fertility rates was marriage. In early modern Europe there was still little fertility outside marriage. We are now extensively informed about illegitimacy rates throughout western and northern Europe. Rates—measured in this period commonly by the number of illegitimate baptisms per 100 live births (both legitimate and illegitimate)—kept below 2 percent for long periods in many parts of France before the mid-eighteenth century. In most countries illegitimate births seldom rose to as high as 5 percent of all births, though it should be borne in mind that most of the information available to us at the moment is based on rural rates; it is unfortunate that the difficulties of detailed demographic work in an urban context have prevented more than isolated explorations of this differential. What little information we have about urban illegitimacy rates before the eighteenth century suggests, however, that though higher than rural rates, they were still low enough not to become a substantial element in overall fertility.

The corollary of an extremely low level of illegitimacy was the key role of marriage rates in the determination of fertility levels. Within marriage, in many ways and for reasons that will be examined more closely in the next chapter, births tended very generally to follow a very regular pattern in the early modern period. In this way general fertility levels were determined quite simply by the proportion of women of reproductive age who were married. If all women were married throughout the whole span of the reproductive period set by nature—a period of about thirty-five years—it is clear, and it was equally clear to early modern European society, that fertility would so greatly have exceeded mortality that a quite unsupportable rate of population growth would have resulted. So the first check—Malthus later was to call it the "preventive" check—to population growth was some limitation on marriage. To assess marriage rates we need two basic measures, and it is unfortunate that most of the reconstitution studies have been obliged to confine themselves to only one of these. The first is the age at which women commonly married for the first time. Results of reconstitution studies indicate that there was a considerable degree of conformity across western Europe in the mean age at which women married for the first time.

Though figures of under twenty at one extreme or over thirty at the other may be found in some parishes, the range of mean ages of women at first marriage for all parts of *ancien régime* Europe for which we now have calculations is generally much narrower, and national means based on all available figures within countries all fall within little more than a two-year range between 24 and a half and 26 and a half. We need also to know what proportion of women ever married, since clearly 50 percent of women under fifty marrying at the mean age of twenty-five would produce fewer children in the aggregate than 100 percent of them marrying at the same mean age. The absence, in all but a few random cases, of figures of the proportion of women ever married at given ages is a serious gap in our knowledge. There was no custom in western Europe obliging all women to marry, and the proportion of those not marrying before age fifty could vary within quite wide limits — anything between 2 percent or 3 percent and 30 percent, though somewhere in the range of 10-20 percent was more common.

Once married, European women before the mid-eighteenth century showed an extremely consistent reproductive behavior. The determinants of this pattern were complex. They were partly physiological and partly responses to influences that varied with changing economic circumstances. They are examined in chapter 3. For the moment it must suffice to notice that although the number of births to individual married women could range from none to over twenty, for the great majority of women the range was much narrower. National means of the now fairly large number of studies of marital fertility available show variations only within quite narrow limits.

When all the constraints on mortality and fertility levels are taken into account and net intergenerational replacement or overall population growth rates are estimated, we see that there remained in early modern Europe a very modest capacity for growth. The many very disparate societies that made up the whole arrived at a strikingly similar system of balances and checks. The realities of the early modern epidemiological situation and the limitations of available agricultural technologies and of prevalent systems of economic and political organizations set mortality, not, as we have seen, at steady, predictable levels, but erratically and unpredictably. It was left to these societies to find a matching reproductive behavior nicely calculated, on the one hand, to ensure the survival of society and, on the other, not to swamp society with a rate of growth that, in the circumstances of the day, could only invoke even more severe culling by famine crises; and to do this, not gradually, in response to steady, predictable shifts in mortality levels, but quickly and urgently in the face of sudden disruption of the normal demographic pattern.

Broadly, populations were maintained in the face of the depredations of the short-run crises in several ways. There is some evidence, but not a lot, that the heavy mortality of the crises was offset by lower-than-normal mortality in a short period immediately succeeding a crisis. The weaker members of communities had succumbed to the pressures of starvation or disease, and those who had recovered from diseases at least had some protection against renewed infection: crises, in other words, both brought forward and delayed some of the normal mortality of the post-crisis period. But the principal mechanism for recuperation lay through marriage. Dupâquier [*345*] has drawn attention to the way in which the mortality crises provoked a lowering of the age at marriage, and he has illustrated this from a count of marriages in one hundred parishes in the Paris basin during the acute crisis of the early 1690s. These parishes averaged 382 marriages per year during the 1680s, a level that fell off in the crisis years of 1693 and 1694 to 314 and 303, respectively. But in 1695 they achieved 590 marriages, and in the following year 499. The bulge of births that would inevitably follow this great drive to the altar would ultimately go a long way towards making good the losses of the crisis. The plethora of marriages was made possible by the remarriages of bereaved spouses and by the availability of an "establishment" — a holding, a living, a homestead, a set of machines and tools in domestic industry — without which marriage in peasant societies was unthinkable. Perrenoud described this capacity for recuperation as "an unsuspected reserve of reproduction" [*693*, 288]. In a parish of central Marseilles in 1721, after the last great plague epidemic there, 63 percent of marriages involved widows or widowers as one or both partners. In that year, marriages in two Marseilles parishes were about three times as numerous as in a normal year [*483*, 572-7].

In a minor crisis it was quite possible for this post-crisis bulge in the birth rate to make good the losses of the crisis; the short-run effect of the crisis would have been no more than the temporary arrest of "normal" population growth. If all crises were of this kind, arresting population growth for a single year and occurring, say, once every ten years, then the effect of the recurring crises would merely be to reduce the normal secular population growth by 10 percent. Many crises, however, were more severe than this, some much more. Livi Bacci [*554*] has suggested as a criterion for a *grande crise de mortalité* that it was one in which the loss of population either directly from mortality or indirectly from births lost exceeded the natural capacity for recovery of the "rising" adult cohort already in existence at the start of the crisis — that is, those less than fifteen years of age. Such a crisis certainly occurred in Scotland between 1695 and 1699, when a succession of terribly deficient harvests led to an exceptionally high level of mortality. Though the regional impact of the famine varied, all of Scotland was affected to a greater or lesser extent, and it has been estimated that the net loss of between 10 percent and 15 percent for the whole country was barely made good in the following half-century [*633*, 200]. With "normal" non-crisis growth of less than 0.5 percent per annum, it might take twenty-five years to make good a 10 percent loss of population in a *grande crise*. In some cities and regions, the bubonic plague epidemics of the seventeenth century led to losses of between 30 and 50 percent of population. This simple arithmetic explains why the varying levels of severity of crises were, far beyond any other demographic variable, the prime determinants of the rate of growth of population in early modern Europe.

Within this global system of demographic equilibrium there were small subsystems of adjustment. The implication of many of the mechanisms I have been describing is that each community worked in a kind of self-equilibrating isolation. This was far from being the case, of course, because there was an enormous amount of movement (which is examined in chapter 5).

One such flow, however, must be looked at here, before closing this survey of equilibrating mechanisms. It has long been established that virtually all towns in early modern Europe over a certain threshold of size were net consumers of population: that is to say, deaths normally exceeded births, so that the towns could maintain their populations and grow only by constant replenishment from rural areas. The drain of populations to towns, in its turn, was a means by which rural areas were able to rid themselves of the surplus population arising from natural increase and thus avoid having to submit to even more stringent operation of the positive or preventive checks to growth. The limits to the extent of this exchange were set by the capacity of the areas supplying towns with food to generate agricultural surpluses. Bairoch [20] has suggested that for this reason urban populations in early modern Europe could never have exceeded 25 percent of the whole. Though the difficulties of the study of urban demography limit the possibilities of systematic urban-rural comparison, there are enough calculations of urban mortality rates to put beyond doubt the general assertion that it was high urban mortality that created the permanent urban deficit. Problems of urban sanitation, water supply, overcrowding, and poverty offer obvious enough explanations of these relatively high mortality rates. In a well-known and telling article, Wrigley [276] demonstrated how it was possible, even likely, for London to have taken up in this way a substantial share of the whole natural increase of English population during its period of fast growth in the seventeenth and early eighteenth centuries. It was easy to conclude from this that, in Wrigley's words, "in many cases. . . urban populations only held their own by immigration" [58, 97], or, as Mols put it rather more extremely, "immigration to the towns was vital if they were to be preserved from extinction" [49, 49].

More recently, however, Sharlin [53] has argued that this interpretation misconceives the ecological role of towns. Urban populations before the late nineteenth century, he suggests, should be disaggregated into their component parts — the permanent residents and the immigrants.

Underlying his argument are the assumptions that the residents were (*a*) wealthier and better housed than the immigrants and thus less subject to an adverse health environment; (*b*) more resistant to the going diseases through long exposure to them and thus subject to lower mortality rates than the immigrants; and (*c*) mostly in occupational groups not subject (as were servants and apprentices) to restrictions on marriage and thus in a position to marry earlier and produce higher fertility rates. Conversely, the immigrants, living in crowded environments most favorable to the transmission of infection, and least protected, because of nonexposure, by antibodies against the—to them—new, urban diseases, succumbed easily and speedily to infection. Sharlin tested this hypothesis against the few European cities—Frankfurt-am-Main, Basel, Vienna, and Prague—for which the extant vital data differentiate for the seventeenth and eighteenth centuries between permanent residents and immigrants, and he found that the facts amply bore it out. His illustrations are also confirmed in many details by Garden's study of Lyons [*357*]. Sharlin then had no difficulty in showing that in spite of the relatively adverse health conditions of any modern town, and even in the larger cities, the permanent residents managed to achieve some natural increase—their fertility normally exceeded their mortality. But the immigrants who compounded their high mortality by low fertility rates because of restrictions on marriage showed such a heavy excess of deaths over births that, though they were normally a smaller proportion of the total population than the permanent residents, their high natural decrease more than offset the small natural increase of the permanent residents and led to the overall natural decrease that is observable in virtually all large towns of the early modern period. In these circumstances, therefore, the usual generalizations about towns requiring immigration to sustain their populations is clearly misleading: without immigration the towns would have had little difficulty in sustaining their populations; it was the immigrants themselves that caused the overall excess of deaths over births. In this light, rural outmigration became just one way of slowing down high growth rates by increasing mortality and reducing fertility in the section of the excess rural population that chose to migrate to the towns.

The balance, evidently, was precarious; but it held, to maintain a slightly unstable equilibrium. At times, as in the sixteenth century and again in the early eighteenth century, the factors favoring growth marginally gained the upper hand. In the seventeenth century, on the other hand, the balance of pressures swung marginally in the adverse direction, leading in some parts to stagnation and even decline. The equilibrium was unstable, however, not merely by virtue of the detailed interaction of changes at the margin in the many variables touched on in this chapter, but, more importantly, because some of the variables were subject to influences and pressures that were capable of causing them to move significantly in the long run. These determinants of fertility and mortality are considered in more detail in the next two chapters.

3   The Instability of Fertility

THE BALANCE DESCRIBED in the preceding chapter showed fertility levels in all parts of Europe running precariously close to mortality levels, often keeping just sufficiently ahead of them for long periods to permit modest growth to occur but here and there and from time to time running behind mortality and allowing population decline to take over. We should be quite clear that an excess of births over deaths was the normal or most prevalent situation, so that for much of the long reign of the *ancien régime* growth—occasionally vigorous but mostly slow or very slow—prevailed. The balance, in the main, was just favorable. But though favorable, it remained precarious because both mortality and fertility rates were themselves the net outcome of an array of pressures that varied in both the short and the long run.

The study of fertility in the *ancien régime* is facilitated a little by being confined very largely to marital fertility. Throughout Europe, as we saw in the last chapter, illegitimacy rates were extremely low. Much effort, and indeed much illuminating writing, by Flandrin [89–90], Shorter [98–100], and others [84] has been devoted to explaining this low level of illegitimacy, and much effort has also been devoted to explaining the relaxation of this social control after the mid-eighteenth century. There were good enough reasons for social controls of this kind. The "one-parent family" is a twentieth-century euphemism for an age-old social security problem. Bastardy and the quest for putative fathers were necessary concerns of all local authorities charged with the relief of poverty. Depauw's study of illegitimacy in eighteenth-century Nantes [335] shows how provincial towns became a focus of the problem and why the inability of eighteenth-century society in the main to cope with the problem provided at least one reason for directing effort at prevention rather than cure. A more powerful, and possibly more humane, reason for discouraging extramarital fertility was, however, that it could so easily disturb the precarious demographic balance locally. Runaway fertility would destroy the delicate balance between man and nature as surely as runaway inflation in the twentieth century can destroy precariously poised monetary systems. If extramarital fertility got out of hand, the annual number of births could rise enormously, and the economies of early modern Europe simply could not cope with uncontrolled demographic growth. To prevent the inevitable nemesis of the Malthusian positive checks, women must be generally discouraged from giving birth outside wedlock.

The struggle to confine sexual relations to marriage and at the same time to keep marriage late was bound, to some extent, human nature being what it is, to be a losing one. That it was so is reflected in the premarital-conception rate, which in most countries ran a great deal higher than illegitimacy rates. This rate defined premarital conceptions, no doubt a little arbitrarily, as births within eight months of marriage and expressed these as a percentage of all first births. Hair has shown [199–200] that as many as one sixth of all first births in sixteenth- and seventeenth-century England were certainly premaritally conceived, and probably one third; but work in other parts of Europe has shown that rates around this level or even higher were by no means uncommon. In Norway, by the mid-eighteenth century rates in the region of 50 percent were recorded [615], and in the eighteenth century generally, as with illegitimacy, there was a tendency for the premarital conception rate to rise. In three villages in the Neuchâtel area of Switzerland premarital conceptions accounted for 21 percent of all first births in the mid-eighteenth century. By the beginning of the nineteenth century the proportion had risen to 64 percent. The increase was attributed to the establishment of textile factories in the area [679]. It was of course recognized that marriage was often precipitated by conception, and there was a range of social customs that determined that marriage should follow illicit sex or even that the latter might legitimately precede the former. Because of the variety of the social customs, of which "bundling" and "zu Licht gehen" are the best known, there were wider variations in levels of premarital conceptions both geographically and chronologically than in many other variables [633, 359–60; 672].

The importance of low illegitimacy rates for the study of fertility is that they place on marriage rates a much more influential role in the determination of fertility rates than they would if fertility outside marriage were high. In an age of very little, if any, deliberate control of fertility within marriage (this is begging an important question that is examined below) and in conditions of very low extramarital fertility, the age at which women commonly married became a key determinant of overall fertility. In nature's design, women are fertile for a period of at most thirty-five years, though this fertility exhibits a rising and falling curve over the whole reproductive period — sharply rising from puberty, remaining at or near a peak throughout the twenties, and declining slowly, though with gathering momentum, from the early thirties until sterility is reached. The pace of growing and declining fertility obviously varies fairly widely from woman to woman, though we must be concerned with means. Given that it takes less than one year to produce a birth, the possibilities for procreation might seem almost boundless with such a long reproductive period and limited access to knowledge and means of the control of births. Though in the twentieth century improved nutrition has produced a lowering of the age of puberty by one or two years, possibly more, there is very little evidence of any significant variation in this particular parameter during the early modern period [41, 214–32; 82]. Demographers take no chances and assume that the woman's reproductive period can stretch from age fifteen to age forty-nine. These ages represent normal physiological limits, but the reconstitution studies, where the data have permitted, have sought the realities of reproductive behavior and calculated for each parish or group of parishes the mean ages of women at their first marriage and of mothers at the birth of their last child.

In a famous article in 1965 [92] Hajnal observed what he called the "European marriage pattern," which he distinguished from an "eastern European pattern." The boundary between the two patterns was, broadly, a line drawn from Trieste to Leningrad. The distinguishing features of Hajnal's European pattern were that a significant proportion of women (up to 15–20 percent) abstained altogether from marriage and that those who did marry did so late relative to the age of puberty. To the east of Hajnal's line, in contrast, virtually all women married, and they did so very soon after puberty. In Hajnal's "European" populations about 45–50 percent of women in the age range 15–50 were married; east of the line the proportion was 60–70 percent.

Given that women's age at first marriage is such an important determinant of fertility, most reconstitution exercises have measured it, with the result that we are now well informed on the subject. (Most reconstitutions have calculated *mean* age at first marriage. There is little doubt that for this purpose the *median* is a better measure. In textual table 3.1 and appendix table 7, however, the *means* have been used, since to have chosen the *medians* would have involved excluding a substantial proportion of all calculations available.) Subject to some variation both geographically and chronologically the results shown in table 3.1 strongly vindicate Hajnal's assertion, at least so far as the West is concerned,

Table 3.1. Mean Age of Women at First Marriage, pre-1750
(Weighted means)

Country	Number of Reconstitutions	Mean Age
Belgium	5	25.0
England	21	25.0
France	18	24.6
Germany	5	26.4
Scandinavia	6	26.7

Sources: See appendix table 7.

while results from the first reconstitutions of three parishes in Hungary, to the east of Hajnal's line, show a mean age at first marriage in the late eighteenth century as low as 18.6 [125]. The lowest national mean age at first marriage for any country revealed by the reconstitutions shown in table 3.1 is 24.6 years in France. Most countries yield means closely clustered around age twenty-five. In particular localities first marriage could be even further delayed. In eighteenth-century Lyons, for example, one third of all women marrying did so for the first time over the age of thirty, while 14 percent were over thirty-five [357, 91]. Providing it did not diverge too far from the female age, the male age at first marriage is of far less significance demographically. It was rare, in fact, for the mean age of males at first marriage to exceed by more than two or three years the corresponding age for their brides.

There is a very strong tendency among demographic historians to attribute the relatively advanced age at first marriage among the women of early modern western Europe to a recognition of the need to maintain the demographic equilibrium, and it is true that customary marriage in the mid- or late twenties substantially reduced the length of the reproductive period in women and also allowed considerable flexibility: there was scope for movement in either direction to rectify dangerously fast positive or negative population growth rates. Olwen Hufton [405, 3-7], however, suggests that, in France at least, there may be a simpler, economic explanation. Women there were expected to make some capital contribution to the establishment of a home, whether in agriculture or domestic industry, and the low levels of remuneration for women's labor necessitated many years of saving — as many as fourteen or sixteen — before an adequate capital sum, the passport to marriage, could be accumulated. It is interesting that a recent study of demographic conditions in post-famine Ireland, where women's age at first marriage was exceptionally high, similarly preferred an economic rather than a demographic explanation for the high marriage age [532, 28].

Table 3.2.   Mean Age of Women at Birth of Last Child, pre-1750
(All ages at marriage; weighted means)

Country	Number of Reconstitutions	Mean Age
Belgium	5	40.9
England	3	38.5
France	4	40.4
Germany	2	40.0

Sources: See appendix table 8.

The high degree of conformity across western and northern Europe to this custom of female marriage in the mid- and even late twenties carried important implications for fertility. Social custom cut out the first ten years of women's reproductive capacity; at the other end of the reproductive span, though some women are physiologically capable of bearing children almost until the age of fifty, menopause is commonly earlier. Attempts to discover whether the age at menopause has changed historically seem not to have been very successful [82], and there is no convincing evidence to show that it differed significantly from the twentieth-century level, though it has been shown that below a certain threshold of nutrition menopause can occur earlier than usual. This threshold may not have been reached occasionally during famines, but mostly it was normally. The proportion of women reaching sterility rises rapidly for women in the thirties: a large number of studies in many countries of early modern Europe show, and table 3.2 confirms, that the mean age of women at the birth of their last child seldom exceeded forty and was often thirty-eight or thirty-nine. Again, this is a European pattern, with surprisingly little interregional variation.

If the mean age at first marriage was around twenty-five and the mean age at the birth of last child was around forty, the average reproductive span practically available to women was fifteen years, somewhat less than the thirty-five years theoretically available. The ages in table 3.2, however, are based on cases where the mothers survived to the age of fifty at least; but many marriages were terminated by the death of one or the other partner before the wife reached the end of her reproductive period. One or two studies of the average duration of the wife's reproductive period have been made (of means, that is, of the periods between marriage and the birth of last child or death of either parent, whichever came earliest). In eighteenth-century Lyons, for example, 33 percent of the women experienced a period of marital fecundity of less than ten years, and only 34 percent one of fifteen years or more [357, 104]. The mean was 12.5 years. Winberg has shown [630, 225] for a group of parishes in late-eighteenth-century Sweden that for peasant wives the duration of marriage averaged 14.6 years, and for the wives of landless workers, only 12.7 years. This contrast between landed and landless families was even greater in early-seventeenth-century Arden (England), where in the period 1600–1624 the mean childbearing span of landless couples was a mere 8.8 years, compared with the landed couples' 12.3 years [*262*, 28]. Mogensen's study of twenty Normandy parishes in the last decades of the *ancien régime* [*448*] showed similar differences. Reproductive losses from marriages prematurely terminated by the death of either party might be offset to some extent by remarriage. Widows, however, remarried at significantly lower rates than widowers, and some period of fertility, however short, was necessarily lost before remarriage.

With a mere nine-month gestation period, however, even twelve to fifteen years allowed some scope for large families. To what use did the married women of early modern Europe put their relatively brief married fertility period? The reconstitution studies have focused their main attention on just this point, since the answer to this question must go a long way towards an understanding of how our European ancestors of the early modern period met the challenge of high, fluctuating mortality.

Two measures have been used in the main to investigate the problem. Age-specific marital fertility aims to show, for each geographical unit studied — parish or group of parishes — and for women married there within a given period — the cohort — how many children were born per 1,000 woman-years lived by married women in each of the seven five-year age groups of the reproductive period. The figure is something of a demographer's artifact, but its universal adoption by the reconstitutors provides a valuable measure permitting interregional and intertemporal comparisons. The second measure is of birth intervals. These are means, measured in months separately for each parity, with separate calculations for the last and penultimate intervals.

Table 3.3 shows that, once again, there is a fair degree of conformity among the mean figures of age-specific marital fertility for all the European countries for which calculations have been made, a homogeneity that enables us to talk about a European demographic system in this period.

Table 3.4, concentrating on mean age-specific marital fertility rates for women married only between the ages of twenty-five and twenty-nine, is a more precise measure and, though there are fewer reconstitutions to draw on, also displays broadly comparable orders of magnitude for this important indicator. (Comparable calculations are available for women married in all the other five-year age groups within the reproductive period.)

Table 3.5, showing national means of birth spacings, illustrates more

Table 3.3. Age-specific Marital Fertility, pre-1750 (All Ages at Marriage of Women)
(Births per 1,000 woman-years lived in each age group; weighted means)

Country	Number of Reconstitutions	Age Groups 20–24	25–29	30–34	35–39	40–44
Belgium	11	472	430	366	317	190
England	14	414	392	332	240	140
France	43	467	445	401	325	168
Germany	10	432	399	358	293	138
Scandinavia	4	447	412	344	287	166
Switzerland	4	509	463	398	321	164

Sources: See appendix table 1.

Table 3.4. Age-specific Marital Fertility, pre-1750 (Women Married at Ages 25–29)
(Births per 1,000 woman-years lived in each age group; weighted means)

Country	Number of Reconstitutions	Age Groups 25–29	30–34	35–39	40–44
France	16	480	415	310	169
Germany	4	426	369	257	115

Sources: See appendix table 2.

immediately the fertility situation in the early modern European demographic system. Before we examine the actual figures, it will be worth considering some of the social and biological influences upon them. First, there were religious pressures for abstinence from sexual relations at certain seasons of the year—Lent and Advent. These, combined with the seasonality of common illnesses and other stresses of the working year, restricted opportunities for procreation and thus tended to reduce births. Second, there were possibilities of amenorrhoea (cessation of ovulation) in consequence of severe undernourishment. Ladurie first drew attention to the lessons for historical demography that might be drawn from the terrible experience of this kind of the starving women of Rotterdam under the Germans in World War II [96], and Frisch has subsequently shown how widespread this form of temporary sterility could have been in the harvest fluctuations of earlier centuries [91]. Third, there were important constraints on the fecundability of women following birth. There was normally a period of amenorrhoea following birth (post-partum amenorrhoea), and this would commonly be extended by the practice of breast-feeding of the infant. There is some uncertainty as to how long this secondary amenorrhoea lasted—clearly, many months but not indefinitely, even if breast-feeding was prolonged well into the second year. A lot of statistical work has been done in respect both of historical experience and of the contemporary world on the effects of breast-feeding on birth spacing [for example, *95, 499*]. High rates of infant mortality make it possible to compare normal birth intervals, when maternal feeding could be presumed, with birth intervals following the death of an infant, when, clearly, breast-feeding would cease. Though there are some variations in the findings, calculations in all parts of Europe show a fairly consistent reduction of birth intervals of between four and eight months in consequence [*350*, 138; *413*, 189–90]. By delaying the next birth, therefore, regular and fairly prolonged breast-feeding clearly played a part in lengthening the birth intervals and reducing overall fertility. Though very little is known about the duration of breast-feeding in early modern Europe, there are a few indications that practices may have varied significantly from one part to another. Knodel has illustrated substantial variations among districts within early-twentieth-century Bavaria in respect both of the duration of breast-feeding and of the proportion of mothers feeding their own children at all [*499*, 301]. It appears that in southwestern France in the eighteenth century the persistence of multigenerational households permitted a division of household tasks among the generations of women, so that the mothers were in a position to continue feeding their own children longer. In this area birth intervals tended to be longer than the French average for the period [*352*, 171–72]. One study of contemporary *recommendations* for suitable periods of breast-feeding that surveyed the surprisingly large number of handbooks on health and childcare in seventeenth- and eighteenth-century England revealed a remarkable diminution of the mean recommended period from two years in the early seventeenth century to nine months in the later eighteenth century [*253*]. Changes of this magnitude, even if observed only in part, must have had some consequential effect on birth spacings and hence overall fertility. Breast-feeding, by providing the ideal, correct diet for infants, also contributed to the reduction of infant mortality. Feeding by other means was invariably associated with higher infant-mortality rates.

Since a previous birth and its subsequent amenorrhoea were missing, the interval between marriage and first birth was invariably the shortest of all intervals. The surprise is perhaps that it was as long as the fourteen to sixteen months that table 3.5 shows prevailed in France and England. These figures, of course, include both pre- and post-marital conceptions: if only post-marital conceptions are taken into account, the delay was, of course, longer.

After the first birth, however, greater regularity prevailed. In table 3.5 only the French figures are based on a sample large enough to inspire

Table 3.5. Birth Intervals, pre-1750
(In months; all ages at marriage; weighted means)

Country	Number of Reconstitutions	Interval				
		0–1	1–2	2–3	Ante-penultimate–penultimate	Penultimate–last
England	4	14.2	28.4	31.3	–	43.6
France	20	16.1	22.9	26.2	30.3	35.4
Germany	1	–	20.9	22.4	32.6	44.7
Switzerland	1	–	20.3	23.8	27.4	34.9

Sources: See appendix table 3.

confidence. They show that the general tendency, whatever the total number of births, was for birth intervals to lengthen marginally with increasing parity. The last two intervals, therefore—mostly calculated from families of six births or more—were substantially longer than lower-parity intervals. The striking fact to emerge from this study of birth intervals is the great length of the interval following the first birth—averaging nearly two to two and a half years for lower-parity births, rising from two and a half to three and a half years or more for higher parities. And these intervals must be related to the average reproductive period available to women in this period. This average, as we have seen, was twelve to fifteen years commonly. It was not possible, on average, to fit in more than five or six births. And if the average age of women at first marriage crept up to twenty-eight or twenty-nine, as it did in some areas, at least one possible birth would be lost.

These relatively low numbers of births should be seen in the context of high infant- and child-mortality rates, since from the point of view of long-run population growth what mattered was the replacement of one generation of reproductive age with another of reproductive age. We have seen that on average broadly one quarter of infants born failed to survive the first year of life, and another quarter the next nine years. Probably one birth in every two must be regarded as wasted as far as producing the next generation of adults was concerned. The average marriage, therefore, would produce at best two and a half to three children that survived to adulthood. Since this was an average, however, it might still seem an ample margin over and above what was necessary to maintain a population. If an average generation is twenty-seven years in length, a replacement of two parents by two and a half adults in the next generation represents an annual growth rate of only a little below 1 percent per annum—probably sufficient to double a population in sixty to seventy years. But, as we have seen, not all women married, and not all women who married did so below the age of fifty, when marriage lost its significance for fertility. Studies of the proportion of women at age fifty who had never married show that figures between 10 percent and 20 percent were common. This failure to utilize the full reproductive capacity of society further eroded an already slight positive margin of intergenerational replacement levels.

However, a significant proportion of women never marrying before age 50, combined with the relatively high mean age of women at first marriage—both important characteristics of the western European demographic system in the early modern period—created a degree of flexibility in the system that permitted quick responses to short-run catastrophes. In the event of the sudden loss of population in a crisis, there was a reserve of both younger and older unmarried women to take the place of the married women lost in the crisis to provide the necessary boost to marriage and fertility rates that would make good the crisis losses. There is little doubt that these possibilities of short-run variations in marriage rates were extensively used as means of quick adjustments to permit communities to recover from crises. By these means communities were able to recover surprisingly quickly from the less severe crises.

It was, of course, also open to societies to use these controls of marriage rates and the various influences on birth spacings in a more gradual way to vary their fertility (and hence their overall population growth rates) in the long run. Wrigley has suggested [274] that this was indeed how the people of Colyton, in southwestern England, responded to secular changes in their economic and social conditions in the late seventeenth and early eighteenth centuries. The median age of women at first marriage rose by over eighteen months between the marriage cohorts 1560–1646 and 1647–1719 and fell again by nearly two years by the following cohort, 1720–1769. Age-specific fertility fell and rose with the same pattern, and birth intervals lengthened and shortened accordingly. Unfortunately, as in many of the reconstitutions, limitations of the raw data prevented the calculation of the proportion of women married in particular age groups with a view to seeing whether this variable changed in a corresponding way also. Other subsequent English reconstitution results have not so far provided much national confirmation of this local trend, and it is similarly hardly possible to discern any general secular trends in marriage and fertility rates in the results of reconstitutions in other countries before 1750, though most show some secular movement. In short, we do not yet have sufficient evidence to confirm the suggestion that women's age at first marriage, the proportion of women married, and fertility within marriage were used systematically by European societies before the mid-eighteenth century as a control for the adjustment of their secular population growth rates. But the question should be regarded as still open to confirmation or rejection by further research.

The foregoing analysis of the human reproductive pattern of early modern western Europe is based on means; and means, of course, conceal variations—in these contexts, differences between regions, between town and country, and between social and occupational groups. Much work has been done recently in an endeavor to trace some logical pattern in these divergences from the means, but on the whole it has so far achieved very little beyond the illustration of diversity. One obvious possible variation appears to have been the contrast between peasant agricultural holdings, often tightly controlled by inheritance customs or landlord regulation that required late marriage and extensive celibacy, and domestic industrial communities, which had every encouragement to early and very general marriage. Much attention has been focused on this problem in many countries. In spite, however, of some statistical evidence, it is more difficult than is generally believed to arrive at any very useful generalizations on the subject. There is, firstly, too little consistency between the forms of measurement used. Some writers calculate mean ages at first marriage, and others medians; some contrast rates for parishes in which certain occupations predominated with those in which different occupations predominated, though in all cases some mixture is involved. Where writers have succeeded in making a clear occupational breakdown, their occupational groupings do not coincide with those used by others. In other cases where family reconstitution is not possible, measures other than age at first marriage or age-specific fertility are used. Not all writers distinguish between first and all marriages. Some writers have no statistical evidence at all and are obliged to rely on literary or indirect evidence, which is seldom reliable. Even where the same occupational groupings are distinguished and the same measures are used, studies in different countries or regions yield disparate trends. Very few researchers have succeeded in calculating the important measures of the proportion of women ever marrying and birth intervals in the key occupational divisions.

But in spite of the difficulty of deriving valid generalizations in this important area, many writers in isolation have thrown much useful light. A picture is gradually being built up of a distinctive "peasant" marital and reproductive pattern. The requirements of a peasant household, and, in the east, of its feudal overlords, were very specific. There was a traditional allocation of tasks between the sexes and among age groups, and the continued functioning of both holding and estate called more than usually for the maintenance of the same delicate balance as we have seen was a feature of the whole demographic equilibrium of the *ancien régime*. The desideratum was the maintenance of a constant number, age structure, and sex structure within the family and the community—the realization in practice of the theoretical stable population. Direct regulation by the landlord played an important part in the regulatory process, and there were many reasons why it was in his interest to do so, as, for example, Kula has shown for Poland [145]. Movement into and out of the estate might involve litigation or loss of assets represented by dowries or workers, while anything other than minimal population growth might lead to expense in the relief of poverty or the more serious economic insecurity resulting from the subdivision of holdings. Conversely, a decline of population could lead to vacant holdings, a decline of rent, or labor services unfulfilled.

A principal weapon in the hand of the landlord was his ability to prevent the fragmentation of holdings. This was a prime object of the regulations of many Polish estates in the eighteenth century. Berkner [491] has provided an instructive contrast in seventeenth- and eighteenth-century Germany between two regions in Hanover—Calmberg, where impartible inheritance ruled, and Göttingen, were partible inheritance was permitted. In impartible Calmberg, population grew between 1689 and 1766 by 30 percent, and the number of households was increased by 15 percent. There was a high celibacy rate. Non-heirs were driven out of families to take positions as servants in other households where marriage was not possible. Only one third of sons over age fourteen lived at home, nearly half being away as servants. In partible Göttingen, on the other hand, population rose in the same seventy-seven-year period by 60 percent, and there was a 40-percent increase in the number of households. Half the sons over age fourteen stayed at home, and only 14 percent were servants elsewhere.

In contrast with this picture, however, evidence from some areas shows the landless rural population marrying even later and having lower age-specific fertility rates than occupants of landed holdings. A recent study of Shakespeare's Arden [262] showed that in the early-seventeenth century English midlands age-specific fertility rates for the landless were lower than those for the land-occupying class, particularly when mortality rates were high. Gaunt, studying a diverse group of parishes in central Sweden during the seventeenth century, found a similar situation [589]: the parishes dominated by manorial organization and the most rigid agrarian structure showed relatively low rates of celibacy among women and first-marriage ages no higher than in more mixed and semi-industrial parishes. Nor have comparisons of marriage habits of farmers and laborers been very instructive. In a study of an English rural area in the eighteenth century Jones [213] found that women marrying agricultural laborers tended to be significantly older than those marrying farmers (mean 28.1 against 26.5), but the results of the study of age-specific fertility and birth intervals are so inconsistent as not to help in the elucidation of the problem. Very similar results emerge from Palli's study of seventeenth- and eighteenth-century Estonia [151], from Winberg's study of the Dala district in eighteenth-century Sweden [630-31], and from Thestrup's study of the Danish parish of Glostrup between 1677 and 1770 [617-18]: cottagers' brides in Glostrup were much older than farmers' brides (29.4 years against 25.7), but there were few significant differences in age-specific marital fertility. Peasants must have been as concerned to ensure the continuity of their families in the holding as they were to guard against an excessive progeny, which would undermine the basis of subsistence. Wrigley [102] has shown, for example, by means of a simulation exercise, that 20 percent of all couples in pre-industrial Europe would have had no surviving heirs, and another 20 percent only one. There may have been real meaning, after all, in the old French couplet:

Ma mère couche avec mon père
Ce n'est pas par agrément.
C'est pour faire un petit frère,
Qui gardera les vaches aux champs.

[Quoted in 648]

The clearest contrast to the rigid peasant pattern, in theory at least, was the pattern associated with domestic industry, both rural and urban. Where income from domestic industry was available there was little if any need for land to support a family. Subdivision of existing holdings became practicable, as did the occupation of land too poor for traditional agriculture. Since both land and capital were only minor requirements, the constraints on marriage were minimal. Chambers was one of the first, as far back as 1957 [167], to illustrate the higher fertility (measured here by the number of baptisms per marriage) in domestic industrial villages of midland England than in wholly agricultural villages. Over the whole of the eighteenth century baptisms per marriage in these industrial villages were 19 percent more numerous than in the agricultural villages. A similar pattern was found by Braun in Switzerland [672]. In the Canton of Zürich highland areas were settled during the eighteenth century by families whose income derived largely from domestic textile manufacture. Braun quotes persuasively from contemporary sources to illustrate how this economic system encouraged early marriage, high fertility, and rapid population growth. The sources do not permit him, however, to establish actual rates (and how these compared with those in peasant agricultural areas) with statistical precision. Where age-specific rates have been established, as, for example, by Knodel for quite a large sample of parishes in Germany, landless laborers (his occupational grouping, which must include domestic workers) do not show consistently higher fertility rates than farmers with self-sufficient holdings [502].

The contrast between the demographic behavior of landed peasants or farmers and that of domestic industrial workers has been most thoroughly explored in the English midlands by Levine [224], who investigated, by means of reconstitution studies, the demographic behavior of the population in two Leicestershire villages of contrasting economies. Shepshed was mainly an industrial village: from the early eighteenth century a high and increasing proportion of its inhabitants made their living in domestic frame-knitting. Bottesford, on the other hand, in the rich Vale of Belvoir, was grazing country, with large farms and a population divided between farmers and laborers. In Shepshed, increasing opportunities during the eighteenth century for earning a living, albeit a poor one, in domestic hosiery manufacture, led to declining ages at first marriage for women, while even within the village the wives of frame-knitters married earlier than others. Population grew by immigration as well as by natural increase. In Bottesford, on the other hand, women's age at first marriage remained steady at the moderately high figure of about twenty-six years. Age-specific marital fertility is difficult to compare, not least because even in a unified comparative study of two communities the author has not used identical cohorts. For most of the period when domestic industry prevailed in Shepshed, age-specific marital fertility was indeed noticeably lower than in pastoral Bottesford. In the second half of the eighteenth century, however, Shepshed rates were higher in most age groups (though not in the important 25–29 group): in particular, the fertility of the 20–24 age group was significantly higher in industrial Shepshed, and this was a key group, since an increasing proportion of women in this age range married there as the eighteenth century progressed. It can be shown that in eighteenth-century Flanders, where farm fragmentation was high, the demographic behavior of domestic industrial workers was closely responsive to conditions in the industry. Mendels [116] has illustrated the positive correlation between real income (measured by the ratio between linen and rye prices) and marriages. As incomes rose, marriages, with a one-year time lag, increased. There was no corresponding decline of marriages when real incomes fell. This asymmetry, observed by Levine in Shepshed, as well as by Mendels, could, in Mendels's words, "tend to promote irreversible population growth as long as the relevant prices continued their stimulating fluctuations."

The conclusions from these occupational studies of marriage and fertility are obviously important in the context of the acceleration of population growth in the eighteenth century. There is little doubt that in many countries a principal feature of economic development, particularly during the late eighteenth century, was a considerable expansion of domestic industry—a possibility, that is to say, of a growing proportion of the population with earlier marriage and a larger number of births than the average. Such a trend may well have occurred; but the studies we have to date have not yet put the matter beyond doubt. [In addition to the studies quoted, see also *121; 324; 410; 415; 448; 509; 688.*] There is only a limited amount of evidence that age-specific marital fertility was higher among domestic workers, and though Levine, for example, shows that women in this group tended in the later eighteenth century to marry earlier, he has also shown a corresponding reduction in the mean age at which they bore their last child, so that the net gain to fertility from the earlier marriages must have been slight. Most of the investigators of occupational fertility differentials have also noticed that infant and child mortality was markedly higher in domestic industrial than in peasant and other agricultural households, thus reducing the net gain to intergenerational replacement rates. Nor is faster population growth on its own, or even a higher ratio of baptisms to burials, as used by Chambers, a sufficient indicator of higher fertility, since opportunities for employment requiring little skill attract immigrants, and immigrants in the fertile age range (as they usually were) will boost baptisms even while age-specific fertility remains constant. There were, further, as several studies have shown, occupational differentials in urban fertility, but here, too, it is difficult to determine, apart from a tendency for the middle classes to display the lower rates, any very meaningful pattern.

The possibility remains, however, of significant occupational differentials, and further detailed studies may throw more light on this important question. So far only certain occupational contrasts have been studied, and these may not necessarily have been those most important in producing changes in national or regional population growth rates: in an eighteenth-century context the demographic behavior of miners, of workers in heavy industry and in textile factories, and of landless agricultural laborers may have been more significant in shifting overall marriage and fertility rates, and these groups are particularly difficult to isolate in historical demographic studies. For the moment we must simply note that fertility may have been to some extent a function of occupation or tenurial status and that since no economic structure or agrarian system is unchanging, overall fertility rates in early modern Europe were capable of being shifted by changes in occupational structure.

So far we have examined the normal reproductive pattern in early modern Europe. In France, however, and to a lesser extent in other countries, this pattern was disturbed—in a way that was capable of significant chronological variation—by the custom, now little known in late-twentieth-century western society, of wet-nursing. It is known that the custom was practiced also in England [*192*] and Italy [*543*], but, to my knowledge, no attempt has yet been made to assess its extent in these countries. The practice may well have existed in other countries, but so far we are without detailed information. In France, where the custom and its demographic consequences have been widely studied, it was the practice for mothers in a fairly wide range of social groups in towns to send their infants shortly after birth to be breast-fed by other women in the surrounding countryside. If this custom had been confined to the middle and upper classes, it might have had only a small demographic significance. It commonly extended, however, into the artisan and shopkeeper classes, and in the French towns in the seventeenth and eighteenth centuries up to 50 percent of mothers put their infants out to wet-nursing. In a study of over three thousand *nourrissons* (infants put out to wet nurses) dying in the Beauvaisis district of northern France during the eighteenth century [*356*], Ganiage showed that 45 percent came from artisan families, mainly in Paris. In Lyons during the 1770s, 22 percent of the *nourrissons* came from middle-class families, 34 percent from silk-workers' families, and 18 percent from miscellaneous artisans' families [*357,* 136]. The practice seems not to have been confined to the large towns: it was, for example, widely used in the little town of Thoissey (which had twelve hundred inhabitants in 1786), a town that itself took *nourrissons* from large towns in the region [*298*]. Generally the wealthier parents used wet nurses in the immediate rural vicinity — in the case of Paris, within a radius of twenty to thirty kilometers, in the case of a smaller town like Lyons, probably no further than twenty kilometers. It was the ability of the *nourrices* within a short distance of the towns to command relatively high fees for their services that drove the lower-income groups further afield, and infants from less wealthy families in Paris were taken as far as 100–150 kilometers in search of *nourrices.*

In addition to the infants voluntarily surrendered by their mothers to distant foster mothers, there were, in all towns and some villages and in other countries as well as in France (there is good evidence, for example, from Fiesole, outside Florence [*543*]) a large number of infants that were put at birth into institutional care, and for the first year or so of life, this, too, involved wet-nursing. There were several categories of these infants in institutional care. Foundlings were infants, mostly newborn, often, but by no means invariably, illegitimate. They were left by their mothers, who were unable or unwilling to keep them and care for them. Often they were left on the steps of the hospitals or infant-caring institutions with little or no attempt to conceal the identity of the mother. Sometimes a note was left to say that the mother would reclaim the child when it was older. Where we have evidence, the number of abandoned infants in early modern Europe appears to have been tragically great — 500 per year in Rouen in the eighteenth century, for example [*288*]. There was also a category of infants that technically were not abandoned but were brought to the hospitals by the parents on the grounds that they were too poor to cope with an additional child: the practice was for the hospital to look after the child until such time as the parents were able to take it back again, perhaps as other older children grew up, or died. In one way or another the hospitals received a significant proportion of the births from the very poorest sector of society, and for these infants, too, wet nurses had to be arranged for and paid. In Lyons, the inability of the hospital, catering for hundreds of foundlings every year, to pay more than half the rate offered by private citizens drove its placements further from the city, up to a radius of sixty to a hundred kilometers from the city from the 1730s [357, 120]. Only the middling poor, probably a substantial proportion of rural society, though a more modest proportion of urban society, nursed all their own infants.

The eighteenth century in France witnessed a quite remarkable development of this practice. The principal vehicle for this expansion was the Hôpital des Enfants-Trouvés in Paris. Founded in 1670, the great majority of its admissions in the late seventeenth century were genuine foundlings — infants left in the streets, at church doors, and on the doorsteps of doctors and accoucheurs. During the eighteenth century, however, the number of foundlings admitted diminished while admissions of legitimate children sent direct to the hospital rose. In its early years the hospital took about five hundred foundlings each year; by the mid-eighteenth century admissions were more than ten times that number. In the single year 1772, 7,672 infants were admitted, of whom over 3,000 came from outside Paris. The business of transporting infants to the hospital, in some cases from several hundred kilometers away, was undertaken by specialist full-time carriers who carried the infants three in a box on their backs. The carrier fed the children with unsuitable cow's milk during the journey of many days, leaving behind those that died and picking up replacements. The mortality en route and on arrival was enormous. The scale of the operation may be gauged by the fact that in the mid-1770s admissions to the hospital from Paris represented 22 percent of all baptisms in Paris [333]. The practice of importing infants into Paris was prohibited from 1773 and probably largely died out during the 1780s, but the traffic outwards from Paris continued. By the 1770s the government of Paris, in an effort to reduce abuses, had institutionalized the traffic through the creation of the Bureau des Nourrices [480]. Garden [357, 122] stresses the role of Rousseau's Emile in influencing the reduction in the custom from the 1760s. He believed that its impact was rapid and great, though putting infants out to be nursed was still a major, if declining, industry in the early nineteenth century. Elsewhere the trade seems not to have abated during the eighteenth century. Corsini takes the view that the abandonment of children increased progressively in Italy from the sixteenth to the mid-nineteenth century, declining thereafter with the diffusion of birth control [543]. There was certainly a sharp rise in abandonments in Lyons during the second half of the eighteenth century — from 3,640 during the 1750s to 8,522 during the 1780s [357, 86].

Regulation might have prevented the worst abuses, but it could have done nothing to alter the fundamental harm to newborn infants of a wagon or rucksack journey that might take several days. Inevitably a proportion of the *nourrissons* failed to survive the journey, but the real slaughter occurred only when the nursing began. The extensive study of burial registers in the receiving parishes has shown that the treatment of the *nourrissons* by the foster mothers was clearly less careful than the natural mothers were likely to have provided. In spite of nature's limitations, some foster mothers can be shown to have taken on, for the sake of the fees, more infants than they can possibly have fed adequately. Of the *nourrices* employed by the hospital of Rouen in 1789, nearly one quarter took four babies or more during the year — 5 percent took eleven babies or more. Catherine Hiard, in the village of Maucomble, took no less than nineteen, of whom only two survived to their first birthday. In contrast, for the infants sent to *nourrices* taking only one baby in the year, the survival rate to age one was as high as 22 percent [288]. The inevitable result was mortality rates among the *nourrissons* enormously higher than among even those infants kept by their own mothers. In Rouen in the 1780s, 91 percent of babies abandoned only a few hours after birth died under age one [288]. In Paris and its suburbs during the years 1773–77, of 21,537 abandoned infants, 18,124 (84.2 percent) died in the course of their first year after admission to a hospital [449, 462]. The sharp contrast between mortality rates of *nourrissons* and of infants kept at home cannot have escaped the mothers who sent their infants away. Either they regarded the higher mortality as a reasonable price to pay for the convenience of avoiding frequent feeds or for the freedom to resume income-producing economic activity; or the practice may be seen as a quite deliberate form of family limitation verging on infanticide.

The corollary of high infant mortality in consequence of the custom of putting newborn infants out to rural wet nurses was the withdrawal of the natural immunity to conception offered by maternal feeding. On the one hand, the *nourrice* herself probably gained some additional contraceptive protection beyond what the normal feeding of her own children would provide, and this probably contributed to some of the long birth intervals and relatively low age-specific fertility rates found in parts of rural France. On the other hand, the urban mothers would be exposed to higher risk of conception, and urban birth intervals in consequence might be much reduced. The classic example of this is the wives of the butchers of Lyons in the eighteenth century, who normally sent their infants immediately after birth to wet nurses in the surrounding Lyonnais. As a distinct occupational group, their mean birth intervals were as low as twelve months. In this group, twelve to sixteenth births per woman were common [357, 96].

So far we have considered the following possible influences on fertility levels: illegitimacy; premarital conceptions; age of women at first marriage; proportion of women ever marrying; age of women at the birth of their last child; temporary interruptions to "normal" marital and reproductive patterns by war, famine, and epidemics; and various influences on marriage and fertility, including occupation and post-partum amenorrhoea prolonged by breast-feeding. Although we have tended to assume that once married, couples in early modern European society submitted themselves necessarily and inevitably to the reproductive pattern dictated by these variables and varied only by specific environmental circumstances, there remained the possibility of defying nature by the employment of some artificial method of birth control. The whole massive influence of the church was brought to bear against this possibility, but the very frequency with which churchmen felt obliged publicly to decry the practice, and the specificity of their references to the practices objected to, suggests that offences against the canon were not unknown [85].

Having regard to well-known references to the use of birth control by mid-eighteenth-century writers like Moheau, and to the very considerable body of writing on this subject in the seventeenth and eighteenth centuries surveyed by Flandrin and others [84–90; 98–100], demographic historians have set out quite specifically to look for clear demographic evidence of the deliberate practice in the early modern period of family limitation within marriage. From the start it was realized that mere fluctuations in marital fertility rates were not in themselves adequate proof of deliberate fertility control: there were too many ways in which, as we have seen, these rates could have been influenced by economic circumstances or other demographic factors. Much ingenuity has been shown in devising ways of detecting deliberate intervention as distinct from fortuitous variation. One uses age-specific marital fertility rates. In the normal circumstances of uncontrolled fertility, age-specific fertility is briefly low in the first, teenage years of female fecundity. It rises rapidly to a peak in the twenties and then falls off with slowly gathering momentum to disappear completely at an age somewhere between the mid-thirties and the late forties, but on the average, as we have seen, at about forty. Apart from brief periods at the very beginning and end of the reproductive period the curve is convex. If, however, the normal pattern is distorted by deliberate birth control, then fertility in one or more age groups will be lowered, and the naturally convex curve will become concave.

Concavity of the age-specific fertility curve is taken as evidence of the employment of deliberate birth control.

Another method has been developed more recently by Dupâquier and Lachiver [348]. Its starting point is birth intervals. The birth intervals shown, for example, in table 3.5 are means of many fairly disparate birth intervals of many individual couples. In any community there will be some couples whose physiology or social and economic circumstances will tend to lead them to produce births at fairly short intervals and others whose circumstances equally naturally will conduce to long intervals. Couples deliberately controlling births, however, will, even if they are not 100 percent successful, at least succeed in lengthening the intervals between the births of their children. If birth intervals in any community are classified into four spacings — under 18 months, 19–30 months, 31–48 months, and over 48 months — a marked increase in the percentage of all birth intervals in the third and fourth classes (particularly the fourth) will indicate an increase in the number of couples deliberately attempting to control their fertility. Note that it is only changes in the proportion of birth intervals falling in each class that matters, not the absolute levels.

A third method looks at the mean age of women at the birth of their last child, on the assumption that attempts to limit family size are more likely to operate at the end rather than at the beginning of the reproductive period [81, 7]. For most of the early modern period in Europe the mean age of women at the birth of their last child kept very close to age thirty-nine or forty. Figures substantially below these, such as one of 28.7 for women married under the age of thirty in Flins-sur-Seine between 1815 and 1839 [349, 9], must indicate deliberate use of birth control. Generally speaking, the earlier women married, the earlier they tended to give birth to their last child. In late-eighteenth-century Sweden, for example, there was a significant difference between the mean age at the birth of the last child of women married under the age of twenty-five and that of women married over twenty-five — a difference of over two and a half years: between 38.0 for those marrying earlier and 40.6 for those marrying later [630]. Since this phenomenon was widespread in all periods and places, it would probably be unwise to ascribe it to deliberate birth control. Thus, the safest test classifies the married female population by age at marriage and compares the proportion of last births over, say, age thirty-six or forty at different periods. A substantial diminution will indicate deliberate restriction at the top end of the age range.

All these detective devices have been employed in the search for deliberate birth control in early modern Europe, and they have indeed shown that the churchmen's concern at the ineffectiveness of their teaching was not misplaced. Most of the examples of the use of birth control before the late eighteenth century that have come to light have been largely confined, however, to fairly narrow social groups among the aristocracy and bourgeoisie. The very first work effectively to employ the technique of family reconstitution—Louis Henry's 1956 study of the Genevan bourgeoisie [683]—revealed all the signs of widespread use of deliberate birth control among this relatively wealthy urban group: very long birth intervals, particularly in the higher parities; an abnormally high proportion of childless couples; and age-specific fertility curves that were consistently and markedly concave.

Henry's Genevan study was followed by studies of the aristocracies of both France [438] and Britain [208-9]. These studies showed the extensive, growing use of birth control from the late seventeenth century producing fertility rates and birth intervals substantially at variance with those of the general population as revealed in parochial studies. With mortality substantially below national rates, the aristocracies could afford to reduce their fertility; indeed their desire to preserve estates intact and their custom of huge dowries created a certain compulsion to do so. In both France and Britain the employment by the aristocracies of birth-control practices within marriage was supplemented by very low proportions of both men and women marrying. More recently, Perrenoud has shown [688] that the practice of birth control was not confined, as Henry implied, to the bourgeoisie of Geneva, but went right through Genevan society. In the first half of the eighteenth century, when 35 percent of the birth intervals of upper-class families in Geneva were in the longest class (forty-nine months or longer), 32 percent of middle-class birth intervals also were in that class, as were 30 percent of lower-class intervals. Blacker [303] believed that the French bourgeoisie, too, was already practicing birth control within marriage by the early eighteenth century and quoted (in translation) from a play of 1706:

All excesses are fatal to us bourgeoisie.
We must on occasion from pleasure abstain,
Having only those children we well can maintain.
Tis better to nurture with care just one child
Than produce half a dozen and let 'em run wild.

Knowledge of methods of birth control and the economic justification of their use were obviously not confined to the upper classes in the late seventeenth and eighteenth centuries, and historical demographers have naturally directed their analyses very deliberately towards the detection of the possibility of its existence in wider social contexts. Generally speaking, they have satisfied themselves that the use of birth control within marriage did not exist extensively, at least in rural society, before the later decades of the eighteenth century. In almost all rural and urban reconstitution studies, fertility rates and birth intervals are consistent with normal uncontrolled fertility within the parameters discussed earlier. Age-specific fertility curves were firmly convex, and, apart from the periodic short-run crises, the only variables for regulating fertility were the age at marriage and the proportion of women marrying, with an unknown, but perhaps very small, extent of abortion and infanticide (in its various forms) as additional, post-conception aids to family limitation. If the presently available evidence does not support the widespread use of birth control in rural Europe before the later decades of the eighteenth century, some reconstitution studies have nonetheless led their authors to believe that birth control was practiced within marriage in some areas. Winberg [630, 340–41] finds some evidence for its employment in a part of rural Sweden in the last quarter of the eighteenth century, and Andorka believes that it was employed in late-eighteenth-century Hungary [125–27].

How were births controlled in earlier centuries? The mechanical and pharmaceutical contraceptive devices widely employed in the late nineteenth and twentieth centuries can be ruled out. It is commonly assumed by demographic historians that coitus interruptus was the most widely used practice. This is notoriously unreliable, however, and it is quite possible that abstention, which is, after all, 100 percent reliable, was more generally the means. Abortion and infanticide (mainly by exposure) were also employed, but unless in the latter case the birth was concealed, the practice would not show up in fertility statistics.

The weight of evidence at the moment suggests very strongly that all these regulators were employed exclusively in the service of the maintenance of the short-run balance. That did not, of course, preclude the possibility that in making their own demographic adjustments to their understanding of their immediate economic and social situation, individual couples might not have adopted a pattern of demographic behavior that, when aggregated into the demographic trends of whole communities and nations, would result in changes in the secular trends. This possibility will be examined in chapter 6.

4

The Instability
of Mortality

THE PREVIOUS CHAPTER SHOWED that short-run movements of fertility in early modern Europe were primarily responses to disturbances of the demographic equilibrium brought about by the mortality crises; their function was the speedy restoration of "normality." With mortality, on the other hand, short-run instability was endemic and at the mercy of exogenous forces. This chapter will examine the principal features of mortality behavior—dramatic short-run fluctuations, low expectation of life, high infant and child mortality, and a high endemic and epidemic incidence of infectious diseases—which were common to the whole of *ancien régime* Europe and in sharp contrast with the conditions that ultimately evolved in the nineteenth and twentieth centuries.

The demographic crises of the early modern period have already been mentioned frequently without any attempt at a serious definition. As so often happens in the quantitative approach to history, however, the minute we attempt to define our concepts, we run into difficulties. No one seriously disputes that a mortality crisis involves a short period when the number of deaths sharply exceeds the normal. But in an era of sharp, short-run fluctuations, what is "normal" mortality is hard to define. Various suggestions for establishing "normal" levels have been made [*67; 256; 557*]. Each has its merits, depending on the preference given to practicality or precision. They all involve striking some means of burials in a short run (between five and ten years) of non-crisis years before, or before and after, the crisis year or years. This sounds simple enough until one realizes that there is little agreement about the ideal "year" for this purpose. When the study of mortality crises was initiated by Jean Meuvret's famous article of 1946 [*442*], there was an assumption of a close correlation between crises and harvest fluctuations, and a virtue was seen in relating the number of burials, not in the calendar year, but in the harvest year, from August round to July, with grain prices as the most obvious indicator of the plenty or scarcity of food. But as other causes of crises assumed greater importance and the varying seasonality of different killing epidemics was appreciated, the limitations of harvest-year measurement became apparent. A crisis originating exclusively in a harvest failure might well make its impact on burials neatly within the twelve months of a harvest year; but one originating in an epidemic of, say, dysentery, which struck commonly between June and September, would show a much lesser impact when divided between two harvest years than when located in a single calendar year. In recognition of the diminished role nowadays accorded to harvest failure on its own, most crisis studies have reverted to the use of the calendar year.

When problems of "year" and "normality" have been resolved, there is still the question of how large an increase of mortality constitutes a crisis: some annual fluctuations of even "normal," non-crisis mortality must be expected. Livi Bacci has suggested that not less than a 50 percent increase above normality should qualify as a *petite crise,* reserving the heights of a fourfold increase and more for the *grandes crises* [554, 10]. Fixing the normal mortality, however measured, as 100 allows severity to be measured simply as a percentage of the normal: a figure of 200 indicates a doubling, 300 a trebling, and so on.

It is realized, of course, that the impact of crises on demographic growth or decline was determined as much by the frequency of crises as by their severity, and any attempt to assess the role of the crises must take account of scale in both dimensions. Here again, measures have been devised, and some assessment is possible. For example, Schofield showed [256] that out of a sample of fifty-four English parishes throughout the long period 1540–1809, four never experienced a crisis (defined here as an annual mortality of twice the "normal"); at the other extreme, two parishes experienced such crises no less than fourteen times. Half of the parishes suffered such crises between two and five times in the two-and-a-half-century period. Every long series of burials, however, illustrates its individual pattern of recurring crises. Two examples at random from the many hundreds now available will illustrate this diversity. The parish of Os in Norway experienced an annual average of fifty-seven deaths in the non-crisis years between 1669 and 1735. There were nine crises in this sixty-six year period when mortality increased by not less than 50 percent. In the most acute of these crises, that of 1733, mortality was three times the normal, while in two others it doubled. Though the crises came irregularly, they averaged once every eight or nine years [577, 33]. At the other end of Europe, in the town of Talavera de la Reina in the province of Toledo in Spain, for which there are very comprehensive data, crises involving at least a doubling of the number of deaths occurred three times during the seventeenth century, in 1622, 1658–59, and 1699, and there were seven lesser peaks [654].

Where, however, the assessment of the changing impact of the crises has largely failed is in not taking account of the third — the spatial — dimension. Indeed, few of the students of crises seem to worry about this dimension very much, yet it is a very vital dimension. Every crisis will follow its own unique geographical pattern. The very nature of disease etiology will ensure more widespread infection in some areas than in others, while climatic variation at both micro and macro levels will ensure an uneven incidence of harvest failure. The result must be a possibility of mortality being more severe the smaller the area studied, simply because a wider area will inevitably involve some averaging of more severely affected areas with less severely affected ones. And given that the basic unit of measurement is almost always the parish, one would expect a small parish to show more acute crises than a large one but possibly to be affected less frequently, since some areas always escape some infections. Similarly, one would expect less drastic fluctuations in a town comprising several parishes than in a one-parish village. Since the survival of registers and the quality of extant registers is quite erratic, it is rarely possible to study mortality fluctuations comprehensively in a wide area, so it is rather unlikely that we shall ever be in a position to assess the total impact of the mortality crises on population growth, in spite of the apparent wealth of information. One valuable exercise taking account of this dimension, has been undertaken, however [554, 51–52]: for the crisis of 1590–91 in Tuscany, burial series in eighteen parishes have been studied. In sixteen of these series mortality rose during these two years by 40 percent or more compared with the "normal"; in four, burials rose to four times the normal or more; in another four to three times; and in three to twice. In the crisis of 1648–49, for which thirty-six burial series were available in the same region, thirty-two showed at least a fifty-percent rise, and in twenty mortality rose to at least three times the normal. These are valuable indicators of extremely widespread rural incidence of mortality crises. In the serious famine crisis of Scotland between 1695 and 1699, for example, mortality as measured by a national index rose 44 percent between the "normal" years of the early 1690s and the peak crisis year of 1697; but in the badly hit rural eastern lowland region mortality in a group of nine parishes rose more than threefold in the peak year for that area, 1699, while in the same year the single parish of Spott suffered almost a tenfold rise in the number of deaths [633, 164–86].

Crises arose in early modern Europe from a variety of causes. Fundamentally, people died in a crisis either from sheer starvation or from illness probably of infectious origin. There has been a tendency recently, initiated by Baehrel in his classic study of Basse-Provence [287] and supported colorfully by Chaunu [325, 1162–63], to argue that actual starvation was rare, that the agricultural system of early modern Europe was, in fact, capable in all but the rarest exigencies of feeding its people. It is true, of course, that people rarely died of actual starvation and that the cause of death in a *crise de subsistances* was generally some specific illness; but there is little doubt that in many situations of serious food shortage the disease causing death was induced by desperate undernourishment. In the context of mortality crises the issue was the variability of harvests from one year to another. The nature of peasant agriculture seldom allowed for production much in excess of normal needs. Cash to pay rents or meet the few needs that could not be satisfied domestically was generally raised by separate cash crops or animal production. The result was that harvests not too severely subnormal were met by consuming the cash crops and running into debt, or, *in extremis,* consuming the next year's seed. But in the Irish potato famine of 1846 there was even a reluctance to broach the cash crop set aside for rent payment lest nonpayment led to eviction, a real possibility in an overpopulated country: people actually starved with stocks of food at hand [532]. One way or another, however, the ill effects of one inclement year could generally be countered. What was really damaging was a succession of subnormal harvests — in two successive years, or, as in Scotland in the 1690s, in three or four years out of five. In Finland, poor harvests in 1693 and 1695 left the country ill-prepared for a disastrous harvest in 1696. In one area of 217 villages, only 12 had a normal crop in 1696, 158 reported a poor crop, and 47 (more than 20 percent) were almost without a crop or had none at all. In the whole county of Tavastland-Nyland investigated by Jutikkala, the crop in general was hardly one third of normal. A population of nearly one hundred thousand was at risk, and seed stocks were consumed as food, so that in spite of favorable weather in 1697, very little food was available that year. Jutikkala estimates the loss of population in that county in the single year 1697 at not less than one third, and he suggests that food supplies sufficed for the winter 1697–98 only because by then the demand for grain had been so reduced by the sheer decline in the number of consumers. Contemporary comment makes it quite clear that though epidemic diseases may in some cases have been the proximate cause of death, the root cause of the mass mortality in Finland in 1697 was plain starvation [602].

A sufficent number of parish registers, mostly relating to small towns, have survived for Scotland in the early 1620s to illustrate the course there of the terrible famine of 1623. In this case, too, a deficient crop in 1621 reduced stocks of both food and seed and the health and strength of the poorer people, so that the disastrous harvest of 1622 left the population with very little support until the 1623 harvest was avail‑ able. The situation was exacerbated by cattle murrain. In 1623, in the words of one contemporary, "many died in the streets and on highway sydes for verie want of food, famished." Another commented that "in the end there was a greath death of persons of all ranks, but speciallie of the poore, which dyed through famine in the fields and the hie ways." In Dunfermline there were 442 burials in 1623 compared with 28 in the nor‑ mal year 1620. Kelso, with less than 100 deaths in a normal year, experi‑ enced over 400 in 1623, while Dumfries suffered a fivefold increase [633, 116–26]. Appleby [159] and Rogers [252] have shown how this famine afflicted northwestern England similarly, while Drake's figures [186] also show 90-, 64-, and 94-percent increases in burials, respectively, in three areas of the West Riding of Yorkshire in the same year compared with the averages of the preceding five years; but there is little evidence of this famine crisis affecting English districts further south.

Famine in early modern Europe was certainly a cause of death, and it is merely playing with words to insist that death from starvation was unknown or rare. It is absurd to deny the existence and killing effect of *crises de subsistances* when there was a close and exact correlation be‑ tween food prices and mortality.

Subsistence crises, then, were one kind of crisis. They might well be associated with some kind of epidemic, a particular or varied infection; but clearly food prices show that many crises were quite independent of harvest fluctuations. Epidemics of infectious diseases struck quite ran‑ domly; their irregular attacks were independent of the irregular harvest cycles. Occasionally, inevitably, the two cycles peaked at the same time, and some of the most severe crises, like those in Spain in 1597–1603 and 1647–52 and in France in 1672, resulted from this coincidence. Not infre‑ quently, of course, severe famines allowed an epidemic of a kind that a well-nourished community might have resisted to take hold.

The demographic effects of epidemics, like those of crises of all ori‑ gins, were determined by their spatial spread as well as by their severity and frequency. Few epidemics have ever reached a continental scale. The early modern period in Europe was sandwiched between two such epi‑ demics — the Black Death of the mid-fourteenth century and the cholera of the 1830s — but, curiously enough, there are no such major episodes during the intervening centuries. Bubonic plague epidemics moved around Europe throughout most of the period, and Biraben's recent comprehensive survey [62] has shown that there were few years when the disease was not attacking somewhere. But after the initiation of the great pandemic in the late 1340s one can hardly talk of a *European* epidemic: on the European scale one might say that the disease became endemic but that particular countries, regions, or places experienced the disease as periodical epidemics. There was no single year or group of years like the late 1340s, when it was possible to see it as a general European phenomenon. But below the continental scale there were many local and regional epidemics, and every country from the south to the north of Europe and from the east to the west experienced them. But epidemics at even the national level, such as the influenza of England in 1557–59 or the bubonic plague of France in 1623, were rare. Most epidemics were quite local, killing perhaps a significant proportion of the population, but in a relatively restricted area. The last great bubonic plague epidemic in Scotland, for example, in 1644–49, struck Edinburgh and its immediate neighborhood with terrible severity but otherwise afflicted only some isolated areas like Kintyre, whither it was certainly carried by military movements [*633,* 133–49].

Military activities, as the example just cited of the Scottish plague of the 1640s illustrates, were also great creators of crises. Armies and their camp followers provided one of the most regular forms of migratory movements in early modern Europe. With their lax camp discipline and their habits of billeting, their wanderings — the map of seventeenth-century Europe, above all, was crisscrossed with a myriad zigzagging of marchings and countermarchings — might have been calculated to pick up whatever disease was going and to disperse it with maximum efficiency. Bacteria need carriers, but peasants, even townsfolk in the early modern times, moved little and then mostly short distances; but wars put civilians on the move as refugees, and refugees, undernourished and disease-prone, were good carriers of infection. Not only did armies infect, but they also deprived civilians of foodstuffs. Armies expected to live off the land, and the effects of requisitioning for soldiers' rations were doubled by the voracious demands of the cavalry and transport horses. In 1658 Polish, German, and Austrian armies moved to the support of Denmark to drive out a Swedish army under Charles X. The Polish Army, in particular, established itself during 1659 in an area of southern Jutland and northern Schleswig. Apart from engaging in sporadic fighting against their allies the Brandenburgers and the local Danes for the possession of the limited stocks of food in the area, the Poles also brought with them typhus, which they spread quickly through the civilian population. "The Poles drove us from house and home," recorded one local source for 1659, "treated us brutally, and took away all we had, cattle and corn and everything we possessed, so that many were doomed to die of hunger; and so...there are only two, three, four persons left alive in every parish, and many corpses are eaten up in the houses by dogs." Parish after parish reported the death of almost all their inhabitants. By means of an examination of parish registers and other documents, Lassen has shown how the parishes in a triangular area bounded by the towns of Vejle, Ribe, and Haderslev (about thirty to forty miles distant from each other) suffered population losses averaging 80 percent and in some places approaching 100 percent. Nearly thirty years later 10–20 percent of the holdings in some of these parishes were still vacant, while four parishes in the center of the area had not recovered their 1650 level of population by 1769. The Danish civilians died from starvation and disease imposed on them by an alien army: there was no serious fighting, no battles, merely a military occupation [605]. Similarly, in 1527–29 most of northern Italy suffered from famines caused by marauding armies requisitioning and destroying crops or by the cutting of supply routes for grain imports, as well as from epidemics of plague spread by invading armies [558]. In France, Benedict [293] attributed Rouen's population decline of more than a quarter between 1562 and 1594 largely to the wars of religion, and Parker similarly ascribed the depopulation of parts of the Netherlands in the late sixteenth century to the war arising out of the Dutch Revolt [518]. Examples of this phenomenon from Germany during the Thirty Years' War have not been quoted only because this tragedy is generally much better known [494]; but it remains the classic case study of the military causation of mortality crises.

It is seldom possible, of course, to subdivide population losses of this kind into their component parts of death at the hands of the military, death from disease brought in by the military, death from starvation created by the depredations of the military, and population loss by the flight of refugees. Undoubtedly the last was important, and statements about population loss due to wars should be examined carefully to see how soon after a catastrophe they were made. The depopulation of a district by death and the temporary out-migration of the refugees in time of war created a vacuum that attracted the return of population with the coming of peace or the moving on of the armies. Gutmann has shown recently [107–8] that there were wide variations in the capacity of communities or regions to recover population quickly from war losses. In a detailed study of an area of southern Belgium much visited by the armies of the seventeenth century, he has shown how quickly in some cases the populations made good their war losses. Gutmann saw good land, markets, and attractive tenurial conditions as the keys to the speed with which populations returned and made good their war losses.

There were, then, three distinct sources of mortality crises: famine, epidemics, and war—Malthus's three positive checks. In reality, however, whatever the basic cause of a crisis, epidemic disease generally took over, so that mortality crises of all kinds very commonly appear as great increases in the number of deaths from infectious diseases.

A mortality crisis interrupted normal population growth in a rather complex way. Obviously the initial check to growth came from the sudden increase in the number of deaths, but these deaths, in their turn, directly affected other determinants of the rate of population‚ growth. Initially, marriages declined, owing to the death or serious illness of one or both partners to a prospective marriage or to an unwillingness to enter this kind of long-term commitment to the future in such disturbed times. In the severe crisis year of 1759, for example, in a group of parishes around Giessen in Germany, marriages declined by 40 percent [497, 120]. In the famine year of 1694 in Tourouvre-au-Perche, a small town of less than two thousand inhabitants to the west of Paris, when mortality rose threefold, marriages were a mere one third of the usual number [324, 246–47]. In two Staffordshire towns in midland England marriages ceased altogether in several crises of the late sixteenth century [241]. But as heads of households died, the pressure for new marriages recovered and increased, and, perhaps even before the crisis had run its full course, marriages might pick up. As the need to reequip vacant holdings or domestic industrial units with the necessary family teams reasserted itself, they might for a period even run at higher than normal rates. Once the wave of crisis-induced marriages was over, however, marriages had to fall once again to subnormal levels, given the decimation of the relevant age groups during the crisis.

Births, too, inevitably declined in a crisis, adding to the loss of population and increasing the task of recuperation in the post-crisis period. Expectant mothers died; starvation and illness increased the number of miscarriages and stillbirths; there was an increase in the abandonment of infants, a form of infanticide, given the extremely high rate of mortality of *enfants trouvés;* starvation induced amenorrhoea and prevented conceptions; and even couples not so seriously affected physiologically by the crisis showed a natural reluctance to conceive with the future so uncertain. In due course, the wave of crisis marriages would combine with a desire to replace children lost during the crisis to produce a post-crisis "bulge" of births. Perrenoud has shown [693] how even during a plague epidemic in Geneva in 1636–37 the desire of parents to make good the plague losses actually produced a greater-than-usual number of births during the crisis. Generally speaking, births tended to fall off rather more during a famine than during an epidemic unaccompanied by food scarcity.

While recent research has thrown up innumerable examples of particular crises and has been able to show just how marriage and fertility responded to the sudden upsurge of deaths, it remains extraordinarily difficult to arrive at an assessment of the role either of any particular crisis or of crises in general in determining the rate of growth or decline of populations. In individual parishes or towns it often is not difficult to assess the net loss of population and, by relating this to the total population and to "normal" rates of growth, to calculate how many years were required to make good the effect of a crisis. Livi Bacci has suggested [554, 9] that the duration of the period of recuperation is the most realistic measure of the seriousness of a crisis, since crises may be liable to affect the capacity of a community to recover in different ways perhaps through variations in the age- or sex-incidence of the mortality. But in contexts wider than those of single parishes or towns the effect of crises on demographic growth is determined by the combination of the three scales of severity, frequency, and geographical spread, and, as we have seen, we are less well-served with data on the second and third of these scales. It is reasonably clear, however, that in most, if not all, parts of western Europe in "normal," non-crisis times throughout the early modern era there was normally some excess of births over deaths: growth, in other words, was the normal demographic condition. Without crises, growth must have been continuous, though of course in early modern Europe continuous growth, even at low rates, would itself have been a disequilibrating condition. To an extent dependent upon their severity, frequency, and ubiquity, crises checked population growth and may therefore be regarded as the checks set in motion by the disequilibrating character of "normal" growth. Whether increasing, stagnating, or declining, population in early modern Europe progressed in sawtooth fashion, which is why isolated census counts in this period taken at a specific moment in time carry less meaning than do those of today and why vital rates (crude birth and death rates) dependent upon them are also unreliable guides to trends in anything other than the extremely short run.

Even when epidemic disease was not the originating source of a mortality crisis it was, as we have seen, mostly the proximate cause of the mortality. The key to population growth or decline in early modern Europe lay, beyond doubt, both in the ebb and flow of epidemic tides of particularly infectious diseases and in the secular shifts of endemic levels of diseases. Of all the infectious diseases taking part in these processes bubonic plague was the preeminent arbiter of population growth rates. Until the middle of the seventeenth century this terrifying disease was seldom absent on an epidemic scale from any part of Europe for much more than a decade and was mostly present permanently at a low endemic level, at least in the great cities. More than any other single factor, the comings and goings of bubonic plague determined whether and where population would grow, stagnate, or decline.

We are dealing in early modern Europe with a wave of plague epidemics that exploded initially in the fourteenth century with the Black Death and lasted in western Europe (barring one or two isolated outbreaks) until the mid-seventeenth century and in eastern Europe until the mid-nineteenth century. There had been earlier epidemic waves in the fifth and ninth centuries, and the wave starting in the fourteenth century lasted within and outside Europe into the twentieth century. It is believed that within the half-millenium of its European history there was some variation in the severity of the recurring epidemics. Livi Bacci [554, 46–47] is of the opinion that after the initial ferocity of the fourteenth century there was some diminution of the intensity of attacks in the later fifteenth and sixteenth centuries. It should not be thought, however, that this implied a steady decline in the virulence of the infection after the Black Death: the epidemics of the first half of the seventeenth century matched once again the ferocity of those of the second half of the fourteenth century.

How was it possible for a single disease to remain the most active killer of humans for so long a period? We should concentrate on the bubonic form of plague because other known forms of the disease were not common, although the pneumonic form probably occurred during the Black Death itself. Bubonic plague, the least lethal of the known forms, nonetheless killed 60–80 percent of those it attacked. This fact alone goes a long way towards explaining why plague dominated the mortality crises of the fourteenth to seventeenth centuries in western Europe. To say that it is highly infectious is to beg a very important question that has not yet been entirely satisfactorily resolved. Broadly, there are two schools of thought over the problem of plague etiology. Ladurie [70, 632] called them recently the "English rat flea school" and the "French human flea school." Plague is primarily an epizootic of rodents, principally, though not exclusively, rats. The issue at debate concerns how the infection is transmitted from rat to man and from man to man. Rats have always been close companions of man: they have shared his houses, ships, and food stores. The agent of plague infection is the bacillus *Pasteuralla pestis,* which is injected into the bloodstream of both rats and man through the bloodsucking bite of a flea. The rat flea, primarily *Xenopsylla cheopis* (though other flea vectors are known), picks up the *P. pestis* by gorging on the blood of an infected rat. The bacilli breed rapidly in the flea's stomach until they fill it, leaving the flea unable to take in its customary food. To increase the flea's problems, its rat host dies of plague and goes cold. The starving flea looks for a new host of correct temperature and finds one on one of the rat's human neighbors. As it attempts to feed on human blood, it disgorges plague bacilli into the victim's blood, and the infection is transmitted.

If this is the whole story of the chain of infection, then certain limits impose themselves. The most common form of European rat in the early modern period, the black rat, *Rattus rattus,* was very restricted in its movements. It was extremely domesticated, nesting mainly in crevices and thatches of human habitations and requiring human aid in the form of wagon or ship transport to move further than a few hundred yards. This last fact is important to remember when considering the spread of the disease, since without human agency the rat fleas, dependent on the rats themselves for transport, would have great difficulty in moving from one human settlement to another. Thus an etiology restricted to rat fleas requires the transmission of rats or their fleas in human baggage or transport — not an impossible requirement, but a limiting one.

The French school, most recently exemplified by Biraben's magnificent treatise [62], allows additionally for the transmission of the bacillus by the human flea, *Pulex irritans*. The human flea, microbiologically speaking, is a far less efficient vector of the plague bacillus, but it is said to have compensated in numbers for what it lacked in capability. Humans were obviously more mobile over longer distances than rats. An etiology that allowed the human flea to carry *P. pestis* from human to human imposed no barriers on the spatial spread of infection wherever there was human, commercial intercourse. There was a possibility of an infection chain from rat to human via rat flea, from human to human via the human flea, and, if necessary, back to rats again via the rat flea. It seems extremely unlikely that a plague epidemic could be initiated, however, without the prior existence of an epizootic [73].

Once an epidemic is started, either etiology will explain the spread of infection, though the French human-flea school, supported as it is with appropriate caution by the leading plague epidemiologists, allows an easier, less restricted passage of infection. There are, in any case, a number of climatic limitations on both etiologies: both fleas and bacilli are selective with regard to the temperatures at which they flourish, and it seems that human fleas may be more or less effective in this role in certain types of climatic conditions. Both types of flea flourished, in varying degrees, in most parts of Europe, with the exception of the extreme north, and in the Mediterranean region.

The easier it becomes to understand the persistence of plague infection once initiated, the harder it becomes, however, to understand how the repetition of epidemics was ever halted. There was, throughout the early modern period and until the introduction of the antibiotics in the 1940s, no known cure for bubonic plague. The only hope of countering it lay in prevention and limitation. Effectively to prevent or limit disease of this nature, however, calls for some understanding of its etiology, and this was not available until the late nineteenth century. Yet, apart from a limited number of isolated outbreaks, which did not gain a wide footing, bubonic plague ceased to be a killer in all western European countries from various dates in the seventeenth century between the 1640s and the

1670s. Given the major role of plague in determining secular mortality levels in late medieval and early modern Europe, this disappearance is of the first demographic significance. How, then, is it to be explained?

Various hypotheses have been put forward — the replacement of the black rat, *Rattus rattus,* by the brown rat, *Rattus norvegicus;* the cutting of east-west trade routes by the Ottoman advance into southeastern Europe; some change in the virulence of the bacillus itself; a gradual build-up of protective antibodies in the western European human and rat populations. None of these is convincing, on account of chronological facts, the heightening of the virulence of the attacks of the early and mid-seventeenth century, or the persistence of plague in eastern Europe and the non-European Mediterranean well into the nineteenth century.

There is a growing body of evidence to show that the defeat of bubonic plague may well have been a triumph of human organization. It is true that so long as plague was assumed to be a manifestation of God's anger at man's sinfulness there was really nothing man could do about it beyond prayer, propitiation, and exhortation to a reduced level of sin: these were, of course, urged with commendable persistence by the church, with total ineffectiveness, though, miraculously, with surprisingly little loss of face. Some civil and medical authorities, however, observing the process of infection, in particular its arrival in a community after some indication of its prior existence in some other place with which the community shared a boundary or had a commercial connection, proposed various forms of isolation in an effort to break the chain of infection. It is interesting that even at the first outbreak of the Black Death in Italy in 1348 some cities, drawing on experience gained in earlier epidemics of other infectious diseases (notably leprosy), attempted to impose quarantines [*541*]. Though ineffective during the Black Death, the quarantine idea persisted in later epidemics.

It took a long time to develop the techniques of effective *cordons sanitaires* and quarantine management. It called, firstly, for a degree of efficiency of civil government that barely existed in much of late medieval Europe. Perhaps more important, however, was the clash between mercantile interests, often the source of urban political power, and the effects of quarantine. A quarantine involved an interruption of trade either with particular places where plague was known to exist or with the entire outside world for anywhere between a few months and a year or more. This was not good for business, and, human cupidity being what it is, there was a reluctance on the part of the local authorities (often themselves merchants) to take the drastic step of ordering a quarantine and on the part of merchants to comply with one if ordered. As plague epidemics recurred, however, and, particularly from the early seventeenth century, as epidemics were seen to be selective rather than universal, quarantines and *cordons sanitaires* were continued, and management techniques evolved. Even merchants began to see the wisdom of preferring life to profits. Local health boards were widely created in towns, which had the advantage over villages of potentially effective local-government institutions. The Black Death led to their creation in a few Italian cities, and the ensuing plague epidemics of the late fourteenth and fifteenth centuries stimulated their establishment more generally. Initially these boards were ephemeral, becoming permanent later. By the end of the sixteenth century all major Italian cities had permanent health boards. Similar boards appeared in France later, mainly during the sixteenth century, while it was the seventeenth century before they appeared in Switzerland and the Low Countries. Health boards had two main functions: the management of measures taken in anticipation of and during an epidemic, which might include the establishment of a *cordon sanitaire* and quarantine lazarets; and the operation at all times of an intelligence service, the object of which was to acquire prior knowledge of the arrival of plague infection in the neighborhood or in any place near or distant with which the town had trading links. Correspondents were appointed in all relevant foreign ports or land centers to keep the health board informed as to the state of the plague infection [*541*, 18–31]. Cipolla [*540*] has provided a dramatic example of the activities of the health board at Prato in Italy during the epidemic of 1630, while there are numerous examples of the operation of the intelligence systems at work in Italy, Switzerland, and France.

Of course, these urban efforts at infection control were not always successful. But we are finding examples of success—witness the experience of Bern in 1669 [*684*, 138–39] and Lourmarin in Provence during the isolated Marseilles outbreak of 1720, superbly described by Sheppard [*478*, 116–27]. However vigorously urban governments of the seventeenth century tried, the odds were against them so long as they worked in isolation. Plague epidemics would march across Europe in the baggage or on the persons of soldiers or merchants or by sea or river in ships. An individual town might, if it were sufficiently vigorous, determined, ruthless, and efficient, keep the infection out. And ruthlessness was not always wanting: when an epidemic struck the small Provence town of Digne in 1629, the inhabitants of the surrounding villages encircled the town with guards, which Biraben describes as having more the appearance of a siege than of a *cordon sanitaire*. There were even, he reported, those among the people of the surrounding villages who went so far as to advocate the destruction of the town with all its inhabitants by means of an incendiary bombardment [*62*, II, 167].

But all this frightened ferocity amounted to no more than local, partial prevention. Without action on a scale wider than anything within the scope of local government, the epidemics must continue. This kind of governmental intervention was made available, for example, on a massive scale when a particularly crass example of human cupidity allowed the Marseilles *cordon sanitaire* to be breached in 1720. The French government ultimately deployed one quarter of the cavalry of the entire French Army and one third of its infantry in the erection of a new *cordon sanitaire* around the province, and the epidemic was contained [*302*]. One hundred years earlier an epidemic of the kind experienced by Marseilles in 1720 would inevitably have spread to the rest of France and, through maritime and overland trade, to many other parts of Europe as well. In the face of a new epidemic in North Sea and Baltic ports in 1711, the English Parliament enacted, and effectively enforced, a severe quarantine for all vessels arriving from infected areas. It repeated this during the Provence outbreak of 1720–22, and on both occasions succeeded in preventing the import of infection [*236*]. Similar rigorous action in Spain kept plague out of that country while it was raging in Marseilles – a port with which many Spanish ports had intimate trading relations – in 1720 [*24*, 221–22].

The tendency for plague infection to spread across Europe from east to west during epidemics had not escaped attention: whatever its ultimate origin, infection entered western Europe from Ottoman territories. When, following the Peace of Passarowitz in 1719, the boundary between the Ottoman and Habsburg empires was newly stabilized further back from the Habsburg heartland than it had been for two hundred years, and the *Militärgrenze* established, the final act of the drama of western European plague was begun. Acting on medical advice, in a series of decrees (the *Pestpatente*) of 1728, 1737, and 1770 the Habsburg government turned the whole nineteen-hundred-kilometer military frontier between the Habsburg and Ottoman empires into a gigantic, permanent *cordon sanitaire*. Movement across the frontier was controlled by the permanent force of *Bauernsoldaten*: the peasants offered settlements in the newly conquered lands in return for a five-month frontier service each year. What may well have been the largest *cordon sanitaire* the world has ever known was underpinned by an intelligence service that alerted the Habsburg government to the state of plague infection in all parts of the Ottoman Empire. In normal times the *Militärgrenze* was permanently manned by a force of four thousand men. On receipt of information about the existence of plague in any part of the Ottoman Empire the force was immediately stepped up to seven thousand. When it was known that plague was present in any part of the southern Balkans, on the Moldau, in Wallachia, Serbia, or Bosnia, the manning was increased to eleven thousand, at which level each watch post along the nineteen-hundred-kilometer frontier was within sight of the next by day and within hearing by night. The quarantine period for any person, transport animal, or goods wishing to cross the frontier was twenty-one days in normal, plague-free times; forty-two days when there were rumors of plague in the Turkish empire; and eight-four days when plague was known to be present in the Balkans. There were elaborate disinfestation programs for travelers, their animals, and their goods during their quarantine in specially built lazarets. Guards were under orders to shoot to kill anyone attempting to evade the control [*146*].

With modifications, this system was maintained until 1873. It was not 100 percent successful in preventing the infection from crossing the frontier, but these occasional inroads were rare and relatively easily contained by the kind of local measures that had been used for centuries.

It is likely that bubonic plague was extinguished in western Europe during the seventeenth century by vigorous local action that prevented the disease from spreading once it appeared and during the eighteenth century by national governmental action that hindered and ultimately prevented the international migration of infection. The key centers for control were the ports, above all the Mediterranean ports, and it was here that failure of control in the eighteenth century led to the last major western European outbreaks—in parts of northern Europe in 1710–11, at Marseilles in 1720, at Palermo in 1743, and at Cadiz in 1800. All these outbreaks were prevented from spreading far, though not without considerable governmental determination and local loss of life. But so long as plague continued to flourish in the Turkish Empire unchecked by communal action, there was a permanent risk of a renewal of epidemics. Only the great Habsburg *cordon sanitaire* of the *Militärgrenze* and the watch at the Mediterranean ports confined the western European outbreaks after the late seventeenth century to manageable proportions.

Bubonic plague continued its periodic culls of human populations in the Turkish Empire because the Porte took no action at either the local or the imperial level of the kind that ultimately proved effective in western Europe on grounds of indifference, religious principle, or sheer governmental incompetence. In 1840, however, almost two hundred years after local action in western Europe had initiated the retreat of the plague, and one hundred years after the iron curtain of the Austrian *Militärgrenze* had set a limit to the age-old east-west drift of infection, the Porte, following a press campaign and the employment of European experts, decided suddenly to begin to apply vigorously and severely throughout the length and breadth of the Turkish Empire anti-plague regulations of the kind elaborated in western Europe over the preceding centuries. Within twelve months plague was virtually eliminated from its last major human reservoir in the European and Mediterranean region [*62,* II, 175].

Ignoring the eighteenth-century aberrations, the disappearance of plague from western Europe was a phenomenon broadly of the second half of the seventeenth century. All other things being equal, the removal of such a major, albeit varying, check on population growth since the fourteenth century ought to have inaugurated a new acceleration of the European population growth rate. In nearly all western European countries the evidence suggests that this did not happen. The great acceleration that initiated the high nineteenth-century growth rates was delayed for a further century. Apart from some compensatory fall in fertility, of which there is some, but far from widespread, evidence, the only explanation can be an offsetting rise in mortality from other causes. The most likely candidates are typhus, smallpox, and tuberculosis, but unfortunately very little indeed is known about the chronology or the changing incidence of any of these diseases. Typhus is believed to have been a virtual newcomer to the European nosology in the very late fifteenth century, and there is evidence that it had achieved the status of a major killing infection by the seventeenth century. Smallpox, too, though known in the Middle Ages, was effectively a new menace in the sixteenth century. There is little doubt that it reached its apogee in the eighteenth century, and there is every sense in talking about a European smallpox pandemic of about 250 years duration, rising in the sixteenth century, reaching a peak in the eighteenth century, and being suppressed and finally conquered, as was plague, by human organization, during the 100 years from approximately the 1760s to the 1860s. Tuberculosis is more of a mystery. There is evidence that this disease accounted for a higher proportion of all deaths in some European countries than any other cause of death by the early nineteenth century, so that it is clear that already by the eighteenth century it was a major killer, if not *the* major killer. Yet very little is known about its rise — assuming that it was not always the major killer it became — during the seventeenth and early eighteenth centuries.

McNeill [71] has singled out two processes to explain in purely biological and ecological terms the changing character of the infectious diseases and the gradual substitution of endemic for epidemic disease during the early modern period. The first was what Ladurie has called the *unification microbienne du monde* [70], accomplished largely by the great expansion of commerce by sea during the early modern period, which, in McNeill's phrase, tended to "homogenize infection" by about 1700. In this process diseases hitherto confined to one region of the world were exchanged among the Old World, the New World, and the East, leading initially, with each new exchange, to what McNeill has disarmingly called "die-offs," of unprotected populations. The Black Death was such a "die-off," as was the holocaust of the natives of the New World in the early sixteenth century on the arrival of the conquerors from the Old. But, as developing commerce gradually established regular contact between all principal world centers of population, possibilities of transmitting "new" diseases to unprotected populations diminished. While much of this traffic involved the infection of hitherto isolated peoples outwards from the European base, Curtin has illustrated the reverse of this coin: Europeans exposed themselves, particularly in the West Indies and West Africa, to the hitherto unfamiliar diseases of these "white Man's graves" [65].

The second, allied process was the human capacity to develop antibodies and establish a modus vivendi with new bacteria; this does not mean that all diseases must ultimately become innocuous as man's protection is acquired, but that after the initial success of a new infection a more stable relationship is gradually created in which the bacteria attack as before, but the degree of immunity acquired is sufficient to restrain mortality to proportions that may permit population growth. Neither of these processes nor their chronologies are susceptible to proof, but they should not be ignored on that account.

Thus, in the broad 150-year period from about 1630 to 1780, though population growth rates accelerated in only a very few countries and even in these only marginally, some important changes were occurring in the character and behavior of mortality. Mortality crises continued in almost all parts of Europe, but their character was changing. War began to play a much reduced part in them, particularly after about 1660. Sheer famine was less obvious, particularly after the 1690s, though severe, often prolonged hunger remained the lot of many of the poorer Europeans. The last great plague epidemics, some of them among the most devastating experienced in the whole pandemic, took place during the 1630s, 1640s, and 1650s. Death from these various causes tended to be concentrated in the great periodic crises. Of course there was "normal" mortality of a non-crisis nature from what might be described as "old age" and endemic diseases that affected all age groups, while infant mortality ran at high levels at all times, though it responded additionally to crises. Of the new diseases only typhus retained largely the same epidemic character. Smallpox mortality fluctuated, but it was primarily of an endemic character, adding recurring epidemics to a high and regular incidence above all among the very young. In the early eighteenth century smallpox was found to be causing 10–15 percent of all deaths in many countries: 80 percent of these deaths were of children under ten, 70 percent of children under two. Smallpox clearly was a major component of the high rates of infant and child mortality in the eighteenth century. The mortality pattern resulting from tuberculosis was different again. It was a disease that took many years to destroy human life, in sharp contrast with plague, which required merely a few days. Tuberculosis mortality was incompatible with mortality crises. While deaths from tuberculosis might rise and fall in a long, secular cycle, they were unlikely to fluctuate significantly in the short run.

It is perhaps not too difficult to explain why mortality in western Europe remained high during the late seventeenth and into the eighteenth century in spite of the disappearance of the plague. The circumstances determining the general level of mortality changed without effectively altering the secular level. In consequence, apart from some particular areas like Spain and Germany, where growth was more in the nature of recovery from exceptionally severe setbacks during the first half of the seventeenth century, population growth rates in most European countries continued to be extremely moderate. The removal of plague was certainly a precondition of more rapid growth, but it was not a sufficient cause.

5   The Movement of Population

MUCH OF THE DISCUSSION in the preceding chapters may seem to have proceeded on the assumption that demographic change in early modern Europe took place within closed communities, that each community reacted to external influences on its mortality by adjusting its marriage and fertility rates so far as possible in the light of the extent of its resources. This process may well have underlain much of the demographic development of the period, but its actual operation was both eased and exacerbated by the movement of population.

Until fairly recently there was a tendency to assume that the population of early modern Europe remained relatively static, that the pressures and traditions in predominantly peasant societies necessarily tied most people to their land. Yet some of the earliest demographic research indicated that in some areas there was an astonishingly lively movement of population, and attempts began to be made to find some methods for the quantitative assessment of this movement. The difficulty was, and has remained, that of finding sources for the study of migration. It is often possible to trace certain kinds of once-for-all migrations—a woman migrating at marriage to her new husband's location, a young person taking up an apprenticeship, an elderly person moving into an urban hospital for care during what may be a final illness. Each of these kinds of movement has been comprehensively recorded in particular types of records—parish marriage registers, apprenticeship indentures kept by guild or borough, admission registers of hospitals—and all these have recently been used widely to illustrate the extent and distances of migration, as well as in attempts to assess chronological variations in the scale and pace of movement. But there were, of course, many other reasons for migration, while many of the migrants whose movements were recorded in these archives may have moved on occasions other than those captured in these sources.

A glance at the bibliography of this book will show that migration in early modern Europe has been widely studied in recent years. The source principally used has been the parish registers, particularly the marriage registers, where it was often the custom to note the parish of origin of a bride or groom not of the recording parish. But apart from permitting study of the catchment area from which spouses were drawn, this source can tell little else about migration. On the other hand, some Swiss burial registers that recorded burials of natives of the parish dying outside the parish as well as within have been particularly valuable in revealing the extent, and often the direction, of emigration [682]. Other valuable studies have been made of another class of parish records: listings of inhabitants, where two or more such documents reveal changes over time in the personnel of a village. Rich, using Elizabethan militia muster rolls [251], was the first to illustrate by this means the rapidity of English population turnover, while two comprehensive listings of the Nottinghamshire village of Clayworth, for 1676 and 1688, respectively, allowed Laslett and Harrison [218] to reveal a turnover of population in twelve years far in excess of that arising merely from deaths and births. For the rest, any kind of document that recorded the presence in one place of someone originating in another has been pressed into service for the purpose of this study. Many towns in early modern Europe kept rolls of burgesses, and in registering admissions to the roll, noted their place of origin if it was outside the town. Some English researchers [172; 182; 203] have made effective use of depositions in ecclesiastical courts, documents in which witnesses notified their place of birth as well as their present residence.

Most of the sources, however, suffer from one vitiating weakness: they rarely indicate more than a single change of residence — the birthplace of someone now resident elsewhere. But many — possibly most — of those who took the decisive step in life of an initial move from their birthplace moved more than once. The record of a death away from a birthplace, however, offers no indication of migrations between the original move away from the birthplace and the place of death, while a record of a new residence during a lifetime — an apprenticeship indenture, say, or a burgess roll — is no guarantee that this was the migrant's last move in life. This difficulty is almost insuperable, and in tracing migration in the past from the extant documentation, we can only make the reservation that our findings must inevitably involve a severe understatement of the extent of movement.

Broadly, the study of these sources has revealed two contrasting types of communities — extremely immobile peasant communities, on the one hand, and much of the rest of the society of early modern Europe, which displayed a remarkably high degree of mobility, on the other. It has always been assumed that peasant society was immobile, since the attachment of families to holdings, and of serfs to estates, inhibited migration beyond that of short-distance interparochial movements of brides or bridegrooms. In remoter parts of Norway, for example, this degree of localization was almost complete: in a mountainous area of central Norway both partners in marriages between members of landowning families were residents of the same parish in all but 2 percent of marriages [612, 93]. In an area of Normandy in the eighteenth century almost three quarters of the small landholders were resident in the parish of their birth at the time of their marriage [448, 348], a degree of immobility confirmed by another study of the same part of France, which showed 70 percent of the males dying in the parish in which they had been born [387, 327].

There can be little doubt that in extensive parts of Europe a very substantial proportion of the population remained rooted to the parish of their birth generation after generation. We should not, however, allow this solid block of immobility to distract our attention from the high mobility of those less directly tied to a particular plot of land. Even the immobile peasants generated more movement than is often suspected, not least because ties with land were ties for a fixed household size. Studies of peasant societies almost always overlook the tendency of their populations to grow except in times of mortality crises: in the long run rural populations grew faster naturally than urban populations in the early modern period. For the natural increase of these populations — the younger sons and daughters — there was usually no livelihood at home: in conditions of virtually unchanging agricultural technology a given acreage of land could not support an increasing population. So even the most static of societies generated some movement. Further, in the southeast the extremely unsettled conditions of the shifting frontier areas of the Ottoman Empire obliged landlords to permit or encourage or even enforce movement of peasants in the process of resettling reconquered territory. For these reasons, assessments of immobility based on the proportion of those buried in a parish who were also born there can be misleading: movement into such parishes (which would be indicated by the burials of those born elsewhere) could be significantly less than movement out.

Many of the rural surplus naturally made their way to the towns — the men in search of apprenticeships to industrial occupations or of the casual employment that was principally available there, the women in search of employment in the textile industry or in domestic service. In many instances these migrations took place along well-worn routes and with the aid of kin who had made a similar move earlier. In France, some extensive rural areas like Flanders, Normandy, the Dauphiné, and the

Massif Central generated permanent surpluses that flowed regularly towards Paris, Rouen, Nantes, Bordeaux, and Lyons [382, 46]. Switzerland, similarly, with a very finite capacity to support population in this era, had a long tradition of emigration northwards and westwards to southern Germany and eastern France: there were always Swiss settlers in Strasbourg, for example. A classic example of this type of movement is the recruitment of London's population during the seventeenth and eighteenth centuries [267; 276]. A net immigration of several thousand a year was necessary to account for the growth of the city in normal times, and the influx accelerated when mortality crises created more vacancies. "The City hath been repeopled," wrote John Graunt in 1662 in respect of the plague epidemics of 1603 and 1625, "let the mortality do what it will."

In migrations of these kinds movement was heavily concentrated among young adults. In the English village of Cardington, in Bedfordshire, about forty miles from London, for example, 84 percent of boys aged ten through fourteen were still living at home in the year 1782, and 91 percent of girls; but of those aged fifteen through nineteen, these percentages had fallen to 22 percent and 71 percent respectively. In this village, clearly, girls stayed at home longer than boys: it was only in the age group 25–29 that the percentage of girls staying at home fell to 22 percent. Many of those that left home remained in another household in the same parish, but more moved out of the parish. Among the males aged 25–29 belonging to families in the parish, 18 percent went to London, half as many again as those who remained at their parents' home [254, 272]. For young adults in eighteenth-century northeastern France mobility rose rapidly in the teens and early twenties to reach a peak at age twenty-five, falling steadily thereafter until the early forties; but in one Italian parish studied where a similar age structure of initial migration was revealed there was a revival of mobility in the fifties [484].

Many English studies have been made of the distances moved by migrants. With the exception of migrants to London, most of these studies bear out Ravenstein's "law" that the number of migrants is in inverse proportion to the distances traveled. From the study of over seven thousand witnesses' depositions in diocesan courts in southern and central England between 1660 and 1730, Clark found that slightly more than half of those who had moved between birth and the time of making their depositions had migrated less than ten miles: only 3 percent of those living in rural parishes at the time of their deposition had traveled more than a hundred miles; the proportion was somewhat higher, as might be expected — 8 percent — for those living in urban parishes [172, 68]. By reason of its size relative to the population of the whole country, London necessarily attracted its immigrants from a wider catchment area. A study of the origins of deponents in London between 1580 and 1639 shows that only 26 percent had been born within London itself and the adjacent counties and that 15 percent had been born as far away as the north of England or further [*182*, 58]. In a group of German parishes in the eighteenth century just over half of entries in marriage and burial registers were of people born in the immediate locality (within 8 kilometers); 12 percent were of people born more than fifty kilometers away, and 4 percent more than one hundred kilometers away [*497*, 660]. Of those born in the seventeenth century and dying over age sixty in the central Swedish parish of Västerfärnebo only 3–4 percent of men and women had been born more than fifty kilometers away, but in the nearby village of Lovö, almost 50 percent had such distant origins [*592*, 73]. The great disparity between these two places seems to have lain in their different economic character. The former was an area of small-scale farming in which an important source of earnings was haulage and the grazing of transport animals; in the latter the location of a royal palace provided employment for specialized labor recruited widely, and the area also became a haven for refugees from the Åland Islands off the Finnish coast during the Great Northern War in 1719–20.

These and many other detailed studies have illustrated the existence in most parts of Europe of a very considerable mobility arising out of what one might call the normal circumstances of social and economic life. While certain classes of documents enable us to assess the extent of the movement, however, they may necessarily be less explicit about the reasons for movement. Marriage, particularly for females, was an obvious and important source of movement, though it might be expected that moves for this reason would be short- rather than long-distance. Most of the remaining causes of movement are related to the search for a livelihood, but the circumstances that impelled people to move in this quest were so varied that they call for closer examination.

The practice of apprenticeship embraced a wide range of economic circumstances, from the pull of the possibility of a lucrative career to the push of rural overpopulation. Whatever the motivation, however, most sets of apprenticeship records studied have revealed that long-distance movement was surprisingly common in this context. Hammer's study of Oxford apprentices in the period 1538–57 revealed [*202*, 201] that 40–45 percent came from the distant areas of Wales and northwestern England. In the seventeenth and eighteenth centuries smaller proportions of apprentices to the cutlery industry around Sheffield in the north of England came from far afield, but this should not surprise us, given the poor returns from employment in this mainly rural domestic industry [*164*, 305]. The larger the town, observed Patten [*243*, 128], the wider its net for catching apprentices.

With the attraction of greater wealth, it is not surprising to find merchants moving greater distances, not least internationally. In a study of the sixteenth-century merchant community of Nantes, Croix found a very wide international group embracing not only Spaniards, Portuguese, and Italians in the fairly large numbers that one might expect to find in an Atlantic port but also some Greek, German, Flemish, Scottish, and African (both Moorish and Negro) merchants [331]. Scottish merchants were prominent also in Sweden, and Scottish names of firms, many originating in migrants of the seventeenth and eighteenth centuries, still catch the eye in Gothenburg today.

Turning from the pull of industry and commerce to agriculture, only new land, or newly available land, could exert quite the same kind of pull. Land drainage was one way of creating such a movement, and this clearly occurred: for example, in Holland in the first half of the seventeenth century newly drained polders drew population from other parts of Holland or even from across the border in Germany [24, 273]. An interesting example of this type of movement is revealed by a Scottish listing of inhabitants. In 1768 a landlord, Lord Kames, moved into the newly drained Kincardine Moss, near Stirling, 170 families mainly from the overcrowded Perthshire highlands. With these highland migrants went also their livestock, including no less than 168 cats, 8 dogs, and 1 sheep [633, 28, 72]. On a larger scale, Chaunu has described [24, 274-5] the colonization from 1766 of the Sierra Morena of southern Spain by several thousand Germans to open up land deserted since the thirteenth century.

Much of the land colonized in this way in the early modern period was made available as a result of war, either through conquest or through the resettlement by newcomers of land long rendered uninhabitable by war. Alsace, for example, ravaged by the Thirty Years' War, attracted a vast immigration after the mid-seventeenth century [411, 157]. So, too, in Hungary, as land was recovered by conquest from the Turks in the late seventeenth and eighteenth centuries, large-scale projects of resettlement were organized by landowners [129, 70-71]. The most striking example of this form of movement was the settlement, after the Peace of Passarowitz in 1719, of new "frontier" zones by the *Bauersolda-ten*, peasants allocated new holdings in reconquered territories on condition of substantial annual military service in defense of the new frontier [146]. These frontier settlements were strengthened in the 1730s and 1740s by large numbers of Wallachian refugees from Turkish rule. Further east many attempts were made during the eighteenth century to settle lands to the north and west of the Black Sea that had been depopulated by centuries of intermittent warfare. There were successful settlements during the 1760s of the Ukraine by immigrants from Poland and other parts of Russia. After the Seven Years' War an estimated eleven thousand German families — mainly those of discharged soldiers, supplemented by others from Lorraine, Belgium, and Italy — settled in the Banat area of present-day Hungary and Romania [*147*, 191–213].

Military activities, scarcely ever absent from wide areas of Europe during the early modern period, were therefore responsible for many large-scale, long-distance movements of population. But military service itself created many individual migrations. Corvisier has estimated that for various reasons, including death and hospitalization, over 60 percent of those who enlisted in the French Army in the eighteenth century never returned to their home parishes [*329*, 193]. Many of the Swiss and Scottish soldiers (up to eight thousand Scots were estimated to have been fighting on the European mainland in the Thirty Years' War) who enlisted in the service of foreign armies never returned to the land of their birth, while in France it was common for young men of military age to leave home in order to avoid the lottery of the call-up. It was possible to do this legally, since in some periods the household staffs of gentry and clergy were exempt from the call-up [*329*, 188–89].

If war and military service were major movers of population, the churches and religious hostility were close seconds. Many of the major migrations resulting from religious differences are well known, such as the flight of protestants from France mainly to Switzerland and England in the sixteenth century and again after the revocation of the Edict of Nantes in 1685. The Anabaptists who fled from Dutch persecution in the sixteenth century settled in Germany, England, Poland, and Russia [*149*, 309–12]. The largest such movement was certainly that caused by the expulsion of the Moriscos from Spain initiated in 1609. Even before the mass expulsion, Castille had shifted some 80,000 Moriscos to other parts of the joint Spanish kingdom in 1569–70, and it has been estimated that about 275,000 of the Moorish population were driven to North Africa between 1609 and 1614 [*655*, 53]. The timing of the expulsion could hardly have been worse, since as a result of the plague epidemics of the late sixteenth and early seventeenth centuries and other setbacks, the population of southern and eastern Spain was already in decline. The province of Valencia took more than a century to recover its pre-expulsion population level, while in most formerly Morisco settlements the influx of Christian population was achieved only at the expense of other areas of Spain, thus setting up a secondary migration at a time of general population stagnation or decline.

Spain chose to rid itself of this active and numerous section of its population at a time when, in any case, it was also experiencing a steady and not insubstantial drain overseas through emigration to its American empire, mainly from Castille. Similar, though certainly smaller, transatlantic emigrations were experienced throughout the early modern period by England, France, and Portugal. Fourteen thousand Scots are reliably estimated to have colonized Ulster in the early seventeenth century, and more crossed the narrow seas between 1688 and 1715 [*633*, 8]. Although some of these subsequently moved on across the Atlantic, enough remained to lay the foundations of some of Ireland's twentieth-century problems.

Though it is possible to categorize each migratory stream according to whether it resulted from religious persecution, war, colonization, or the pursuit of commercial profit or a livelihood, at the root of many of these situations was overpopulation with its consequent threat of poverty and inadequate food supply. Rural populations (which accounted for over three quarters of early modern Europe) tend to prefer the security of land to the uncertainties of wider economic possibilities. The attachment to the land that characterizes small farmers the world over is so fierce that a decision to desert a family holding can only signify a very serious imbalance between land and people. Without steady improvement in agricultural technology, however, sooner or later the population of individual settlements or holdings must outstrip the yield of the land. In this situation the subdivision of holdings, frequently resorted to, provides no answer: very small holdings yield no more per acre than do small holdings. When this imbalance is reached, two things generally happen: the absence of any safety margin, even in years of a normal or good harvest, exposes the population to starvation in the recurring years of subnormal harvests; and there begins a movement out of the area of the natural surplus of population. It is true that agricultural yields were most likely to rise on large farms with easier access to capital and markets, and where larger units began to predominate, as in England, the checks to population growth imposed by subsistence crises were probably least. There may also be some truth in the suggestion that population pressure is a powerful and, in the long run, effective pressure for agricultural improvement: in anything less than the long run, however, population growth has not always stayed its hand until agricultural yields advanced.

There is no shortage of evidence—especially from the seventeenth century—either of the periodic subsistence crises, as we saw in chapter 4, or of migration enforced in this way by overpopulation. The mountainous regions of central and southern France long provided a good illustration of this situation. Nadal and Giralt have traced the very considerable movement of French migrants from the central Pyrenees and the western side of the Massif Central through to Spain. It was a stream that reached its maximum flow in the middle and later sixteenth century. Between 1570 and 1620 from 10 percent to 20 percent of the male population of Catalonia was of French origin. Nadal and Giralt show how, in the French Pyrenean region, pressure of natural population growth in the sixteenth century first drove settlement and cultivation up to heights of 3,000–5,000 feet above sea level and then forced the emigration of the demographic excess. Catalonia, the first province of Spain across the Pyrenees, offered immigrants from southwestern France agricultural conditions closely resembling those they had left behind [657, 58–101].

Goubert [382, 46] shows that other parts of France also experienced out-migration from this cause, but it was Switzerland, whose mountainous character imposed strict limits on the availability of cultivable land, that provided a clear case of the enforced migration of the demographic surplus. During the seventeenth century one major stream led migrants from most Swiss cantons into a fairly concentrated area of Alsace. This movement, comprising mainly very poor peasants and laborers, often took the form (as did emigration from the Scottish highlands in the following century) of parties from particular areas accompanied by their pastor or schoolmaster. Since Alsace itself was not untouched by the wars of the seventeenth century, the Swiss migrations tended to be concentrated in the intervals of peace, above all after 1648, when Swiss overpopulation was exacerbated by the return of mercenaries from the war [411, 173–79]. Perrenoud has described this emigration, which was directed towards Franche-Comté and southern Germany as well as Alsace, as "traditional," insofar as its origins throughout its course lay in the sheer insufficiency of resources under normal circumstances in the regions of the emigrants' birth. He contrasted this type of population movement with "accidental" movements, arising out of war or religion [687, 252]. Anne-Lise Head has succeeded in quantifying the movement out of the single canton of Glaris. Her calculations, which include all emigrants from the canton whether or not they left the country, show emigration running high in the early decades of the eighteenth century, when the economic situation in the canton was unfavorable; much lower between 1740 and 1780, as a developing textile industry contributed to the retention of the natural surplus of population growth; and extremely high, and rising, during and after the French wars of the revolutionary and Napoleonic period, as the demand for mercenaries rose, the textile industry languished, and possibilities of transatlantic emigration were opened up. In the early eighteenth century up to 12–13 percent of the survivors to age sixteen of each generation born in the groups of parishes studied were leaving the canton, a proportion that fell to 6–7 percent in the 1760s but rose again to around 20 percent by 1820 [682, 187].

Another area of out-migration originating fundamentally in overpopulation was northern and western Scotland in the later eighteenth century. Poor, rocky land here permitted grain cultivation and cattle-raising in only minimal areas and set an absolute ceiling to population. As in Switzerland, the availability of military service in the wars of the mid-eighteenth century allowed the population to sustain its normal economy within these limits, but the peace of 1763 created a situation in which overpopulation could be relieved only by extensive emigration. Some migrants moved south to the Lowlands, but many went in organized parties to North America. Unlike in the canton of Glaris, in this remote region there were no possibilities of industrial development to provide the wherewithal to purchase imported food, and the problem of overpopulation was even exacerbated by the actions of "improving" landlords in shifting population from inland straths to the coast to make way for sheep-farming, which yielded higher rents. It was the crowded coastal parishes that by the early 1770s yielded such high quotas of emigrants that James Boswell, touring Skye with Samuel Johnson in 1773, was driven to comment on "the present rage for emigration" [*633*, 443–46; *634*].

We should be under no illusions about the forcible nature of migrations in these circumstances. People rarely leave their homes, holdings, and families for good willingly: only the direst pressures drive them to it, and the loving precision with which emigrant communities recreate their native life style in the reception areas indicates that the decision to move must be made with heartrending difficulty. The sheer misery and desperation of migration enforced by inadequate resources of the homeland in the poorer, mountainous, and over-populated districts of France in the last decades of the *ancien régime* were vividly illustrated by Olwen Hufton. She showed that there was much seasonal migration—an interlinking of the mountain and plain economies—as the inhabitants of the Pyrenees, the Massif Central, and the Alps swept down to pick up earnings in the grain fields, vineyards, and mulberry fields of the plains. There was the less regular movement of pedlars, craftsmen, and odd-job men. Temporary migration, however, merely mitigated and sustained the poverty of overpopulation. Lifting the ceiling a little does not solve the ultimate problem, and permanent out-migration was the only alternative to starvation at home. The excess population of the overpopulated mountain regions of France—the *pauvres montagnards*—flowed out in a continual stream to find livings as domestic servants, casual laborers, industrial workers, dockers, chinmey sweeps, and beggars. It was they who fed the growing towns and cities, filled the hospitals, and overwhelmed the insufficient charities [*404*, 69–106].

Olwen Hufton believes that this movement accelerated in France at least until the 1780s. Clearly, as Anne-Lise Head's study of Glaris shows, every region experienced its own individual chronology of mobility, though no doubt the widespread wars of the seventeenth and eighteenth centuries set up rhythms that rippled through large areas of the continent. Without doubt, research into migratory movements, particularly research employing quantitative methods, will continue; but enough has already been done to indicate that mobility was a very widespread characteristic of European populations of the early modern period. Nor was this movement without important wider demographic consequences. Migration was an essential means of making effective use of new resources in agriculture and industry without which populations could grow but little, and at the same time it relieved pressures in areas of constant or only very slowly growing resources. Without this equilibrating movement the "positive" checks of famine and disease would certainly have operated even more efficiently to curb an already slow rate of population growth. While migration served in this way to assist in the accommodation of the existing population growth rates, it also contributed to modifying the rates themselves. Migrants, whether seasonal or permanent, were heavily concentrated in the younger adult—the reproductive—age range, and their movements, often sex-specific in composition, served to reduce opportunities for marriage. Populations left behind by migrants often displayed marked sex-imbalances, particularly in the age groups in which marriage was most common. Any movements that in these ways involved delaying marriage or raising the mean age at first marriage necessarily contributed, in an age of low illegitimacy rates, to the lowering of fertility and the slowing down of population growth rates.

These effects, however, were unlikely to have been anything other than marginal. Migration was more frequently a consequence of prior population growth rates than a cause of alteration of them. While it remained a permanent element in the demographic system of early modern Europe, it would be extremely difficult to demonstrate causal links between variations in the pace of migration and changes in the overall rate of population growth. For this reason there are few references to population movements in the final chapter, which concentrates on the varying dynamics of the European population in the early modern period.

6   Breaking Out of the System

BY THE EARLY EIGHTEENTH CENTURY the population of Europe was significantly greater than it had been two hundred years earlier, but even so, it is doubtful whether it had recovered its levels of the fourteenth century, so severe had been the damage caused by the first century and a half of the plague pandemic. We have no need, in other words, to regard the halting growth of the early modern period as anything other than a recovery from an unusually severe and prolonged crisis. The growth of the sixteenth and seventeenth centuries is unlikely to have amounted to much more than 50 percent. This implies annual growth rates averaging barely 0.2 percent — less than one tenth of the growth rates achieved by some developing countries in the later twentieth century, though, of course, this is a mean growth rate of what was in reality a growth distributed chronologically and regionally very irregularly.

In the nineteenth century, in contrast with this slow growth, growth rates in most European countries were substantially greater. At 0.5–1.5 percent per annum, European populations were growing at rates many times the secular rates of the preceding two centuries. It is true that rates approaching these higher levels were achieved from time to time for short periods during the sixteenth and seventeenth centuries, but they were never sustained at regional and national levels for more than a decade or two at most, and when they were, they were frequently offset subsequently by the sharp retribution of crises. What was new about the nineteenth century was not so much the high level of the rate of growth as its being sustained virtually unchecked. At a growth rate of 1.5 percent per annum, a population will double itself in roughly fifty years, and quadruple in one hundred. Population growth at these rates carries implications for agricultural, industrial, urban, social, and political developments of the utmost historical significance, but far beyond the scope of this brief survey. What is important is the discontinuity between the re-strained, constrained system of the *ancien régime* and the unchecked growth of the nineteenth century.

But before we look at ways in which recent work has so far contrib-uted to the understanding of this key change, the impression must not be left that the demographic system of the *ancien régime* left the sixteenth and seventeenth centuries a homogenous, undifferentiated period. Hel-leiner, whose 1955 survey [*34*] was our starting point, distinguished sharply between a sixteenth century of dynamic growth and a seven-teenth century of stagnation almost everywhere. Work in the quarter-century since Helleiner wrote has not so much discarded this dichotomy as it has rather heavily blurred it around the edges. Almost every country has its own unique chronology, which researchers have been busy sharp-ening during the 1960s and 1970s.

In England, for example, there is growing agreement that there was little if any recovery from the decline of the late fourteenth and early fif-teenth centuries during the mid- and later fifteenth century [*205*]. One writer [*161*] even sets 1520 as the earliest date for the beginning of the six-teenth-century growth. The large-scale aggregation exercise of the Cam-bridge Group indicates that the principal period of growth lay between 1540 and 1640. After 1640, possibly for the next hundred years, the ex-cess of births over deaths generally narrowed. Absolutely nothing is known about trends in Scottish population of the sixteenth century, but enough is known of emigrations, famines, and epidemics to indicate the unlikelihood of there having been much net growth throughout the seventeenth century [*633*]. In France the small amount of work that has been done on the sixteenth century leaves the chronology vague. There is evidence of quite significant growth in the first half of the century, but the Wars of Religion seem to have checked this growth during the third quarter of the century. There was a resumption of growth during the 1580s but further checks by famine and epidemic in the 1590s. Different parts of France showed some renewed growth in the early decades of the seventeenth century, but from the Fronde of the 1650s stagnation and, in some parts, decline seem to have become more general. What spasmodic growth there was in the last third of the century was offset by the fearful losses of the widespread famines of the mid-1690s [*51; 339*].

Very little of the very recent work in Scandinavia has touched on the sixteenth century, and we are still left with no more than vague assump-tions of some growth. Even for the seventeenth century there were few guides other than the reconstitution work, which suggests that conditions in the later part of that century did not differ very markedly from those of the early eighteenth century and that these produced only the most modest growth. There were major mortality crises, like those created by war in Jutland in 1659 or by famine in Finland in 1697, which must have contributed to restraining the secular growth rates. Similarly, the sixteenth century remains largely an unwritten chapter in German demographic history, but there is plenty of evidence of the catastrophic demographic effects of the Thirty Years' War on many parts. There seems little ground for supposing that such recovery as occurred in the second half of the century did more than, if as much as, make good the losses of the first half. There can hardly have been any secular growth of German population during the seventeenth century. In Belgium, war, famines, and epidemics combined to make the second half of the seventeenth century a period of decline, but growth seems to have resumed after 1710 [*115, 147*].

Further south, there has been much effort to establish the pattern of secular growth in Spain and plenty to show that, in spite of a vigorous emigration to the New World, there was a fairly strong, if intermittent, growth throughout most of the sixteenth century until the late 1580s. This growth was effectively checked by the famines and epidemics of the 1590s. There is less agreement about the seventeenth-century chronology but some ground for believing that the stagnation that set in in the late sixteenth century may not have endured beyond about 1660. Nonetheless, such growth as reappeared later in the century must have been slight, and the best current estimates still leave the Spanish population of the early eighteenth century at a slightly lower level than it had been towards the end of the sixteenth century [*641–42; 645–47; 655; 665; 667*]. Evidence from Italy shows growth for much of the sixteenth century but, as in Spain, checks by epidemic holding growth back from the 1590s [*536; 539*].

With so much divergence among national chronologies, it must seem impossible to arrive at any generalizations that could hold good for the whole of Europe, even western Europe. However, it seems clear that most countries experienced some moderate growth for substantial periods of the sixteenth century. Checks to this growth seem generally to have become more widespread from the 1560s, and to have become fairly general from the 1590s. Only in the peripheral northwest did halting growth continue into the early decades of the seventeenth century. There was probably even greater diversity in the chronologies of the resumption of what we should consider "normal" growth. In Spain this recovery may have been initiated as early as 1660, as in Germany, which was recovering quickly from the losses of the Thirty Years' War. After a significant decline in the first half of the seventeenth century, Italy, particularly northern Italy, also showed signs of recovery later in the century, as did Switzerland; but Scotland and Scandinavia may have shown little growth until the devastating famines of the 1690s were behind them. France continued to suffer serious setbacks periodically throughout the second half of the seventeenth century, and secular growth must have been negligible until the early decades of the eighteenth century, possibly even until the 1740s. The evidence from England suggests a less volatile pattern of development, with moderate growth continuing throughout the later sixteenth and seventeenth centuries. Probably this growth slowed down between the mid-seventeenth century and about 1730 or 1740. Only Holland seems to have displayed trends seriously counter to the broad European pattern of some slowing down or stagnation for a substantial part of the seventeenth century: there, growth continued vigorously throughout most of the seventeenth century until about 1680, when the signs are that it ceased, and a decline began that ran on until at least the middle of the eighteenth century.

How are we to explain this contrast in trends between the body of the sixteenth and a substantial part of the seventeenth century? Unfortunately, while we have some information, if rather patchy, about demographic behavior in most countries for some periods in the seventeenth century, certainly for the later seventeenth century, we are almost totally lacking in firm measures of the basic variables of fertility and mortality in the sixteenth century, which are the necessary foundation of any real understanding of changes in secular trends. There are a few isolated examples of declining fertility in the middle or later decades of the seventeenth century — Colyton in England [274], Geneva in Switzerland [688], Giessen in Germany [497, 412] — but evidence is generally too deficient as yet to determine whether the variations in rates of demographic growth in the sixteenth and seventeenth centuries were brought about by fertility changes or not. We are on slightly firmer ground so far as mortality is concerned, though not much. There is enough evidence of short-run mortality fluctuations in the seventeenth century to explain the absence, or at least the low level, of secular growth, but it is not possible, except in a handful of cases, to go the necessary stage further and compare this fluctuating mortality with the corresponding pattern for the sixteenth century. The causes of the mortality crises — wars, epidemics, and famines — were certainly also present in the sixteenth century, and if the explanation of contrasting growth patterns in the sixteenth and seventeenth centuries lies in the behavior of mortality rather than of fertility, then it might well lie in some slightly lower incidence of the frequency, severity, and ubiquity of these crises in the sixteenth century. Such attempts as have been made so far [256; 554] to measure the frequency and severity of the crises from the sixteenth century show no lesser impact of crises in the sixteenth century than in the seventeenth, even the reverse, but, in the very general absence of parish registers for the first few decades of the sixteenth century, we must remain ill-informed about mortality fluctuations in a key period. Some escalation of crises must therefore remain a possible explanation of the lower growth rates of the seventeenth century.

The most probable explanation of the contrast in growth rates between, broadly, the sixteenth and seventeenth centuries — that towards the turn of the centuries population in many parts of western Europe, after perhaps a century of solid growth, was once more nearing the limits of what could be fed, given the land then available and the going levels of agricultural technology — is equally difficult to substantiate. Certainly there is evidence of this kind of pressure arising at this time in northern and midland England [159; 262]. We would not expect to observe this kind of pressure exerting itself gradually so much as through an intensification of the periodic subsistence crises, since the unfavorable relationship between population and food supplies would manifest itself initially in periods of subnormal harvests rather than in normal or good years. If this is what was indeed occurring, we would expect subsistence crises to become relatively more frequent than the other forms of crisis as the pressure of population on food supplies made itself felt; but in spite of the amount of work that has been done on sixteenth- and seventeenth-century crises, it is scarcely possible yet to confirm that the evidence supports this view of trends unequivocally.

We are far less handicapped by absence of information when we turn to the dynamics of the eighteenth century. Here the issue is not mere variation in what was at best a very slow rate of growth, but entirely novel phenomena of faster growth rates that were not quickly reversed. Unlike in the seventeenth century, virtually every country experienced uninterrupted growth in the second half of the eighteenth century, and this continued in most countries throughout the whole of the nineteenth century. The absence of censuses or even good estimates of total populations makes it difficult in many cases to achieve any certainty about the exact chronology of growth, but the growth itself is mostly unmistakable. The English case is a good illustration of this problem. A reliable estimate by Gregory King in 1695 may be set beside the figure from the first official census of 1801 to show a growth of about 70 percent during the intervening century; but there is no firm evidence to show how this growth was distributed over the century. With mid-century censuses we can plot growth at varying rates in all Scandinavian countries after 1750, but in the case of Ireland it is almost entirely a matter of guesswork, since even the first official census in 1821 is probably unreliable. With an excellent private census of 1755, we can be reasonably sure of an increase in Scotland's population of just under 30 percent up to the first census of 1801. For Spain and Italy there are a number of estimates derived from quasi-censuses, which permit some rough plotting of the growth and reveal, in both cases, some mid-century acceleration of growth rates [647, 104]. The acceleration appears to have been least in France, which achieved only 32 percent of overall growth over the century, though there, too, growth was significantly faster in the second half of the century than in the first, with the highest growth rates being achieved in the third quarter of the century [305; 339].

By the early decades of the nineteenth century many countries in Europe were experiencing population growth rates in the region of, or in excess of, 1 percent per annum. In some cases—in England, Scotland, Ireland, Scandinavia, the Low Countries, Germany—the rate rose to over 1.5 percent. For Europe as a whole without Russia, Biraben has recently estimated [23] a doubling during the nineteenth century compared with growths of 17 percent and 35 percent for the first and second halves of the eighteenth century, respectively, and 7 percent for the whole of the seventeenth century. Since this acceleration in the growth rate has transformed Europe, its explanation has necessarily become, and remained, the single most important problem in the whole field of modern demographic history. Given that net migration at the intercontinental level is more likely to have been outwards than inwards, the explanation of this acceleration must be in terms of either falling mortality or rising fertility, or some combination of both.

What evidence is there, first, of rising fertility? In spite of the difficulties both of evolving satisfactory measures of fertility and of producing data to utilize the measures, a very high proportion of all the effort that has gone into reconstitution studies in recent years has been channeled into the study of fertility in the eighteenth century; and though we may wish for many more studies in most countries, if only to resolve the problem of regional variations, there is beginning to be enough information available already for several countries to set the main trends beyond serious dispute. For France, above all, we really can say that we are well informed in this area.

Perhaps the sharpest trend in the whole field of fertility measures was in illegitimate births. In every single country where eighteenth-century illegitimacy has been measured (as can be seen from table 6.1), it rose, if not between all three periods, at least between the last two, and must therefore have tended, all other things being equal, to increase overall fertility.* The contribution was slight, however, since even in the early decades of the nineteenth century illegitimacy accounted for only a very small proportion of total births—mostly between 4 percent and 7 percent, in spite of the great rise during the eighteenth century. Clearly

*For the method of allocating data to periods, see pp. 11–12 above.

Table 6.1.　Illegitimate Births
(Number per 100 live births, both sexes; weighted means)

Country	Period	Number of Reconstitutions	Number per 100 Live Births
England	pre-1750	24	2.6
	1740–90	24	4.3
	1780–1820	24	5.9
France	pre-1750	8	2.9
	1740–90	12	4.1
	1780–1820	6	4.7
Germany	pre-1750	11	2.5
	1740–90	15	3.9
	1780–1820	8	11.9
Scandinavia	pre-1750	2 parishes	3.8
	1740–90	3 countries	2.5
	1780–1820	4 countries	6.8
Spain	pre-1750	3	5.4
	1740–90	2	5.1
	1780–1820	1	6.5

Sources: See appendix table 5.

Table 6.2.　Premarital Conceptions
(Births within eight months of marriage per 100 first births; weighted means)

Country	Period	Number of Reconstitutions	Number per 100 First Births
England	pre-1750	14	19.7
	1740–90	3	37.3
	1780–1820	2	34.5
France	pre-1750	9	6.2
	1740–90	9	10.1
	1780–1820	6	13.7
Germany	pre-1750	12	13.4
	1740–90	15	18.5
	1780–1820	8	23.8

Sources: See appendix table 6.

this development can have made no more than a marginal contribution to the acceleration in population growth rates. A similar sharp upward trend has been revealed by the statistical study of premarital conceptions (table 6.2). Whatever this may mean for the history of morals, however, by definition these births fall within the sphere of marital fertility and are duly taken into account in all calculations of that variable. The only possible demographic effects of an increase in the proportion of births premaritally conceived would be some marginal increase in the number of births per married woman (but we must be aware of any corresponding reduction in the mean age at birth of last child, which could offset such an increase) and some marginal reduction in the mean age at first marriage in consequence of marriages being precipitated by conceptions. Calculations of mean age at first marriage would, of course, embrace this effect.

In conditions of low illegitimacy other principal determinants of fertility are marriage rates. Broadly, two rates determine the proportion of women in the fertile age range that is exposed to the risk of childbearing: the mean or median age at first marriage of those who marry and the proportion of women in any of the fertile age groups that ever marry. Changes in either of these variables could influence fertility in ways not directly reflected in standard measures like age-specific marital fertility, in which births are related only to the number of married women.

Mean age at first marriage, on its own, is a measure of limited value, since in early modern Europe there tended to be a correlation between age at marriage and age at birth of last child: the earlier a woman married, the earlier she tended to produce her last birth. This phenomenon has never been properly explained, though it seems likely that there is an inverse correlation between coital frequency and duration of marriage irrespective of age at marriage. Thus, a fall in the age at marriage, which, in an age of largely uncontrolled fertility ought logically to lead, all other things being equal, to a greater number of births per marriage, would in fact do so only if there were no corresponding reduction in the age of wives at the birth of their last child. The relationship is, of course, a complex one, since age-specific fertility is appreciably higher in early than in late marriage, so that to compensate fully for a reduction in age at first marriage, the fall in the age at birth of last child has to be somewhat greater – possibly as much as twice as great.

Table 6.3 shows data, where we have them, for age at first marriage. There was a clear, though small, reduction in this age in England between the last two periods, but not elsewhere. This fall, however, was more than offset by the fall in the mean age at the birth of last child (table 6.4), so that the mean length of the reproductive period decreased from 12.9 years to 11.7. Apart from that for England, there is not a lot of evidence of a lowering of the age at first marriage during the late eighteenth and early nineteenth centuries. There is, indeed, much more evidence of a contrary trend: in France, Scandinavia, Germany, and Belgium, on the evidence at present available, the trend in mean age at first marriage during the later eighteenth century was upwards rather than

Table 6.3. Mean Age of Women at First Marriage
(Weighted means)

Country	Period	Number of Reconstitutions	Mean Age
Belgium	pre-1750	5	25.0
	1740–90	6	24.8
	1780–1820	1	27.9
England	pre-1750	21	25.0
	1740–90	12	25.3
	1780–1820	10	24.2
France	pre-1750	18	24.6
	1740–90	21	26.0
	1780–1820	9	26.7
Germany	pre-1750	5	26.4
	1740–90	4	26.9
	1780–1820	15	27.5
Scandinavia	pre-1750	6	26.7
	1740–90	3	25.5
	1780–1820	3	29.8

Sources: See appendix table 7.

Table 6.4. Mean Age of Women at Birth of Last Child
(All ages at marriage; weighted means)

Country	Period	Number of Reconstitutions	Mean Age
Belgium	pre-1750	5	40.9
	1740–90	2	40.9
	1780–1820	1	40.0
England	pre-1750	3	38.5
	1740–90	2	38.2
	1780–1820	2	35.9
France	pre-1750	4	40.4
	1740–90	9	39.3
	1780–1820	3	36.7
Germany	pre-1750	2	40.0
	1740–90	3	40.3
	1780–1820	3	39.5

Sources: See appendix table 8.

downwards. Unless some more than offsetting rise in the mean age of women at the birth of their last child can be shown, the effect of this upward trend was to reduce the length of the reproductive period. Table 6.4 — based, sadly, on a quite inadequate number of reconstitutions — does not support the possibility of rises anywhere in the mean age at birth of last child, so that, on the extremely limited evidence at present available, the general trend was towards some reduction in the mean length of the reproductive period. In France this was substantial — from 15.8 years before 1750 to 10.0 years after 1780. In England the reduction was of just under two years, and in Germany of one and a half years. In Sweden, on the other hand, though there is not enough standardized information to form the basis of national means, Winberg found some extension of the mean length of the reproductive period in three parishes in Västergötland [*630*, 225].

The proportion of women married in each of the fertile age groups may well have been a more significant variable, but unfortunately it has been too infrequently calculated, and we can generalize only on the basis of scrappy rather than systematic information. In Sweden, for example, the proportion of women aged forty to forty-four who were ever married fell marginally from 87.5 percent in 1750 to 85.1 percent in 1800 and 84.9 percent in 1850 [*595*, 35]. In the remaining handful of isolated series available, however, there are scarcely any discernible trends. In Brittany and Anjou, for example, the proportion of women over fifty never married rose fairly steadily from the 1720s to the 1750s but fell again in the 1760s [*308*]. Until more evidence of this important variable is forthcoming, it will probably be wisest not to assume any very significant changes during the eighteenth century.

If marriage rates offer very few possibilities of increases in potential fertility, what of marital fertility? Two good measures of marital fertility have been employed in the recent reconstitution studies: age-specific marital fertility and birth spacings. (Means derived from these calculations are set out in tables 6.5, 6.6, and 6.7.) At the moment only in Belgium can there be said to be strong evidence of rising marital fertility towards the late eighteenth and early nineteenth centuries. Elsewhere the evidence is either equivocal or of falling fertility. In England there was a small increase in age-specific fertility in the two highest age groups but no clear upward trend in the younger age groups. The only three English studies of birth intervals so far available show some reduction, so that we may conclude tentatively that there is some evidence of very gently rising fertility; there is hardly enough, however, to explain fully what may have been one of the faster accelerations of growth rate in all Europe. The evidence from Germany is also equivocal. Age-specific fertility remained fairly stable in all but the youngest age groups, in which it rose somewhat; but the same measure for women married between ages twenty-five and twenty-nine shows quite decisive upward trends (table 6.6). The small number of calculations of birth intervals, however, are not entirely consonant with these trends, and it may well be that any rises there were in age-specific fertility were offset by the reduction in the mean length of the reproductive period. There is a similar problem, arising probably

Table 6.5. Age-specific Marital Fertility (All Ages at Marriage of Women)
(Births per 1,000 woman-years lived in each age group; weighted means)

Country	Period	Number of Reconstitutions	Age Groups				
			20–24	25–29	30–34	35–39	40–44
Belgium	pre-1750	11	472	430	366	317	190
	1740–90	6	494	476	385	313	204
	1780–1820	4	543	464	433	329	178
England	pre-1750	14	414	392	332	240	140
	1740–90	3	437	393	301	239	164
	1780–1820	4	427	361	318	261	162
France	pre-1750	43	467	445	401	325	168
	1740–90	58	496	459	400	309	148
	1780–1820	31	458	383	329	245	120
Germany	pre-1750	10	432	399	358	293	138
	1740–90	10	474	456	379	311	180
	1780–1820	9	491	429	367	297	144
Scandinavia Parishes	pre-1750	4	447	412	344	287	166
	1740–90	5	410	362	300	225	122
	1780–1820	4	398	364	283	241	119
Whole countries	1780–1820	3	371	347	312	249	135
Switzerland	pre-1750	4	509	463	398	321	164
	1740–90	2	391	303	285	126	–
	1780–1820	2	476	450	367	297	173

Sources: See appendix table 1.

Table 6.6. Age-specific Marital Fertility (Women Married at Ages 25–29)
(Births per 1,000 woman-years lived in each group; weighted means)

Country	Period	Number of Reconstitutions	Age Group			
			25–29	30–34	35–39	40–44
France	pre-1750	16	480	415	310	169
	1740–90	24	472	394	292	150
	1780–1820	12	429	318	206	99
Germany	pre-1750	4	426	369	257	115
	1740–90	1	508	380	300	150
	1780–1820	3	580	425	314	120

Sources: See appendix table 2.

from inadequate data, with Switzerland. It is, however, not possible to interpret the available Swiss figures in the sense of any significant upturn of fertility. The rather inconclusive nature of the available evidence suggests that it would be unwise to attempt to draw any very positive conclusions about trends in English, German, and Swiss fertility in either direction until further evidence becomes available.

Table 6.7. *Birth Intervals*
(In months; all ages at marriage; weighted means)

Country	Period	Number of Reconstitutions	Interval				
			0–1	1–2	2–3	Ante-penultimate–penultimate	Penultimate–last
England	pre-1750	4	14.2	28.4	31.3	—	43.6
	1740–90	2	16.1	26.2	29.2	—	38.7
	1780–1820	1	13.1	31.2	26.7	—	37.9
France	pre-1750	20	16.1	22.9	26.2	30.3	35.4
	1740–90	23	14.3	22.5	24.5	29.8	37.6
	1780–1820	8	14.6	26.1	27.1	30.7	42.4
Germany	pre-1750	1	—	20.9	22.4	32.6	44.7
	1740–90	4	14.0	23.0	23.5	28.7	37.3
	1780–1820	6	14.2	22.0	22.9	29.2	37.4
Switzerland	pre-1750	1	—	20.3	23.8	27.4	34.9
	1740–90	3	—	19.7	20.7	29.2	34.7

Sources: See appendix table 3.

Clear evidence of declining fertility comes from Scandinavia and France. After an initial quite substantial fall in age-specific fertility in Scandinavia during the eighteenth century, there was a slight recovery towards the end of the century and into the beginning of the nineteenth century. Mean age at first marriage for women also appears to have risen here (table 6.3).

Only in France, for which there is a great deal of evidence from reconstitutions, is the trend in fertility quite beyond doubt. From the middle of the eighteenth century it was unmistakably downwards, and from the Revolution, sharply so. This substantial decline was accompanied by a distinct fall in the mean age at birth of last child (table 6.4) and a rise in the mean age at first marriage (table 6.3), which combined to reduce the average reproductive period between my first and third periods by a staggering 5.8 years—in itself a reduction of 37 percent. There was also (as table 6.7 shows) some, though not very much, widening of birth intervals.

There are of course a number of possible explanations for falling fertility, many of which—prolonged breast-feeding, amenorrhoea resulting from undernourishment, increased miscarriages and stillbirths—may be relevant to the analysis of short-run fluctuations, but it is difficult to say whether they are likely to be equally relevant to long-run changes of the kind revealed by the French figures. The phenomenon has attracted considerable attention from historical demographers, since the only alternative explanation of so marked a trend seemed to be the widespread adoption of deliberate birth control within marriage almost one hundred years before its general use was known in any other European country. The methodological problem was that the mere decline of age-specific fertility, pronounced as it was in France, was not in itself proof of the purposeful adoption of birth control, and the nature of the phenomenon was such that there was unlikely to be any direct evidence available. Given that birth control was more likely to be employed initially by older women anxious not to add to families they judged to be already large enough, the widening of the higher parity birth intervals evident in table 6.6 was assumed to provide some kind of confirmation of its employment.

Of the many statistical tests designed to detect the employment of birth control that were mentioned above in chapter 3, the most ingenious was the one devised by Dupâquier and Lachiver [348]. This test grouped birth intervals into four categories of length and then studied shifts in the distribution of mean birth intervals between these categories as between successive cohorts of married women. Table 6.8 sets out the results of the handful of applications of this test at present available. As might be expected from the other German fertility data in tables 6.5, 6.6, and 6.7, this test shows no significant change over the three periods. In Switzerland, where both Henry [683] and Perrenoud [688] had demonstrated the

Table 6.8.   Classified Birth Intervals
(Percentage of birth intervals subsequent to first occurring
in each of four lengths of intervals; weighted means)

Country	Period	Number of Reconstitutions	Percentage of Intervals			
			0–18 Months	19–30 Months	31–48 Months	48 + Months
France	pre-1750	2	13.8%	57.7%	17.1%	11.4%
	1740–90	3	11.1	42.9	27.7	18.3
	1780–1820	3	2.3	21.7	26.6	49.4
Germany	pre-1750	2	16.0	41.3	33.9	8.7
	1740–90	1	15.1	41.1	33.3	10.5
	1780–1820	1	19.4	42.2	26.5	11.8
Switzerland	pre-1750	1	6.3	44.1	29.6	20.0
	1740–90	1	5.2	30.4	26.3	38.2
	1780–1820	1	0.0	9.0	24.7	66.3

Sources: See appendix table 4.

use of birth control before the late eighteenth century, and in France, the shift towards a greater proportion of longer birth intervals is quite decisive. It is now no longer possible to doubt that the decline in French fertility from the late eighteenth century is to be explained, partly at least, in terms of a growth in the number of married couples consciously controlling their fertility, leading to the reduction in the mean age at the birth of their last child and the wider birth intervals we noticed earlier. The very high proportion — over 80 percent — of couples with birth intervals in the two higher categories (over thirty-six months) in Meulan and elsewhere between 1790 and 1815 encouraged Lachiver [415, 39] to claim that over a fifty-year period up to 1815 family limitation had won over the immense majority of the French population, whether urban or rural.

As in most areas of demographic history, it is even less easy to explain trends than to trace them. At first sight there might appear to be little cause for surprise at declining fertility in eighteenth-century France or elsewhere. Given effective means for controlling fertility, from the late nineteenth century western Europeans seized the opportunity to do so to an extent far in excess of what was called for merely to compensate for the higher survival rates of infants and children: why should eighteenth-century Europeans not also have responded similarly to earlier, albeit less effective, possibilities of curbing their natural fertility? Though the human instinct to give birth and nurture offspring is powerful, too many children are an impoverishing embarrassment. Even with the low fertility levels of late twentieth-century Europe, it is well known that many births are still unwanted: is it not probable that as many, if not more, were equally unwanted when fertility rates were a great deal higher? Is it

not possible that human fertility has always exceeded any rational calculation of optimal family size at all times until the coming of the means of
birth control—that artificial fertility control was seen to provide man
with an attractive alternative to the positive or the preventive checks that
had hitherto been the sole means of keeping population growth within
the limits of what could be fed?

The reality of the eighteenth century does not wholly support this
view. There was, in the first place, nothing new about the methods of
birth control coming into use during the eighteenth century: they had
been equally available, and possibly as widely known, in earlier centuries. What was new in the eighteenth century was a heightened desire to
limit family size. Our admittedly limited knowledge of trends in real income during the eighteenth century does not suggest that there is any
positive correlation, in the long run, between personal income and fertility: that is to say, it is extremely unlikely that this desire to reduce family
size was a function of falling incomes. Indeed, all the evidence shows
that it was the wealthier families—the families least financially embar-
rassed by numbers of children—who first took advantage of the capability
of restricting births. This, however, should not bother us, since fertility
control the world over has been shown to be a function of wealth and
education. Further, as the experience of many developing, mainly peasant, societies in the twentieth century shows us, many occupational
groups in these societies place great value on numerous families: they
raise family incomes and provide a guarantee of support for parents in
their old age in the absence of state welfare provision. Any explanation
of the gradual adoption of birth control in European society must clearly
allows for considerable social and occupational variations. The role of
the church was probably important, too. For centuries the church, a
powerful influence on personal behavior, had strenuously opposed any
interference with natural fertility. In the eighteenth century, however, it
is possible that the church's teaching on this point lost some of its em-
phasis; or more likely, that people paid less attention to its teaching.

It is clear, then, that no single generalization can cover eighteenth-
century trends in European fertility. There is generally very little evidence to support the view that the European acceleration in the rate of
population growth may be explained in terms of rising fertility: there is
indeed more evidence of the reverse happening. Where fertility declined,
as it did unmistakably in France, and more arguably in Scandinavia,
Switzerland, Spain, and Hungary, the rate of population growth rose in
spite of it.

In all countries in which eighteenth-century fertility has been ana-
lyzed, however, there was a fairly wide range of trends among different
communities. In France, for example, in spite of the very decisive down-

ward trend in the national mean between the second and third periods, there were still some age groups in some parishes for which we have age-specific calculations for both periods in which fertility rose, contrary to the national trend. The possibility is now being explored by historians in several countries that different types of communities practiced very different reproductive habits and that an increase in national fertility, which would not be revealed in parochially based reconstitution studies, could be brought about by shifts in the balance between these different types of communities. In particular, the demographic behavior of domestic industrial village communities is being contrasted with that of more rigidly conservative peasant agrarian communities. In the latter, access to a land holding was a prerequisite to marriage; on the larger farms there was a demand for labor, preferably unmarried, of both sexes, and the food needs of a family set a minimum size and therefore a limit to subdivision of holdings. All these circumstances conspired to delay marriage, and delay in marriage, as we have seen, was a form of birth control. In domestic industry, on the other hand, land was not essential and no more than a bonus if it was available, and married couples and their families formed convenient production units. Circumstances here favored early marriage and large families. Where these hypotheses have been tested against the demographic facts, as in the English midlands, Switzerland, Belgium, and Sweden, some of the facts, as we saw in chapter 3, have indeed supported the hypothesis. Since in many areas domestic industry expanded during the eighteenth century, there may have been some shift in the balance between low-fertility and high-fertility groups of communities in society in favor of the latter, which could have contributed to the increase in the rate of population growth. A recent study of pre-famine Ireland by Almquist provides persuasive evidence of positive correlations between the extent of domestic industrial employment, high marriage rates, and large families [701, 711]. Elsewhere, the evidence for differentials in age at first marriage, age-specific fertility, and length of the reproductive period between the relevant socioeconomic groups is not entirely unequivocal. And even if the growing, domestic industrial communities did achieve higher fertility, this was clearly offset in some degree by higher mortality, particularly of infants [224, 68, 99], which must have diminished their possible contribution to the acceleration of the population growth rate.

In spite, therefore, of these possibilities of fertility changes contributing to the rise in the rate of population growth, the likelihood that declining mortality contributed more must remain very strong. Oddly enough, demographic historians have given rather less attention to the measurement of mortality trends in the eighteenth century than to the question of fertility. Problems of measurement are scarcely less acute

Table 6.9.   *Infant Mortality*
(Deaths under age one per 1,000 live births; both sexes; weighted means)

Country	Period	Number of Reconstitutions	Deaths per 1,000 Live Births
England	pre-1750	23	187
	1740–90	8	161
	1780–1820	8	122
France	pre-1750	33	252
	1740–90	47	213
	1780–1820	15	195
Germany	pre-1750	8	154
	1740–90	2	388
	1780–1820	11	236
Spain	pre-1750	2	281
	1740–90	2	273
	1780–1820	3	220
Sweden	1740–90	28	225
	1780–1820	28	187
Switzerland	pre-1750	2	283
	1740–90	2	237
	1780–1820	2	255

Sources: See appendix table 10.

than for fertility. The crude death rate, widely used in the past, is really a very poor guide, not merely because it is influenced by changes in age structure as well as by real changes in mortality levels but mainly because we so rarely have reliable totals of populations necessary for its calculation and because of the sharp fluctuations in the short run of mortality. Some use has been made of expectation of life, but where this is estimated from birth, as it usually is, it is so biased by the heavy infant-mortality rates that prevailed in the early modern period as to be a poor guide to child- and adult-mortality trends. In the absence of widespread calculations of age-specific mortality rates, we are left with two measures that have been used by historians: the infant-mortality rate itself, widely assessed, and survival rates to various ages, unfortunately measured only infrequently. What trends have been revealed by the use of these measures in the eighteenth and early nineteenth centuries?

Infant mortality was so high in relation to birth, and represented such a significant proportion of all deaths, that variations in it must have played an important role in determining the rate of population growth. In nearly all countries for which calculations are available (and shown in table 6.9), there was a fall in the later eighteenth century between the second and third periods. The exception is Switzerland, for which we have as yet too few calculations to place much reliance on. The well-substantiated fall in France was both pronounced and persistent. In England there seems no reason to doubt the trend, though the extremely low absolute levels of some parochial figures must raise some doubts as to the completeness of registration. The downward trend, particularly between the second and third periods in Scandinavia, Germany, and Spain, is very marked. The German figures, however, are too erratic to take very seriously particularly since the very high figure for the second period is derived from only two sources.

There are, unfortunately, far fewer calculations of survival rates, but such as there are are averaged in table 6.10 (in this table, reductions in mortality are reflected in rising survival rates). While this table is too thin to offer a basis for confident generalizations, nonetheless it does indicate an extremely consistent downward trend in mortality, not least for France, where the figures are based on a more respectable number of samples. The downward trend indicated by these figures is also supported by a certain amount of more random information and by some of the less reliable calculations of crude death rate. In the Belgian parish of Meerhout-en-Campine, for example, the mean age of death (both sexes) rose from 28.2 in the second quarter of the eighteenth century to 36.4 in the first fifteen years of the nineteenth century. Infant mortality over the same interval fell from 191 per 1,000 live births to 167 [*115,* 151]. Adult mortality fell substantially in two other Belgian villages between the two halves of the eighteenth century [*105,* 625]. Crude death rates in all parts of Norway show a very persistent decline from the middle of the eighteenth century [*573,* 49], while survival rates for children in Palamós (Spain) showed substantial increases between the mid-eighteenth century and the early decades of the nineteenth century, interrupted only during the decades of the Napoleonic Wars [*663,* 64]. Inevitably, much of the evidence in all countries comes from rural areas. Urban evidence, where we have it, is more equivocal. François [*493*] is able to show very little reduction indeed in the mortality of German towns during the eighteenth century, but quite substantial reductions in child and adult mortality by the early nineteenth century emerge from the studies of Meulan in France [*413,* 203] and Geneva [*694,* 219–21]. Infant mortality in the town of Lucerne fell from around 248 per 1,000 live births in 1755–65 to 220 in 1816–25 [*676,* 139].

Taken in conjunction with data from aggregations of burials in parish registers and in urban bills of mortality, which illustrate the pattern of short-run fluctuations in mortality, and from other scattered, scrappier, information, there is a clear, if less than wholly satisfactory, indication of some widespread decline in mortality in the later eighteenth and early nineteenth centuries. How is this to be explained? Given that population growth before the eighteenth century had so frequently been held

Table 6.10. Survival Rates
(Survivors per 1,000 live births to various ages; both sexes; weighted means)

Country	Period	Number of Reconstitutions	Number of Survivors at Age:			
			1	5	10	15
England	pre-1750	6	799	668	624	—
	1780–1820	1	842	763	738	—
France	pre-1750	10	729	569	516	502
	1740–90	16	780	632	574	542
	1780–1820	5	806	691	652	636
Switzerland	pre-1750	1	766	597	533	506
	1740–90	1	808	679	619	595
	1780–1820	1	833	726	676	700

Sources: See appendix table 9.

in check by recurring short-run crises rather than by a sustained high
level of mortality, some reduction in the frequency, severity, and ubiquity of these crises could have accounted for this lessening of the grip of
the positive check. Chaunu believed [24, 238], for example, that the be-
ginnings of uninterrupted growth in eighteenth-century Europe origi-
nated in the attenuation and spacing of crises: crises, he pointed out, lost
their amplitude and, above all, became less frequent. Evidence that this
was what was happening comes from the careful study of the many long
series of burial aggregations that are now available. Data from these aggregations were systematized a few years ago [67], and the additional information that has since come to hand has not materially altered the
conclusions these calculations pointed to. No elaborate calculations, however, are really needed. Looking at the large number of graphs plotting annual fluctuations of burials in parishes, towns, regions, and countries, the
eye tells one plainly enough that, though with varying chronologies, in all
countries during the eighteenth century the violence went out of the mortality crises: generally they became less severe and less frequent. They did
not, of course, disappear completely. There was an exceptionally severe
one in most parts of Scandinavia in 1773; a prolonged epidemic of dysentery concentrated in northwestern France during the 1780s; one of the
most acute crises ever in Spain in 1809, which combined the three elements of war, famine, and disease; while the failure of the potato crop in
Ireland in the mid-1840s provided a classic example of a subsistence
crisis. Post [75] has recently drawn our attention to what he probably
rightly described as the last great "European" subsistence crisis of 1817,
though by seventeenth-century standards the peaks of mortality on this
occasion in all but a very few places were very moderate. Cholera, starting in eastern Europe in 1829, threatened for a time to presage a return to
the scale and horror of the plague epidemics of former centuries, but in

the event it was mastered fairly quickly, and the increment of mortality it brought, even in the peak years of its most severe attacks, was relatively slight. More serious was the inability of municipal governments to cope with the public-health problems of the burgeoning cities of the early nineteenth century. In Glasgow and other major Scottish cities these conditions produced a return of short-run fluctuations between the 1820s and 1850s of a violence and frequency redolent of the seventeenth century [*633, 369–79*]. Similar trends have been revealed for the same period in the great Italian cities [*557*], and it seems likely that further detailed studies may well show this development to be typical of a wide range of early nineteenth-century cities. But the public-health reforms of the second half of the nineteenth century, aided by the water closet and new technologies of sewerage and water supply, quickly suppressed this return of instability.

Stabilization of mortality was ultimately achieved, in other words, and these last European reminders of the ever-present possibility of flare-ups of mortality can only distract our attention from the underlying trend, which was unmistakably one of stabilization — the gradual diminution of the violence and persistence of short-run crises. Although various dates have been put forward from time to time to mark the disappearance of the crises in different countries during the eighteenth century, the attempt at precision must be misplaced, since the stabilization was a gradual process.

How was the reduction and final elimination of the crises won? This problem is probably best tackled by looking at each of the three main types of crisis separately, even though in reality these types often overlapped. The role of military activities in creating and spreading crises may have been diminished by changes in the organization of armies rather than in the frequency of wars. There probably was, in any case, a diminution in the amount of military activity and movement on land in Europe after the War of Austrian Succession as the switch to naval and colonial wars took the lethal consequences of military activity away from the European civil populations. But more important probably in reducing the impact of armies on civilian mortality were the evolution of the science of military hygiene, the greater discipline of armies, and the development of the use of barracks and cantonments, which reduced contact between military and civilian populations. And we hear far less in the eighteenth century than formerly of the sacking of cities, of putting whole populations to the sword, and of the burning of crops and villages.

The diminution of the *crises de subsistances* is harder to explain. McKeown [*43*], for example, has argued recently that the European rise of population of the eighteenth and early nineteenth centuries can only be explained in terms of nutrition levels, and it is to be regretted that in a field as vast and amorphous as this it may never be possible to establish whether in such a relatively short period as, say, 1740–1820, there were sufficient significant dietary changes in the habits of the rural and urban masses of Europe. Certainly the poverty of peasant diets in almost all *ancien régime* economies has been established, perhaps most vividly of all by Bernard in his 1969 *Annales* article [*294*]. We know too little of how agrarian developments in all countries affected the quantity and variety of food consumed by the masses. The march of agricultural improvement was clearly very uneven across Europe. The agricultural historians have been moderately successful in showing how English farmers kept abreast, if not ahead, of the demand for food in the seventeenth and eighteenth centuries, and Morineau's attempt to discount gains in French agricultural productivity [*452*] has not won universal agreement [*285*]. It is hazardous, if not imposible, to generalize on the European scale in this kind of area, but, very broadly, four kinds of development seem to have contributed to increasing food supplies and evening out their geographical and chronological distribution during the eighteenth century. First, more a feature of eastern than of western Europe, was the settlement and cultivation of new lands. Second was the introduction and spread of new crops, perhaps the New World's principal contribution to the salvation of the Old in these times [*40*]. While maize (corn) and, to a lesser extent, buckwheat were important here, the principal development was undoubtedly the potato. Historians of Ireland [*526–27; 530*], Scotland [*633*, 421–38], the Low Countries [*451; 523,* 216], Norway [*573,* 54–65], Sweden [*583,* 149], and parts of France [*451*] have all testified to the very great role played by the potato. These new crops were important not so much because their higher yields permitted more people to be fed from a given acreage, or because they could be grown on land too poor to sustain regular grain cropping, or because, as with maize in Wallachia in the later eighteenth century, they were not subject to central-government or landlord taxation, as were the traditional grains [*147,* 206]; but because they reacted differently to climatic variations: weather conditions that were damaging to the traditional grains did not necessarily damage the new crops. "A year of scarcity is but rare since potatoes were cultivated in such quantities," observed a Scottish reporter in 1799, while a year later another noted that "since this root came into such general repute the nation has never been exposed to such scarcity as was experienced before that time and which sometimes bordered on famine" [*633,* 428]. In Scotland and Ireland the unreliability of the potato ultimately brought its own problems; but that unreliability was a long time in making itself evident, and in the late eighteenth and early nineteenth centuries the potato contributed significantly, there and elsewhere, to the elimination of famine crises.

Third was the contribution of improved transportation and commercial organization to the distribution of food supplies. After the 1690s, when food scarcity due to harvest deficiencies was very widespread, famine tended to be a local, or at the most a regional, rather than a national phenomenon. Food was mostly available somewhere, not necessarily near at hand, if only it could be got to the deficient area. A wide range of transport developments—canals, harbors, navigational aids, road- and bridge-building technology—all played their parts in this. The construction of the Forth-Clyde Canal, giving the populous west of Scotland access by navigation to the east coast, enabled grain to be brought to the west from Germany and Poland at the time of the grain harvest failures of 1782 and 1783 and, in the words of one contemporary, "prevented a real famine and saved the lives of thousands in that populous country" [*633*, 9].

Fourth, and not least, was a reinvigorated humanity combined with the evolution of more sophisticated social administration. Though the expression "famine relief" may seem more appropriate to the twentieth than to the eighteenth century, this is indeed what was being developed. The new spirit manifested itself in different ways. In England and Scotland it was through a new-found stress on the duties as well as the rights of landowners and through some raising of the level of humanity and acceptance of minimal standards of operation, formerly neglected, within the poor-law system. In France there were extensive interventions in the operation of the market in grain during famines by the intendants. Heightened standards of "caring" by the Société Royale de Médecine may not have actually reduced mortality greatly during the severe epidemics of the 1780s in northwestern France, but they at least demonstrated a new-found desire to save lives [*336; 369*]. In Norway, Sogner has recently claimed, a severe mortality crisis was actually averted in 1783 by vigorous state and church famine-relief operations [*614*].

Clearly the increase in quantity and variety of food, the greater regularity in its supply, and the superior distribution of what was available in all regions and sections of the population were achievements whose explanation is complex and involves almost all sectors of economic development. But by whatever means these results were achieved—and the situation still left much to be desired—the recurring catastrophes of mass starvation in times of peace were largely eliminated from most of Europe during the eighteenth century. Chaunu believes [*24*, 233] that already by the end of the seventeenth century "classical Europe" enjoyed a better food-supply situation than that of the Third World in the 1960s, and there was much progress during the eighteenth century.

French historians believe that what was happening in France during the eighteenth century was not so much an overall reduction of mortality nor a very noticeable decline in the incidence of infectious diseases; rather, the peaks of crisis mortality were being flattened, and their bases spread. By creating the concept of *crises larvées,* they were drawing attention to changes in the pattern of incidence of infectious diseases, which may have underlain such reductions of mortality as occurred. One explanation for this development during the mid- and later eighteenth century might have been the rise in relative importance of diseases that killed more slowly and had lower case-fatality rates than, say, bubonic plague. Plague brought death with a high degree of probability in four to seven days, and an epidemic normally ran its course in a single location in no more than three or four months. At the other extreme, tuberculosis, perhaps the most important of the killing diseases to rise during the eighteenth century, might take ten years or more to cause death. There could be no such thing as a mortality crisis from tuberculosis, no matter how serious its incidence.

We know far too little as yet about variations in the incidence of infectious diseases during the eighteenth century, though given that these were obviously responsible for a high proportion of premature deaths, including infant deaths, it stands to reason that it was these variations that were most likely to explain the late-eighteenth- or early-nineteenth-century decline in mortality. Smallpox was the disease *par excellence* that took over from bubonic plague in the eighteenth century. The fact that it killed about 15 percent of those it attacked contrasted with bubonic plague's 60–80 percent fatality rate. But its incidence in the eighteenth century was far more general than that of plague had ever been, and its importance as a killer — it was probably responsible for 10–15 percent of all deaths, killing principally children under age two — has attracted much attention by historians, not least because it was the only disease in the whole repertoire of the *ancien régime* for which a form of immunization was devised during the eighteenth century. The debate as to the effectiveness of inoculation is probably not yet resolved, but recent work by Razzell [*246–48*] on English inoculation after 1760 is extremely persuasive. He is certainly able to show a strong correlation between the widespread adoption of mass inoculation and mortality decline in some rural areas and small towns during the last third of the eighteenth century, though it seems equally the case that the practice made little impact on the disease in the large cities. The problem now becomes one of determining how widespread were the mass inoculations on which Razzell bases much of his argument. A similar pattern emerges in Scotland, where inoculation may have had some success in the remote western and northern islands but apparently none in the cities [*633,* 290–93].

Debate also still surrounds the equally important question of the role of Jennerian vaccination, introduced in 1798. It is possible to show from some local series, both for rural areas and large towns (there is unequivocal evidence for Glasgow and Carlisle, for example), that in less than ten years the adoption of vaccination led to the substantial reduction of smallpox mortality. Though in these places smallpox crept back in the 1830s and 1840s, it was never again on an eighteenth-century scale, and the coming of compulsory vaccination in the 1850s and 1860s ultimately dismissed it. What is in dispute is the distinction between eighteenth-century inoculation and early-nineteenth-century vaccination. Razzell has argued [249], with a wealth of circumstantial, detailed evidence, that although Jenner and his colleagues believed they were using vaccine drawn from cowpox-infected sources, their arm-to-arm method almost certainly produced a smallpox-infected lymph, so that all that was happening was a continuation of the old form of inoculation. In one sense, this mattered little: whether old-style inoculation or new-style vaccination, what the doctors were achieving in the first decade of the nineteenth century was the popularization and extension of a valuable preventive therapy and a sharp reduction in mortality from a major killing disease that must have played an important part in the decline in overall mortality rates, particularly those of infant and child mortality.

The debate about smallpox has been illustrated mainly from English and Scottish material, partly because most of the statistical work on trends in smallpox mortality in the key period of the late eighteenth and early nineteenth centuries has been done there, but also because it was in an English context that Razzell did his important work. But there is evidence from France [447], Ireland [247], Norway [573, 49-54], Sweden, Denmark [573, 53], and Switzerland [692] that similar, if possibly less dramatic, trends occurred, and it would not be surprising if, when work is done in this area in other countries, further evidence of the same developments is found elsewhere. In Sweden, for example, deaths from smallpox fell from 278 per 100,000 living in the late 1770s to 15 per 100,000 in the late 1810s [595, 59].

The initiation of the conquest of smallpox was largely a triumph for the medical profession. Much attention, in both France and England, has been devoted to the role of the profession and hospitals in the decline of mortality. McKeown and his colleagues [42-44; 228] have demonstrated beyond reasonable doubt, however—and their conclusions in an English context must be equally valid for the whole of Europe in the same period—that however hard doctors tried and however much their numbers increased during the eighteenth and nineteenth centuries, their armories were so devoid of weapons that they could have contributed nothing to the cure of diseases. The French historians who have studied in great detail the work of the French medical profession in the last decade or two of the *ancien régime* have revealed much energy, dedication, and humanity but no effective techniques or drugs for curing the killing infectious diseases [*336; 368-69*]. The great development of hospitals in France from the late seventeenth century and in Britain from the early eighteenth century illustrates well the desire to show compassion; but in the absence of any effective cures, it can hardly have made any impact on mortality levels. It was not until the coming of chemotherapy in the twentieth century that doctors acquired the means actually to cure fatal diseases. The inability of doctors actually to cure diseases once they had taken hold should not, however, be confused with measures they recommended for the prevention of disease. The medical profession certainly played an important, initiating role, for example, in the extensive and ultimately successful measures to contain and eliminate bubonic plague; it must take much, though not all, of the credit for the conquest of smallpox by inoculation and vaccination; and it was the source of most of the measures that gradually improved the public health of cities during the nineteenth and twentieth centuries.

Finally, there was the possibility of secular climatic change [*38*]. This appeals because there seems to be some evidence for it, whether revealed by dendrology (the measurement of tree rings), the advance or retreat of glaciers or of cultivation [*50*], the seasons of vine harvest (the *vendanges*) [*36-37; 418*], or the melting of the ice on Swedish lakes [*625*]. I do not think that this study has yet achieved sufficient precision to sustain the hopes that it has raised and some of the claims that have been made on its behalf. There is much talk, for example, of a "little ice age," which, by causing the withdrawal of cultivation at the margin and a deterioration generally of harvests, would have reduced Europe's overall capability of supporting population — this by way of explaining the setbacks of the seventeenth century. A principal difficulty is that simple secular shifts in mean temperatures — and the most extreme hypotheses in this area seldom go beyond the claim that in this or that long period mean annual temperatures were more than one degree centigrade lower or higher than in other long periods — are inadequate on their own to explain crop responses. It is the presence or absence of heat and rain at particular seasons of the year, rather than mean annual rainfall or mean annual temperatures, that matters; and the climatic-change hypotheses rarely achieve this degree of specificity.

In conclusion, we now know that only in a few areas can rising fertility or earlier marriage effectively have contributed more than very marginally to the acceleration of population growth rates. In most parts fertility either remained constant or actually declined. Where fertility declined, the acceleration has to be explained in terms of mortality falling fast enough both to compensate for declining fertility and to produce a real increase in the rate of population growth. The possibility of overall fertility being raised by shifts in the balance between occupational groups with early marriages and relatively high fertility and those with later marriage and relatively low fertility is currently being explored. The important variables in this context are women's age at first marriage, length of reproductive period, proportion of women under age fifty ever married, age-specific fertility, and infant and child mortality. We need to be satisfied that the net outcome of differentials in all these variables would produce the faster rate of natural increase that we are seeking to explain before accepting the proposition that the rise of domestic industry contributed in a significant way to the eighteenth-century acceleration in the rate of population growth. This is an important possibility for which there is, at the moment, a growing, if not as yet wholly convincing, body of evidence.

The decline in mortality was also, in its turn, a net effect, since there were at least two areas of rising mortality: mortality from tuberculosis was certainly rising in many areas in the late eighteenth and early nineteenth centuries [66], and urbanization—a growing proportion of national populations subject to the more lethal urban environments—must have tended, all other things being equal, to drive overall mortality rates up [226]. Mortality decline in other areas must have been sufficient to more than offset these trends. The explanation of this all-important decline in mortality is likely to be complex rather than simple and must lie in a range of possibilities in two main interacting areas—nutrition, which includes the quality (vitamin diversity) of diet as well as merely the quantity and regularity of food; and the diminution of the incidence of infectious diseases. In the former area the very process of economic development, by which each region became more integrated with its neighbors and therefore less isolated in disaster, must have contributed, as did, surely, administrative advances allied to some primitive humanitarianism. In the latter—the changing pattern of infectious diseases—human action, in the shape of disease control and immunology rather than any specific therapy, may also have contributed. Though ecological developments beyond human control certainly underlay the eighteenth-century demographic developments, social action, in the shape of economic progress and welfare policies, surely helped to accelerate the pace of change.

Appendix: Tables

THESE TABLES PROVIDE THE DATA from which the means in the tables in the text are calculated. The entries are grouped by country and by period. In some instances the individual figures are means of a number of short cohorts. The second column of each table indicates the number of parishes to which the data relate: in one or two instances the researcher has not made it absolutely clear how many parishes were involved, and I have had to do my best to determine the correct figure. Entries in this column within parentheses are my estimates of "parish equivalents" (for weighting purposes) of numbers of families. A question mark in the third column indicates that the source does not state the date of commencement of the reconstitution. The numbers in the right-hand column of each line refer to the corresponding numbered entry in the bibliography and indicate the source of the data in that line.

Table 1.   Age-specific Marital Fertility (All Ages at Marriage of Women)
(Births per 1,000 woman-years lived in each age group; weighted means)

Place	Number of Parishes	Period	20–24	25–29	30–34	35–39	40–44	Source
					Age Groups			
Belgium								
Pre-1750								
Gierle	1	1594–1700	353	364	284	252	108	*121*
Elversele	1	1608–49	571	406	310	343	232	*105*
Herzele	1	1643–1796	454	424	377	328	247	*121*
Elversele	1	1650–99	430	432	407	386	202	*105*
Dilsen	1	1650–1749	420	360	327	255	189	*121*
Mussy-le-Ville	1	1660–1796	454	427	386	331	189	*121*
St. Vaast	1	1666–1740	423	439	413	351	252	*121*

Table 1 — *Continued*

Place	Number of Parishes	Period	Age Groups					Source
			20-24	25-29	30-34	35-39	40-44	
Astene	1	1670-1779	460	440	380	250	130	*121*
Walem	1	1674-1755	594	488	374	326	213	*121*
Elversele	1	1700-1749	542	492	396	348	166	*105*
Kalmthout	1	1700-1749	493	461	376	312	166	*121*
Mean			472	430	366	317	190	
1740-90								
Geetbets	1	1720-79	427	456	341	307	217	*121*
St. Vaast	1	1741-90	438	428	374	343	217	*121*
Elversele	1	1750-96	611	579	452	272	170	*121*
Kalmthout	1	1750-97	524	464	416	338	188	*121*
Dilsen	1	1750-99	438	393	345	278	168	*121*
Desteldonk	1	1765-96	528	537	384	339	264	*121*
Mean			494	476	385	313	204	
1780-1820								
Astene	1	1780-1829	550	480	470	360	200	*121*
Geetbets	1	1780-1832	595	440	370	335	184	*121*
Furnes	1	1790-96	551	506	517	290	129	*121*
Dilsen	1	1800-1849	478	430	376	333	201	*121*
Mean			543	464	433	329	178	
England								
Pre-1750								
Terling	1	1550-1624	427	318	267	258	136	*224*
Colyton	1	1560-1629	467	403	369	302	174	*274*
Arden	5	1575-99	417	424	312	228	175	*262*
Arden	5	1600-1624	393	337	339	204	112	*262*
Bottesford	1	1600-1649	400	368	342	236	162	*224*
Shepshed	1	1600-1699	353	385	304	260	121	*224*
Arden	5	1625-49	432	459	377	258	150	*262*
Terling	1	1625-99	377	305	281	223	76	*224*
Colyton	1	1630-46	378	382	298	234	128	*274*
Colyton	1	1647-1719	346	395	272	182	104	*274*
Bottesford	1	1650-99	579	381	317	244	162	*224*
Terling	1	1700-1744	413	363	299	263	109	*224*
Bottesford	1	1700-1749	417	430	359	333	179	*224*
Shepshed	1	1700-1749	395	368	397	255	112	*224*
Weighted mean			414	392	332	240	140	
1740-90								
Colyton	1	1720-69	362	342	292	227	160	*274*

Table 1 — *Continued*

Place	Number of Parishes	Period	Age Groups					Source
			20–24	25–29	30–34	35–39	40–44	
Moreton Say	1	1731–70	615	474	342	255	200	*213*
Bottesford	1	1750–99	333	364	269	234	131	*224*
Mean			437	393	301	239	164	
1780–1820								
Shepshed	1	1750–1824	447	344	315	256	135	*224*
Colyton	1	1770–1837	441	361	347	270	152	*274*
Moreton Say	1	1771–1840	408	363	289	240	182	*213*
Terling	1	1775–1851	411	376	323	277	178	*224*
Mean			427	361	318	261	162	
France *Pre-1750*								
Paris basin	25	1545–1792	442	431	388	309	164	*345*
Villepreux	1	1590–1680	386	425	287	228	198	*89*
Marly-le-roi	1	1596–1695	483	431	380	354	191	*89*
Bayeux	1	1600–1699	490	446	445	421	209	*350*
Cormeilles	1	1610–67	464	442	395	394	177	*89*
Istergues	1	1620–1745	428	442	404	390	328	*89*
Argenteuil	1	1625–69	410	396	413	325	267	*89*
Aubervilliers	1	1634–99	404	460	436	399	173	*89*
Tamerville	1	1640–1710	468	450	426	300	208	*487*
St. André d'Hébertot	1	1643–1792	444	424	401	294	154	*292*
St. Malo	1	1650–1700	517	544	442	326	272	*289*
Sérignan	1	1650–1792	423	392	363	284	143	*89*
St. Pierre Eglise	1	1657–1790	517	500	474	410	237	*432*
Troarn	1	1658–1760	500	485	400	328	149	*313*
Meulan	3	1660–1709	486	465	498	410	159	*413*
Coulommiers	1	1660–1739	519	507	503	379	157	*465*
Tourouvre	1	1665–1714	412	425	378	330	164	*324*
Cormeilles	1	1668–99	515	512	435	423	226	*89*
Arthies	1	1668–1719	419	425	362	283	129	*415*
Chailly-en-Brie	1	1670–1715	573	500	429	302	127	*465*
St. Denis	1	1670–1739	527	487	416	370	145	*415*
Northeast France	11	1670–1769	515	458	405	323	158	*401*
Northwest France	10	1670–1769	447	426	380	293	150	*394*
Crulai	1	1674–1709	422	436	356	310	150	*364*
Honfleur	1	1680–1739	563	496	414	290	130	*323*
Royat	1	1680–1740	346	378	336	306	150	*477*
St. Clément	1	1680–1792	348	378	383	320	191	*475*
Lisieux	1	1690–1729	420	368	327	247	112	*488*
Sainghin	1	1690–1739	512	521	419	402	220	*334*

Table 1 — *Continued*

Place	Number of Parishes	Period	20–24	25–29	30–34	35–39	40–44	Source
					Age Groups			
Les Martres	1	1690–1749	422	412	388	335	192	*477*
Anet	1	1691–1740	535	434	419	343	146	*415*
Boulay	1	pre-1720	492	448	377	355	197	*398*
Alençon	1	pre-1750	619	432	331	240	128	*313*
Boulay	7	pre-1760	417	415	386	325	187	*400*
St. Malo	1	1705–50	602	436	386	386	192	*289*
St. Méen	1	1707–39	478	444	380	322	148	*414*
Meulan	3	1710–39	555	547	508	357	155	*413*
Crulai	1	1710–42	435	426	363	328	92	*364*
Tourouvre	1	1715–65	439	412	379	297	159	*324*
Arthies	1	1720–44	422	452	411	314	135	*415*
Boulay	1	1720–49	474	448	405	347	178	*398*
Ille-et-Vilaine	3	1720–55	560	527	464	379	185	*304*
Ingouville	1	1730–49	450	412	400	279	103	*482*
Weighted mean			467	445	401	325	168	
1740–90								
Bayeux	1	1700–1780	578	474	442	392	197	*350*
Isigny	1	1700–1780	439	468	382	256	108	*350*
St. Vigor	1	1700–1780	419	466	340	278	176	*350*
Trévières	1	1700–1780	517	419	397	340	182	*350*
Bas Quercy	2	1700–1792	392	318	289	222	64	*485*
Bessin	1	1700–1799	458	451	373	291	155	*289*
Caen	1	1700–1799	359	297	260	195	93	*289*
Plaine d'Alençon	1	1700–1799	572	427	319	240	117	*289*
Pont l'Evèque	1	1700–1799	515	460	384	275	149	*289*
St. Hymer	1	1700–1799	414	432	372	297	173	*289*
St. Martin	1	1700–1799	513	473	435	344	188	*289*
Thoissey	1	1700–1799	624	546	440	328	137	*366*
Villedieu-les-Poëles	1	1711–90	491	491	471	366	215	*409*
Tamerville	1	1711–92	496	474	378	256	143	*487*
Rumont	1	1720–90	496	504	444	370	186	*474*
Lisieux	1	1730–79	491	434	354	278	116	*488*
St. Agnan	1	1730–92	403	429	378	242	246	*397*
La Guerche	1	1733–92	507	487	458	270	145	*304*
Suresnes	1	1735–60	564	553	492	383	182	*415*
Bonnières	1	1736–55	490	533	401	397	133	*283*
East Paris	3	1740–64	551	535	420	343	165	*473*
Flins	1	1740–64	582	444	416	342	169	*349*
Meulan	3	1740–64	467	490	420	306	107	*413*
Southwest France	4	1740–64	464	422	368	292	165	*352*
Verneuil	1	1740–64	571	440	461	386	137	*415*
Bléré	1	1740–65	508	433	374	290	133	*414*
Auray	1	1740–69	574	527	438	386	181	*431*
Sainghin	1	1740–69	592	519	472	412	213	*334*
Île-de-France	3	1740–79	573	560	464	386	149	*355*

Table 1 — *Continued*

Place	Number of Parishes	Period	20–24	25–29	30–34	35–39	40–44	Source
			Age Groups					

Place	Number of Parishes	Period	20–24	25–29	30–34	35–39	40–44	Source
Honfleur	1	1740–80	500	400	382	279	154	*323*
Coulommiers	1	1740–89	493	477	403	294	111	*465*
Grenoble	1	1740–89	624	546	440	328	137	*297*
Meulan	3	1740–89	582	520	489	358	–	*413*
Anet	1	1741–80	459	522	420	307	135	*415*
Royat	1	1741–89	390	407	358	352	145	*477*
Arthies	1	1745–69	497	426	373	258	145	*415*
Istergues	1	1746–89	559	463	457	411	200	*89*
St. Aubin	1	1749–89	582	520	489	358	–	*304*
Ingouville	1	1750–70	391	463	418	310	71	*482*
Boulay	1	1750–79	477	459	387	330	179	*398*
Alençon	1	1750–89	666	241	264	174	100	*313*
Les Martres	1	1750–90	434	433	381	300	179	*477*
Lévignac	1	1750–90	396	424	308	253	96	*89*
Tonnerois	4	1750–90	500	491	436	304	138	*338*
Bonnières	1	1756–85	460	453	332	256	128	*283*
St. Méen	1	1756–92	632	591	502	400	262	*304*
Boulay	7	1760–79	420	423	434	354	166	*400*
Sotteville	1	1760–90	564	473	423	322	130	*366*
Troarn	1	1760–92	538	523	414	259	113	*313*
Suresnes	1	1761–89	544	504	425	304	131	*415*
East Paris	3	1765–89	644	501	393	304	172	*473*
Flins	1	1765–89	490	427	356	232	126	*349*
Meulan	3	1765–89	515	465	385	283	115	*413*
Southwest France	4	1765–89	351	351	315	250	165	*352*
Verneuil	1	1765–89	446	418	356	273	139	*415*
Arthies	1	1770–89	431	354	284	212	88	*415*
Sainghin	1	1770–89	417	466	428	289	158	*334*
Châtillon	1	1772–89	509	437	341	247	90	*322*
Weighted mean			496	459	400	309	148	
1780–1820								
Boulay	7	1780–89	440	379	402	312	149	*400*
Boulay	1	1780–89	510	419	405	328	207	*398*
Beauvaisis	3	1780–99	519	431	359	222	109	*355*
Bayeux	1	1780–1810	454	283	162	87	23	*350*
Isigny	1	1780–1815	418	431	346	247	125	*350*
St. Vigor	1	1780–1815	592	413	255	200	55	*350*
Trévières	1	1780–1815	429	348	404	318	108	*350*
Anet	1	1781–1810	430	379	275	150	61	*415*
Bonnières	1	1786–1815	436	328	258	150	59	*283*
Boulay	7	1790–99	449	443	388	340	165	*400*
Boulay	1	1790–99	512	397	350	302	167	*398*
Châtillon	1	1790–99	472	357	298	193	86	*322*
Sainghin	1	1790–99	547	402	385	276	174	*334*
Flins	1	1790–1801	483	377	270	175	96	*349*
Arthies	1	1790–1804	430	333	227	172	58	*415*
East Paris	3	1790–1804	481	383	295	193	73	*473*

Table 1 — *Continued*

Place	Number of Parishes	Period	20–24	25–29	30–34	35–39	40–44	Source
				Age Groups				
Verneuil	1	1790–1804	449	532	329	223	96	*415*
Suresnes	1	1790–1809	508	344	265	183	69	*415*
Meulan	3	1790–1814	433	331	253	159	53	*413*
Southwest France	4	1790–1814	323	358	296	239	132	*352*
Isbergues	1	1790–1825	514	446	406	381	200	*89*
Grenoble	1	1790–1839	535	385	324	229	103	*297*
Donnemarie	1	1793–1809	475	383	277	116	66	*415*
Boulay	1	1800–1809	554	387	397	277	143	*398*
Boulay	7	1800–1809	474	399	394	313	160	*400*
Sainghin	1	1800–1809	586	454	322	298	221	*334*
Flins	1	1802–14	333	223	136	100	27	*349*
Arthies	1	1804–19	318	246	175	115	39	*415*
East Paris	3	1804–19	462	322	230	130	93	*473*
Verneuil	1	1805–19	330	283	263	104	73	*415*
Sainghin	1	1810–19	667	460	360	276	137	*334*
Weighted mean			458	383	329	245	120	

Germany
Pre-1750

Place	Number of Parishes	Period	20–24	25–29	30–34	35–39	40–44	Source
Bavaria	3	pre-1750	460	426	421	396	144	*502*
Grafenhausen	1	pre-1750	478	436	351	277	151	*502*
Öschelbronn	1	pre-1750	468	397	336	268	125	*502*
Waldeck	4	pre-1750	388	374	329	269	146	*502*
Werdum	1	pre-1750	425	357	350	291	134	*502*
Giessen	1	1631–80	424	420	353	297	168	*498*
Giessen	1	1681–1730	466	408	346	242	108	*498*
Heuchelheim	1	1691–1720	431	357	335	234	104	*498*
Anhausen	1	1692–1799	472	496	450	355	173	*500*
Heuchelheim	1	1721–50	379	346	273	169	89	*498*
Weighted mean			432	399	358	293	138	

1740–90

Place	Number of Parishes	Period	20–24	25–29	30–34	35–39	40–44	Source
Boitin	1	1740–1809	410	349	219	162	118	*495*
Kreuth	1	1746–1809	472	488	456	396	201	*495*
Bavaria	3	1750–99	492	534	476	378	200	*502*
Grafenhausen	1	1750–99	493	473	414	326	170	*502*
Massenhausen	1	1750–99	555	589	457	330	245	*509*
Öschelbronn	1	1750–99	479	426	362	289	133	*502*
Thalhausen	1	1750–99	545	540	404	327	264	*509*
Waldeck	4	1750–99	441	392	370	281	178	*502*
Werdum	1	1750–99	471	406	340	270	120	*502*
Heuchelheim	1	1751–80	438	398	328	300	138	*498*
Weighted mean			474	456	379	311	180	

Table 1 — *Continued*

Place	Number of Parishes	Period	Age Groups					Source
			20-24	25-29	30-34	35-39	40-44	
1780-1820								
Heuchelheim	1	1781-1810	467	380	335	212	83	*498*
Bavaria	3	1800-1849	549	476	439	350	156	*502*
Grafenhausen	1	1800-1849	498	420	369	279	138	*502*
Öschelbronn	1	1800-1849	554	512	464	319	150	*502*
Waldeck	4	1800-1849	455	424	374	304	169	*502*
Werdum	1	1800-1849	442	355	286	224	108	*502*
Volkharding-hausen	1	?-1810	490	445	315	284	159	*495*
Boitin	1	1810-39	470	327	248	198	89	*495*
Kreuth	1	1810-39	–	438	312	379	147	*495*
Weighted mean			491	429	367	297	144	
Scandinavia								
Pre-1750								
Möklinta	1	1650-80	408	363	312	260	163	*566*
Tåsinge	1	1660-79	353	421	351	326	214	*618*
Glostrup	1	1677-1790	558	426	380	314	191	*617*
Sejerø	1	1700-1739	471	437	333	248	97	*580*
Mean			447	412	344	287	166	
1740-90								
Etal	1	1715-94	462	401	352	277	190	*576*
Sejerø	1	1740-79	490	414	336	230	119	*580*
Alskog	1	1745-69	363	318	261	260	114	*585*
Tortuna	1	1761-90	363	305	270	155	94	*631*
Alskog	1	1770-94	372	374	279	204	94	*585*
Mean			410	362	300	225	122	
1780-1820								
Dala	1	1776-1830	438	358	322	251	137	*631*
Sejerø	1	1780-99	476	414	323	206	64	*580*
Tärnborg	1	1787-1801	333	348	222	335	185	*580*
Alskog	1	1795-1820	345	337	265	174	90	*585*
Mean			398	364	283	241	119	
All Denmark		1760-1801	495	415	358	326	181	*599*
All Sweden		1776-1800	467	382	323	224	121	*593*
All Finland		1801-5	152	244	255	197	103	*627*
Mean			371	347	312	249	135	

Table 1 — *Continued*

Place	Number of Parishes	Period	Age Groups					Source
			20–24	25–29	30–34	35–39	40–44	
Switzerland								
Pre-1750								
Geneva	5	1625–29	518	425	385	345	184	*693*
Geneva	5	1633–37	532	508	421	344	142	*693*
Geneva	5	1641–50	494	467	431	343	215	*693*
Geneva	5	1700–1772	494	451	356	254	115	*691*
Mean			509	463	398	321	164	
1740–90								
Geneva	5	1750–99	390	287	269	92	–	*684*
Silenen	1	1765–85	397	382	368	296	261	*668*
Weighted mean			391	303	285	126		
1780–1820								
Entlebuch	1	1785–1809	449	435	385	298	202	*674*
Luzern	1	1786–95	503	466	349	296	144	*676*
Mean			476	450	367	297	173	

Table 2. Age-specific Marital Fertility (Women Married at Ages 25–29)
(Births per 1,000 woman-years lived in each age group; weighted means)

Place	Number of Parishes	Period	Age Groups				Source
			25–29	30–34	35–39	40–44	
France							
Pre-1750							
Coulommiers	2	1557–1715	436	454	292	154	*465*
Paris basin	18	1596–1792	472	370	283	147	*345*
Meulan	3	1660–1739	516	514	414	167	*415*
Tourouvre	1	1665–1765	459	411	301	163	*324*
Northeast France	14	1670–89	487	466	321	187	*401*
Southeast France	8	1670–1739	400	416	325	166	*392*
Crulai	1	1674–1742	415	325	333	90	*364*
Honfleur	1	1680–1780	557	390	270	66	*323*
Northeast France	14	1690–1719	532	435	312	189	*401*
Sainghin	1	1690–1739	517	388	359	171	*334*
Lisieux	1	1690–1779	485	410	319	150	*488*
Hirschland	1	1698–?	471	388	227	147	*410*
Bléré	1	1707–65	514	432	371	165	*414*

Table 2 — *Continued*

Place	Number of Parishes	Period	Age Groups 25–29	30–34	35–39	40–44	Source
Northeast France	14	1720–39	536	459	352	187	*401*
Southwest France	9	1720–39	373	303	235	158	*390*
Bonnières	1	1736–55	571	444	292	135	*283*
Weighted mean			480	415	310	169	
1740–90							
Villedieu	1	1711–90	483	471	371	186	*409*
Bas Quercy	2	1720–92	328	322	244	77	*485*
Ingouville	1	1730–70	490	440	283	114	*482*
La Guerche	1	1733–92	492	482	275	–	*304*
East Paris	3	1740–64	555	433	375	155	*473*
Flins	1	1740–64	423	376	310	164	*349*
Southwest France	4	1740–64	472	397	283	218	*352*
Auray	1	1740–69	577	522	371	200	*431*
Northeast France	14	1740–69	520	442	350	166	*401*
Sainghin	1	1740–69	577	464	405	206	*334*
Southwest France	9	1740–69	404	329	266	133	*390*
St. Aubin	1	1740–79	601	477	316	–	*304*
Meulan	3	1740–89	524	425	295	107	*413*
Southeast France	8	1740–89	412	401	274	150	*392*
Tonnerois	4	1750–1800	530	462	315	152	*338*
Bonnières	1	1756–85	458	396	252	108	*283*
Sotteville	1	1760–90	565	409	304	148	*366*
East Paris	3	1765–89	606	407	333	187	*473*
Flins	1	1765–89	575	381	241	124	*349*
Southwest France	4	1765–89	392	293	211	188	*352*
Northeast France	14	1770–89	495	413	285	135	*401*
Sainghin	1	1770–89	456	423	248	141	*334*
Southwest France	9	1770–89	371	294	237	137	*390*
Châtillon	1	1772–84	503	356	287	47	*322*
Weighted mean			472	394	292	150	
1780–1820							
Bonnières	1	1786–1815	392	298	185	62	*283*
Sainghin	1	1790–99	439	358	222	200	*334*
East Paris	3	1790–1804	514	345	176	91	*473*
Flins	1	1790–1814	366	224	183	64	*349*
Meulan	3	1790–1814	405	315	154	40	*413*

Table 2 — *Continued*

Place	Number of Parishes	Period	Age Groups 25–29	30–34	35–39	40–44	Source
Southwest France	4	1790–1814	383	284	205	153	*352*
Northeast France	14	1790–1819	479	348	216	96	*401*
Southeast France	8	1790–1819	420	331	241	109	*392*
Southwest France	9	1790–1819	359	285	198	89	*390*
Sainghin	1	1800–1809	440	293	229	230	*334*
East Paris	3	1805–19	387	261	161	51	*473*
Sainghin	1	1810–19	637	435	254	136	*334*
Weighted mean			429	318	206	99	
Germany *Pre-1750*							
Giessen	1	1631–80	497	411	366	160	*497*
Giessen	1	1681–1730	462	382	259	119	*497*
Heuchelheim	1	1691–1720	364	376	224	118	*497*
Heuchelheim	1	1721–50	380	308	180	62	*497*
Mean			426	369	257	115	
1740–90							
Heuchelheim	1	1751–80	508	380	300	150	*497*
1780–1820							
Massenhausen	1	1750–1849	642	463	367	147	*509*
Thalhausen	1	1750–1849	665	446	323	125	*509*
Heuchelheim	1	1781–1810	434	365	252	87	*497*
Mean			580	425	314	120	

Table 3. *Birth Intervals*
(In months; all ages at marriage; weighted means)

Place	Number of Parishes	Period	0–1	1–2	2–3	Ante-penultimate–penultimate	Penultimate–last	Source
					Interval			
England								
Pre-1750								
Terling	1	1550–1724	14.9	29.5	37.0	—	—	*702*
Colyton	1	1560–1719	10.8	27.2	32.5	—	44.1	*274*
Moreton Say	1	1681–1740	17.6	32.2	29.0	—	43.1	*213*
Kilmarnock (Scotland)	1	1730–53	13.5	24.9	26.9	—	—	*633*
Mean			14.2	28.4	31.3	—	43.6	
1740–90								
Colyton	1	1720–69	11.9	25.1	29.8	—	40.6	*274*
Moreton Say	1	1740–80	20.4	27.4	28.7	—	36.9	*213*
Mean			16.1	26.2	29.2	—	38.7	
1780–1820								
Moreton Say	1	1780–1800	13.1	31.2	26.7	—	37.9	*213*

Table 3 – Continued

Place	Number of Parishes	Period	Interval					Source
			0–1	1–2	2–3	Ante-penultimate–penultimate	Penultimate–last	
France *Pre-1750*								
Coulommiers	1	1557–1715	—	19.0	23.0	—	37.0	*465*
Paris basin	7	1587–1719	—	24.2	26.5	30.4	34.3	*345*
Paris basin	9	1590–1792	—	23.2	28.5	31.8	36.7	*345*
Bayeux	1	1600–1699	21.2	25.5	26.5	24.4	30.4	*350*
Trois Monts	1	1603–1792	—	26.6	27.7	36.6	47.0	*434*
Tamerville	1	1640–1792	—	22.2	25.7	29.9	35.9	*487*
St. André d' Hébertot	1	1643–1792	—	22.2	29.8	38.6	41.4	*292*
Troarn	1	1658–1792	—	21.8	25.4	31.0	32.7	*313*
Meulan	3	1660–1739	13.1	19.3	21.6	26.4	35.9	*413*
Tourouvre	1	1665–1765	19.7	20.9	24.0	29.5	33.5	*324*
Arthies	1	1668–1719	—	23.9	—	—	32.6	*337*
Crulai	1	1674–1740	16.6	22.4	25.3	30.9	33.0	*364*
Senneley	1	1675–89	12.6	—	—	—	—	*310*
Honfleur	1	1680–1780	14.7	20.0	20.9	24.4	22.9	*323*
Azereix	1	1685–1715	18.7	29.7	33.1	—	—	*489*
Les Martres	1	1690–1739	20.3	25.1	26.3	30.3	36.1	*477*
Lisieux	1	1690–1779	16.1	20.8	22.9	28.9	34.5	*488*
Bléré	1	1707–65	—	—	21.8	27.8	35.4	*414*
Arthies	1	1720–44	—	20.9	—	—	39.3	*337*
Senneley	1	1730–44	13.8	—	—	—	—	*310*
Weighted mean			16.1	22.9	26.2	30.3	35.4	

Table 3 — *Continued*

Place	Number of Parishes	Period	Interval					Source
			0-1	1-2	2-3	Ante-penultimate–penultimate	Penultimate–last	
1740–90								
Bayeux	1	1700–1792	15.1	21.5	23.0	31.3	37.8	*350*
Thézels-St. Sernin	1	1700–1792	16.7	25.4	30.0	33.7	38.3	*485*
Villedieu	1	1711–90	14.9	18.1	19.4	26.3	32.6	*409*
Rumont	1	1720–90	16.0	23.2	22.5	31.7	35.7	*474*
St. Méen	1	1720–90	–	20.8	22.2	26.3	33.0	*304*
Tonnerois	3	1720–1800	–	20.5	22.0	27.8	33.5	*338*
St. Agnan	1	1730–92	–	25.5	25.2	–	32.0	*397*
Azereix	1	1732–91	16.0	29.0	31.0	–	–	*489*
East Paris	3	1740–64	–	19.7	22.5	27.3	47.4	*473*
Flins	1	1740–64	12.2	21.9	–	–	–	*349*
Southwest France	4	1740–64	–	25.2	27.2	32.4	42.0	*352*
Grenoble	1	1740–89	–	17.2	19.8	26.0	30.9	*297*
Meulan	3	1740–89	13.4	18.5	20.8	28.5	35.4	*413*
Argenteuil	1	1740–90	–	19.9	21.8	26.0	33.3	*365*
Les Martres	1	1740–90	16.8	23.7	26.7	31.4	35.0	*477*
Ile-de-France	3	1740–92	14.2	19.8	23.4	29.1	35.2	*355*
Arthies	1	1745–69	–	21.8	–	–	38.0	*337*
St. Aubin	1	1749–89	14.7	20.3	21.4	26.6	31.2	*304*
Sotteville	1	1760–90	–	18.1	18.5	27.0	31.6	*366*
Senneley	1	1765–79	12.7	–	–	–	–	*310*
Flins	1	1765–89	11.2	27.7	–	–	–	*349*
Southwest France	4	1765–89	–	29.0	31.9	34.9	40.5	*352*
Arthies	1	1770–89	–	22.9	–	–	47.4	*337*
Weighted mean			14.3	22.5	24.5	29.8	37.6	

Table 3 – *Continued*

Place	Number of Parishes	Period	Interval					Source
			0-1	1-2	2-3	Ante-penultimate–penultimate	Penultimate–last	
1780–1820								
Flins	1	1790–1801	13.6	27.0	–	–	–	*349*
Arthies	1	1790–1804	–	23.2	–	–	43.8	*337*
Southwest France	4	1790–1814	–	26.6	28.7	35.7	40.2	*352*
Grenoble	1	1790–1839	–	18.9	22.8	29.3	34.1	*297*
Meulan	3	1790–1839	15.0	20.6	23.6	29.3	41.9	*413*
Flins	1	1802–14	14.5	39.8	–	–	–	*349*
Arthies	1	1805–19	–	30.2	–	–	45.9	*337*
East Paris	3	1805–19	–	27.9	30.0	25.9	47.0	*473*
Weighted mean			14.6	26.1	27.1	30.7	42.4	
Germany *Pre-1750*								
Heuchelheim	1	1701–50	–	20.9	22.4	32.6	44.7	*497*
1740–90								
Massenhausen	1	1750–99	14.8	20.5	21.4	–	–	*509*
Thalhausen	1	1750–99	14.2	22.6	25.7	–	40.3	*509*
Coblenz	2	1751–97	13.5	22.9	23.4	–	–	*492*
Heuchelheim	1	1751–1800	–	26.1	23.5	28.7	34.4	*497*
Weighted mean			14.0	23.0	23.5	28.7	37.3	

Table 3 – *Continued*

Place	Number of Parishes	Period	Interval					Source
			0–1	1–2	2–3	Ante-penultimate–penultimate	Penultimate–last	
1780–1820								
Massenhausen	1	1800–1849	15.4	18.7	20.6	—	—	509
Thalhausen	1	1800–1849	13.1	19.2	20.7	—	31.4	509
Heuchelheim	1	1801–20	—	24.3	20.8	28.0	35.1	497
Boitin	1	pre-1810	—	24.0	27.6	31.5	43.7	495
Kreuth	1	pre-1810	—	18.3	20.5	25.2	33.8	495
Volkhardinghausen	1	pre-1810	—	27.5	27.3	32.0	43.0	495
Mean			14.2	22.0	22.9	29.2	37.4	
Switzerland *Pre-1750*								
Geneva	5	1625–1772	—	20.3	23.8	27.4	34.9	694
1780–1820								
Haslen	1	1760–1800	—	16.5	19.2	23.6	28.9	497
Lucerne	1	end 18th c.	—	19.9	19.9	32.1	35.8	677
Marbach	1	end 18th c.	—	22.8	22.9	31.8	39.3	497
Mean			—	19.7	20.7	29.2	34.7	

Table 4.   Classified Birth Intervals
(Percentage of birth intervals subsequent to first occurring in each of four lengths
of intervals; weighted means)

Place	Number of Parishes	Period	Percentage of Intervals				Source
			0–18 Months	19–30 Months	31–48 Months	48 + Months	
France							
Pre-1750							
Meulan	3	1660–1739	14.3%	60.1%	15.9%	9.7%	*348*
Bonnières	1	1736–55	12.5	50.0	20.8	16.7	*283*
Weighted mean			13.8	57.7	17.1	11.4	
1740–90							
Flins	1	1740–89	3.2	53.5	32.6	10.7	*349*
Meulan	3	1740–89	14.1	39.2	25.9	20.9	*348*
Bonnières	1	1756–85	10.0	43.3	28.4	18.3	*283*
Weighted mean			11.1	42.9	27.7	18.3	
1780–1820							
Bonnières	1	1786–1815	4.1	29.6	23.5	42.8	*283*
Flins	1	1790–1814	0.0	12.6	39.0	48.4	*349*
Meulan	3	1790–1839	2.4	22.1	23.5	52.0	*348*
Weighted mean			2.3	21.7	26.6	49.4	
Germany							
Pre-1750							
Giessen	1	1631–1730	19.2	46.2	28.5	₋6.0	*497*
Heuchelheim	1	1691–1750	12.8	36.4	39.4	11.4	*497*
Mean			16.0	41.3	33.9	8.7	
1740–90							
Heuchelheim	1	1751–1800	15.1	41.1	33.3	10.5	*497*
1780–1820							
Heuchelheim	1	1801–20	19.4	42.2	26.5	11.8	*497*
Switzerland							
Pre-1750							
Geneva	5	1625–1727	6.3	44.1	29.6	20.0	*688*
1740–90							
Geneva	5	1745–72	5.2	30.4	26.3	38.2	*688*
1780–1820							
Geneva	5	1800–1810	0.0	9.0	24.7	66.3	*688*

Table 5. *Illegitimate Births*
(Number per 100 live births, both sexes; weighted means)

Place	Number of Parishes	Period	Number per 100 Live Births	Source
England				
Pre-1750				
Various	24	1581–1740	2.6	219
1740–90				
Various	24	1741–80	4.3	219
1780–1820				
Various	24	1781–1810	5.9	219
France				
Pre-1750				
Trois Monts	1	1603–1769	3.6	434
Crulai	1	1604–1749	0.6	364
Tamerville	1	1624–1710	1.2	487
Tourouvre	1	1640–1740	1.4	324
Boulay	1	1670–1739	0.6	398
Bayeux	1	17th c.	0.9	350
Meulan	3	1700–1759	0.6	413
Strasbourg	2	1710–29	10.7	315
Weighted mean			2.9	
1740–90				
Bayeux	1	18th c.	1.4	350
East Paris	3	1740–79	0.5	473
Boulay	1	1740–89	0.9	398
Meulan	3	1741–89	3.1	413
Tamerville	1	1741–90	2.4	487
Crulai	1	1750–99	0.9	364
Dôle	1	1755–70	4.8	430
Reims	2	1760–79	2.6	320
Strasbourg	2	1763–86	18.0	315
Aubenas	1	1768–87	4.1	448
Trois Monts	1	1770–92	4.9	434
Annonay	1	1778–82	2.9	434
Weighted mean			4.1	
1780–1820				
Reims	3	1780–90	6.5	320
Bas Quercy	2	1780–92	3.3	485
East Paris	3	1780–1819	5.0	473
Annonay	1	1788–92	4.7	434
Boulay	1	1790–1819	3.0	398
Meulan	3	1790–1819	4.3	413
Weighted mean			4.7	

Table 5 — *Continued*

Place	Number of Parishes	Period	Number per 100 Live Births	Source
Germany				
Pre-1750				
Anhausen	1	1692–1749	2.3	*500*
Albach	1	1701–50	2.0	*497*
Allendorf	1	1701–50	4.1	*497*
Giessen	1	1701–50	2.9	*497*
Grossen Linden	1	1701–50	2.8	*497*
Heuchelheim	1	1701–50	2.6	*497*
Klein Linden	1	1701–50	2.1	*497*
Lang Gons	1	1701–50	2.6	*497*
Leihgestern	1	1701–50	3.0	*497*
Wieseck	1	1721–50	2.8	*497*
Coblenz	2	1734–57	1.6	*492*
Mean			2.5	
1740–90				
Boitin	1	pre-1800	3.5	*495*
Kreuth	1	pre-1800	6.5	*495*
Volkhardinghausen	1	pre-1800	5.2	*495*
Massenhausen	1	1750–79	4.2	*509*
Thalhausen	1	1750–79	3.5	*509*
Anhausen	1	1750–99	5.0	*500*
Albach	1	1751–1800	3.6	*497*
Allendorf	1	1751–1800	6.3	*497*
Giessen	1	1751–1800	3.3	*497*
Gross Linden	1	1751–1800	3.3	*497*
Heuchelheim	1	1751–1800	1.9	*497*
Klein Linden	1	1751–1800	3.9	*497*
Lang Gons	1	1751–1800	2.1	*497*
Leihgestern	1	1751–1800	3.0	*497*
Wieseck	1	1751–1800	3.6	*497*
Mean			3.9	
1780–1820				
Massenhausen	1	1780–1819	9.4	*507*
Thalhausen	1	1780–1819	11.4	*509*
Coblenz	2	1796	12.0	*492*
Boitin	1	1800–1838	10.1	*495*
Kreuth	1	1800–1838	17.8	*495*
Volkhardinghausen	1	1800–1838	14.7	*495*
Anhausen	1	1800–1849	15.4	*500*
Allendorf	1	1801–20	4.3	*497*
Mean			11.9	

Table 5 – *Continued*

Place	Number of Parishes	Period	Number per 100 Live Births	Source
Scandinavia				
Pre-1750				
Rendalen	1	1730–49	4.1	*615*
Ullensaker	1	1730–49	3.6	*615*
Mean			3.8	
1740–90				
All Finland		1751–60	1.4	*620*
All Sweden		1751–60	2.4	*620*
All Norway		1761–70	3.6	*620*
Mean			2.5	
1780–1820				
All Finland		1791–1820	5.4	*620*
All Sweden		1791–1820	5.9	*620*
All Denmark		1811–20	8.7	*620*
All Norway		1811–20	7.4	*620*
Mean			6.8	
Spain				
Pre-1750				
Talavera	1	1550–1749	3.0	*665*
Pontevedra	1	1600–99	6.1	*649*
Galicia	10	1600–1749	5.6	*665*
Weighted mean			5.4	
1740–90				
Galicia	10	1750–99	5.2	*665*
Talavera	1	1765–69	3.9	*665*
Weighted mean			5.1	
1780–1820				
Talavera	1	1780–99	6.5	*665*

Table 6.   *Premarital Conceptions*
(Births within eight months of marriage per 100 first births; weighted means)

Place	Number of Parishes	Period	Number per 100 Live Births	Source
England				
Pre-1750				
Dymock	1	1538–67	28.0	*200*
Horsham	1	1541–52	13.0	*200*
Aberford	1	1541–64	20.0	*200*
Various	77	1550–1700	20.0	*199*
Various	7	1550–1749	23.8	*41*
Standish	1	1560–89	24.0	*200*
Orwell	1	1570–1643	11.5	*200*
Wimbledon	1	1600–1650	7.0	*200*
Cuckfield	1	1605–12	17.0	*200*
Kirkham	1	1622–28	17.0	*200*
Conway	1	1627–1729	14.5	*200*
Angmering	1	1640–82	8.0	*200*
Blackburn	1	1653–54	26.0	*200*
Medmenham	1	1662–1749	3.0	*200*
Weighted mean			19.7	
1740–90				
Abinger	1	1750–98	46.0	*200*
Various	7	1750–99	35.2	*41*
Medmenham	1	1750–1836	43.0	*200*
Weighted mean			37.3	
1780–1820				
Northumberland	5	1798–1807	29.0	*200*
Various	7	1800–1849	38.5	*41*
Weighted mean			34.5	
France				
Pre-1750				
Tamerville	1	1624–1740	10.1	*487*
Tourouvre	1	1665–1765	5.0	*324*
Arthies	1	1668–1744	9.3	*337*
Northeast France	14	1670–1739	8.1	*401*
Bléré	1	1677–1788	8.0	*414*
Lourmarin	1	1681–1750	1.6	*478*
Northwest France	10	1690–1739	4.9	*393*
Southwest France	8	1690–1739	3.7	*392*
Boulay	1	pre-1749	9.1	*398*
Weighted mean			6.2	

Table 6 – *Continued*

Place	Number of Parishes	Period	Number per 100 First Births	Source
1740–90				
Bas Quercy	2	1700–1792	4.9	*485*
Northeast France	14	1740–89	12.1	*401*
Northwest France	10	1740–89	9.0	*394*
Southwest France	8	1740–89	5.5	*392*
Tamerville	1	1740–90	20.0	*487*
Arthies	1	1745–89	15.9	*337*
Boulay	1	1750–79	13.2	*398*
Lourmarin	1	1751–90	15.4	*478*
Châtillon	1	1772–84	14.7	*322*
Weighted mean			10.1	
1780–1820				
Boulay	1	1780–1809	15.2	*398*
Arthies	1	1790–1819	15.5	*337*
Northeast France	14	1790–1819	15.7	*401*
Northwest France	10	1790–1819	12.7	*394*
Southwest France	8	1790–1819	9.7	*392*
Lourmarin	1	1791–1820	25.3	*478*
Weighted mean			13.7	
Germany				
Pre-1750				
Efrigen-Kirchen	1	pre-1749	6.6	*502*
Schweigern	1	pre-1749	17.9	*501*
Oldenburg	1	1606–1700	21.0	*100*
Heuchelheim	1	1691–1740	6.2	*497*
Anhausen	1	1692–1749	14.0	*500*
Berich	1	1700–1749	7.7	*502*
Grafenhausen	1	1700–1749	15.6	*502*
Ingelheim	1	1700–1749	12.8	*502*
Logabirum	1	1700–1749	20.0	*502*
Massenhausen	1	1700–1749	16.0	*502*
Wetteburg	1	1700–1749	15.8	*502*
Durlach	1	1701–30	6.9	*100*
Mean			13.4	
1740–90				
Oldenburg	1	1700–1780	23.5	*100*
Durlach	1	1731–70	5.3	*100*
Heuchelheim	1	1741–80	10.5	*497*
Anhausen	1	1750–99	17.0	*500*
Berich	1	1750–99	17.1	*502*
Efrigen-Kirchen	1	1750–99	18.8	*502*

Table 6 — *Continued*

Place	Number of Parishes	Period	Number per 100 First Births	Source
Grafenhausen	1	1750–99	32.4	*502*
Ingelheim	1	1750–99	11.3	*502*
Logabirum	1	1750–99	19.0	*502*
Massenhausen	1	1750–99	32.4	*502*
Schweigern	1	1750–99	19.0	*501*
Wetteburg	1	1750–99	19.0	*502*
Boitin	1	pre-1800	28.5	*495*
Kreuth	1	pre-1800	2.7	*495*
Volkhardinghausen	1	pre-1800	20.8	*495*
Mean			18.5	
1780–1820				
Durlach	1	1771–1800	16.1	*100*
Oldenburg	1	1780–1800	11.4	*100*
Heuchelheim	1	1781–1820	15.6	*497*
Boitin	1	1800–1839	32.0	*495*
Kreuth	1	1800–1839	28.6	*495*
Volkhardinghausen	1	1800–1839	34.2	*495*
Anhausen	1	1800–1849	20.0	*500*
Schweigern	1	1800–1849	32.3	*501*
Mean			23.8	

Table 7.   *Mean Age of Women at First Marriage*
(Weighted means)

Place	Number of Parishes	Period	Mean Age	Source
Belgium				
Pre-1750				
Elversele	1	1608–1749	26.6	*105*
North Belgium	(3)	1620–1749	26.5	*114*
Adegem	1	1680–1739	24.3	*105*
Vieuxbourg	1	1680–1739	25.3	*105*
West Flanders	4	1680–1739	23.6	*105*
Weighted mean			25.0	
1740–90				
Vieuxbourg	1	1740–79	23.1	*105*
West Flanders	4	1740–79	22.5	*105*
Adegem	1	1740–96	25.2	*105*
Kalmthout	1	1750–95	24.9	*121*
Elversele	1	1750–96	28.5	*105*
North Belgium	(3)	1750–99	26.9	*114*
Weighted mean			24.8	
1780–1820				
North Belgium	(3)	1800–1849	27.9	*114*
England				
Pre-1750				
Alcester	1	1550–1749	25.7	*264*
Aldenham	1	1550–1749	25.7	*264*
Banbury	1	1550–1749	25.7	*264*
Bottesford	1	1550–1749	26.7	*264*
Colyton	1	1550–1749	28.0	*264*
Gainsborough	1	1550–1749	24.5	*264*
Hartland	1	1550–1749	27.5	*264*
Shepshed	1	1550–1749	27.7	*264*
Terling	1	1550–1749	24.2	*264*
Arden	5	1575–1674	26.5	*262*
Hawkshead	1	1600–1749	26.4	*264*
Southern counties	(1)	1615–21	24.6	*246*
Old Stratford	1	1624–69	26.0	*232*
Napton-on-the-Hill	1	1660–1749	27.5	*232*
Yorkshire	(10)	1662–1714	23.8	*246*
Suffolk	(2)	1684–1723	24.5	*237*
Yorkshire	(6)	1691–1710	23.1	*237*
Birmingham St. Martin	1	1694–1708	28.0	*232*
Bidford-on-Avon	1	1695–1749	27.4	*232*
Nottinghamshire	(3)	1701–10	24.2	*237*
Nottinghamshire	(2)	1701–36	24.5	*246*
Weighted mean			25.0	

Table 7 – *Continued*

Place	Number of Parishes	Period	Mean Age	Source
1740.90				
Colyton	1	1720–69	26.8	*274*
Surrey	(1)	1741–45	24.9	*246*
Moreton Say	1	1741–80	27.3	*213*
Old Stratford	1	1745–79	26.5	*232*
Nottinghamshire	(1)	1749–70	23.9	*246*
Bidford-on-Avon	1	1750–79	27.1	*232*
Shepshed	1	1750–79	25.9	*224*
Napton-on-the-Hill	1	1750–79	26.3	*232*
Bottesford	1	1750–99	26.5	*224*
Nottinghamshire	(4)	1751–60	24.2	*237*
Suffolk	(1)	1751–60	25.5	*237*
Surrey	(3)	1751–60	24.4	*237*
Weighted mean			25.3	
1780–1820				
Colyton	1	1770–1837	25.1	*274*
Terling	1	1775–1851	23.0	*224*
Old Stratford	1	1780–1804	25.7	*232*
Bidford-on-Avon	1	1780–1819	24.8	*232*
Napton-on-the-Hill	1	1780–1819	26.2	*232*
Shepshed	1	1780–1819	23.9	*224*
Sussex	(2)	1796–99	24.1	*246*
Bottesford	1	1800–1851	26.5	*224*
Leicestershire	(6)	1801–10	23.8	*237*
Sussex	(2)	1801–10	22.3	*237*
Weighted mean			24.2	
France				
Pre-1750				
Lorraine	4	1575–1625	22.1	*412*
Tamerville	1	1641–1750	25.7	*487*
St. André d'Hébertot	1	1643–1730	28.0	*292*
Meulan	3	1660–1739	25.1	*413*
Bayeux	1	1660–1750	27.1	*350*
Tourouvre	1	1665–1734	24.5	*324*
Reims	1	1668–1749	25.4	*320*
Boulay	1	1670–1739	27.8	*398*
Trévières	1	1672–1751	27.3	*350*
Crulai	1	1674–1742	24.6	*364*
Sainghin	1	1680–1739	28.9	*334*
Royat	1	1680–1740	21.9	*477*
Les Martres	1	1690–1740	19.5	*477*
Prompsat	1	1690–1790	23.3	*477*
Duravel	1	1693–1720	24.0	*439*
Bas Quercy	2	1700–1739	23.7	*485*
Lyon	1	1700–1750	27.5	*357*

Table 7 — *Continued*

Place	Number of Parishes	Period	Mean Age	Source
Limons	1	1702–58	22.6	*456*
Weighted mean			24.6	
1740–90				
Rumont	1	1720–90	26.9	*474*
Tonnerois	3	1720–1800	25.6	*338*
St. André d'Hébertot	1	1730–92	28.8	*292*
Tourouvre	1	1735–70	26.2	*324*
Boulay	1	1740–79	24.7	*398*
Sainghin	1	1740–79	27.3	*334*
Grenoble	1	1740–89	23.7	*297*
St. Aubin	1	1740–89	27.0	*377*
Meulan	3	1740–90	26.2	*413*
Bas Quercy	2	1740–92	25.1	*485*
Ile-de-France	3	1740–99	24.6	*355*
Royat	1	1741–89	23.5	*477*
Les Martres	1	1741–90	21.0	*477*
Reims	3	1750–74	26.3	*320*
Tamerville	1	1750–90	26.3	*487*
Limons	1	1750–92	23.7	*456*
Bayeux	1	1751–90	26.3	*350*
Trévières	1	1752–92	26.0	*350*
Isigny	1	1753–92	24.2	*350*
Brittany and Anjou	21	1770–79	26.7	*308*
Pont-à-Mousson	2	1774–92	25.6	*471*
Weighted mean			26.0	
1780–1820				
Duravel	1	1770–1800	28.0	*439*
Reims	3	1775–91	26.7	*320*
Brittany and Anjou	21	1780–89	26.8	*308*
Sainghin	1	1780–99	27.3	*334*
Boulay	1	1780–1809	28.1	*398*
Bayonne	1	1789–99	26.1	*470*
St. Esprit	1	1789–99	26.7	*470*
Meulan	3	1790–1814	25.3	*413*
Grenoble	1	1790–1839	26.3	*297*
Weighted mean			26.7	
Germany				
Pre-1750				
Giessen	1	1631–1730	24.5	*497*
Heuchelheim	1	1691–1750	25.6	*497*
Durlach	1	1701–50	25.9	*92*
Massenhausen	1	1740–49	25.3	*502*
Thalhausen	1	1740–49	30.6	*509*
Mean			26.4	

Table 7 – *Continued*

Place	Number of Parishes	Period	Mean Age	Source
1740–90				
Massenhausen	1	1750–89	26.8	*497*
Thalhausen	1	1750–89	31.5	*509*
Durlach	1	1751–80	25.6	*92*
Heuchelheim	1	1751–90	23.7	*497*
Mean			26.9	
1780–1820				
Anhausen	1	1750–1849	28.3	*502*
Bavaria	3	1750–1849	29.5	*502*
Braunsen	1	1750–1849	25.9	*502*
Gabelbach	1	1750–1849	29.0	*502*
Grafenhausen	1	1750–1849	26.5	*502*
Horinghausen	1	1750–1849	27.4	*502*
Kreuth	1	1750–1849	31.5	*502*
Massenhausen (Hesse)	1	1750–1849	27.3	*502*
Öschelbronn	1	1750–1849	25.6	*502*
Vasbeck	1	1750–1849	26.3	*502*
Werdum	1	1750–1849	25.8	*502*
Durlach	1	1781–1800	25.1	*92*
Massenhausen (Bavaria)	1	1790–1819	27.2	*509*
Thalhausen	1	1790–1819	29.1	*509*
Heuchelheim	1	1791–1820	24.0	*497*
Weighted mean			27.5	
Scandinavia				
Pre-1750				
Kolbäck	1	1581–1700	25.2	*592*
Skinnskatteberg	1	1581–1700	25.8	*592*
Västerfärnebo	1	1581–1700	27.4	*592*
Lovö	1	1611–1700	26.8	*592*
Björksta	1	1641–1700	27.1	*592*
Glostrup	1	1677–1740	28.2	*617*
Mean			26.7	
1740–90				
Glostrup	1	1741–90	26.8	*617*
Alskog	1	1745–94	24.1	*585*
Etne	1	1755–94	25.5	*576*
Mean			25.5	
1780–1820				
Sejerø	1	1787–1801	31.0	*580*
Tärnborg	1	1787–1801	33.1	*580*
Alskog	1	1795–1820	25.3	*585*
Mean			29.8	

Table 8.   Mean Age of Women at Birth of Last Child
(All ages at marriage; weighted means)

Place	Number of Parishes	Period	Mean Age	Source
Belgium				
Pre-1750				
Elversele	1	1608–1749	40.9	*105*
Asterne	1	1670–1779	41.1	*121*
Adegem	1	1680–1759	40.2	*105*
Kalmthout	1	1700–1797	40.6	*121*
Vieuxbourg	1	1720–59	41.5	*105*
Mean			40.9	
1740–90				
Adegem	1	1760–96	40.0	*105*
Vieuxbourg	1	1760–96	41.8	*105*
Mean			40.9	
1780–1820				
Landvan Waas	1	1800–1830	40.0	*114*
England				
Pre-1750				
Arden	5	1575–1674	37.8	*262*
Bottesford	1	1600–1749	40.4	*224*
Shepshed	1	1600–1749	39.9	*224*
Weighted mean			38.5	
1740–90				
Bottesford	1	1750–99	37.4	*224*
Shepshed	1	1750–99	39.0	*224*
Mean			38.2	
1780–1820				
Bottesford	1	1800–1849	35.2	*224*
Shepshed	1	1800–1849	36.6	*224*
Mean			35.9	
France				
Pre-1750				
Bayeux	1	17th c.	41.0	*350*
Tourouvre	1	1665–1770	39.8	*327*
Arthies	1	1668–1744	39.9	*337*
Les Martres	1	1690–1739	40.9	*477*
Mean			40.4	

Table 8 — *Continued*

Place	Number of Parishes	Period	Mean Age	Source
1740–90				
Ile-de-France	3	1700–1800	40.4	*355*
Bayeux	1	18th c.	41.9	*350*
Bas Quercy	2	1720–92	39.4	*485*
Tonnerois	4	1720–1800	38.5	*338*
Flins	1	1740–89	38.7	*349*
Argenteuil	1	1740–90	39.9	*365*
Les Martres	1	1740–90	40.8	*477*
Arthies	1	1745–89	38.7	*337*
Châtillon	1	1772–89	36.0	*317*
Weighted mean			39.3	
1780–1820				
Ile-de-France	3	1780–1800	38.3	*355*
Flins	1	1790–1814	34.0	*349*
Arthies	1	1790–1819	34.4	*337*
Weighted mean			36.7	
Germany				
Pre-1750				
Anhausen	1	1692–1749	40.8	*500*
Germany	10	pre-1750	39.9	*502*
Weighted mean			40.0	
1740–90				
Massenhausen	1	1750–79	40.2	*509*
Anhausen	1	1750–99	40.4	*500*
Germany	10	1750–99	40.3	*502*
Weighted mean			40.3	
1780–1820				
Massenhausen	1	1780–1819	38.2	*509*
Anhausen	1	1800–1849	39.9	*500*
Germany	10	1800–1849	39.6	*502*
Weighted mean			39.5	

Table 9. Survival Rates
(Survivors per 1,000 live births to various ages; both sexes; weighted means)

Place	Number of Parishes	Period	Number of Survivors at Age:				Source
			1	5	10	15	
England							
Pre-1750							
Terling	1	1550–1724	869	794	763	741	*702*
London—All Hallows	1	1570–1653	729	574	511	—	*192*
London—St. Mary	1	1570–1653	682	501	452	—	*192*
London—St. Michael	1	1570–1653	796	652	595	—	*192*
London—St. Peter	1	1570–1653	859	699	665	—	*192*
Shepshed	1	1600–1749	859	787	761	—	*224*
Mean			799	668	624	—	
1780–1820							
Shepshed	1	1750–1824	842	763	738	—	*224*
France							
Pre-1750							
Coulommiers	1	1557–1715	731	518	483	—	*465*
Meulan	3	1668–1739	758	520	471	—	*413*
Crulai	1	1674–1742	795	698	644	627	*364*
Mogneneins	1	1675–1739	750	539	475	455	*299*
Tourouvre	1	1690–1739	720	563	520	492	*324*
St. Méen	1	1720–55	752	552	475	—	*304*
St. Trivier	1	1730–39	663	463	417	—	*300*
Britanny and Anjou	21	1740–49	724	586	530	503	*308*
Sainghin	1	1740–49	741	592	572	558	*334*
Thoissey	1	1740–49	689	420	373	351	*299*
Weighted mean			729	569	516	502	
1740–90							
Ingouville	1	1730–90	714	762	495	463	*482*
La Guerche	1	1733–92	715	561	500	—	*304*
Tourouvre	1	1740–69	789	660	615	589	*324*
Auray	1	1740–79	747	576	491	476	*431*
Mogneneins	1	1740–79	788	624	569	549	*299*
Meulan	3	1740–89	774	566	535	—	*413*
Ile-de-France	3	1740–99	788	646	613	—	*355*
Bas Quercy	2	1747–92	809	689	672	661	*485*
St. Aubin	1	1749–89	757	—	578	—	*304*
Brittany and Anjou	21	1750–69	755	623	563	532	*308*

Table 9—*Continued*

Place	Number of Parishes	Period	Number of Survivors at Age:				Source
			1	5	10	15	
Sainghin	1	1750–79	773	683	644	627	*334*
St. Trivier	1	1750–79	731	523	475	–	*300*
Thoissey	1	1750–79	753	580	517	506	*299*
St. Méen	1	1756–92	777	543	451	–	*304*
Sotteville	1	1760–90	756	611	572	557	*366*
Paris suburbs	17	1774–94	823	657	600	–	*354*
Weighted mean			780	632	574	542	
1780–1820							
Mogneneins	1	1780–1819	792	685	656	637	*299*
Sainghin	1	1780–1819	838	749	730	712	*304*
Thoissey	1	1780–1819	774	615	584	558	*299*
Meulan	3	1790–1814	808	665	622	–	*413*
Brittany and Anjou	21	1790–1819	806	696	656	–	*308*
Weighted mean			806	691	652	636	
Switzerland *Pre-1750*							
Geneva	5	1625–1744	766	597	533	506	*694*
1740–90							
Geneva	5	1745–69	808	679	619	595	*694*
1780–1820							
Geneva	5	1770–1820	833	726	676	700	*694*

Table 10. Infant Mortality
(Deaths under age 1 per 1,000 live births; both sexes; weighted means)

Place	Number of Parishes	Period	Deaths per 1,000 Live Births	Source
England				
Pre-1750				
York	6	1538–1601	480	*177*
Alcester	1	1550–1749	179	*280*
Aldenham	1	1550–1749	132	*280*
Banbury	1	1550–1749	183	*280*
Colyton	1	1550–1749	110	*280*
Gainsborough	1	1550–1749	223	*264*
Gedling	1	1550–1749	96	*264*
Hartland	1	1550–1749	84	*264*
Terling	1	1550–1749	133	*264*
Bottesford	1	1550–1774	133	*224*
Willingham	1	1559–1749	180	*250*
Shropshire	9	1561–1760	182	*214*
Arden	5	1575–1674	139	*262*
Ludlow	1	1577–86	215	*280*
Various	16	1580–89	149	*280*
Old Stratford	1	1580–1659	222	*231*
Leake	1	1584–1743	243	*272*
Shepshed	1	1600–1749	140	*224*
Wrangle	1	1604–1743	246	*272*
Various	16	1630–39	157	*280*
London	2	1630–1739	217	*280*
Various	16	1680–89	201	*280*
Various	16	1730–39	161	*280*
Weighted mean			187	
1740–90				
Leake	1	1744–83	214	*272*
Wrangle	1	1744–83	225	*272*
Alcester	1	1750–99	97	*280*
Aldenham	1	1750–99	143	*280*
Banbury	1	1750–99	199	*280*
Bottesford	1	1750–99	143	*224*
Colyton	1	1750–99	94	*280*
Willingham	1	1750–99	174	*250*
Mean			161	
1780–1820				
Shepshed	1	1750–1824	158	*224*
Colyton	1	1750–1837	137	*277*
Shropshire	9	1761–1810	102	*214*
Various	16	1780–89	120	*280*
Leake	1	1784–1823	133	*272*
Wrangle	1	1784–1823	157	*272*

Table 10 — *Continued*

Place	Number of Parishes	Period	Deaths per 1,000 Live Births	Source
Willingham	1	1800–1812	240	*250*
Bottesford	1	1800–1851	115	*224*
Weighted mean			122	

France
Pre-1750

Coulommiers	1	1557–1715	269	*465*
Tamerville	1	1624–1755	151	*487*
Argenteuil	1	1640–1770	256	*89*
St. André d'Hébertot	1	1643–1792	118	*292*
Seine-et-Oise	15	1650–1720	230	*311*
Beauvaisis	4	1656–1735	288	*372*
Tourouvre	1	1660–1749	264	*324*
Meulan	3	1668–1739	244	*413*
La Chapelle d'Aligné	1	1670–1749	316	*423*
La Pommeraie	1	1670–1749	233	*423*
Morannes	1	1670–1749	213	*423*
Trévières	1	1671–1760	134	*350*
Auneuil	1	1675–1700	157	*372*
Beauvais	1	1675–1700	271	*372*
Clermont	1	1675–1700	171	*372*
Mony	1	1675–1700	193	*372*
Mogneneins	1	1675–1739	249	*299*
Bléré	1	1677–1707	200	*414*
Sennely	1	1680–1744	324	*310*
Crulai	1	1688–1719	236	*364*
Lisieux	1	1690–1729	190	*488*
Cerdon	1	1690–1739	281	*463*
Villemurlin	1	1690–1739	356	*463*
St. Laurent des Eaux	1	pre-1750	326	*374*
Challain	1	1710–49	235	*423*
Ille-et-Vilaine	3	1720–55	248	*304*
Tonnerois	4	1726–50	203	*338*
St. Trivier	1	1730–49	329	*350*
Isigny	1	1732–60	165	*350*
Vexin	20	1738–43	264	*339*
Brittany and Anjou	21	1740–49	276	*308*
Thoissey	1	1740–49	311	*299*
Bonnières	1	1741–50	261	*283*
Weighted mean			252	

1740–90

Villedieu	1	1711–90	154	*409*
St. Méen	1	1720–92	237	*377*
Ingouville	1	1730–70	286	*482*
Lisieux	1	1730–79	135	*488*

Table 10 — *Continued*

Place	Number of Parishes	Period	Deaths per 1,000 Live Births	Source
St. Agnan	1	1730–93	193	*397*
St. Vigor	1	1731–92	125	*350*
Azereix	1	1732–72	188	*489*
Argenteuil	1	1740–79	251	*365*
Auray	1	1740–79	253	*431*
Bilhères d'Ossau	1	1740–79	182	*89*
Mogneneins	1	1740–79	212	*299*
Soudeilles	1	1740–79	154	*89*
Grenoble	1	1740–81	259	*297*
Cerdon	1	1740–89	317	*463*
Ille-et-Vilaine	3	1740–89	243	*304*
Ménestreau	1	1740–89	408	*463*
Meulan	3	1740–89	226	*413*
Mezières	1	1740–89	400	*463*
Sainghin	1	1740–89	267	*89*
St. Aubin	1	1740–89	243	*377*
Thoissey	1	1740–89	259	*89*
Villemurlin	1	1740–89	361	*463*
Ile-de-France	3	1740–92	212	*355*
Thézels-St. Sernin	1	1747–92	191	*485*
Vexin	20	1749–79	160	*339*
Tourouvre	1	1750–59	189	*324*
Boulay	7	1750–79	180	*400*
Boulay	1	1750–79	196	*398*
Brittany and Anjou	21	1750–79	245	*308*
St. Trivier	1	1750–79	260	*300*
Challain	1	1750–89	201	*423*
La Chapelle d'Aligné	1	1750–89	259	*423*
La Pommeraie	1	1750–89	182	*423*
Morannes	1	1750–89	156	*423*
Paris basin	41	1750–89	230	*89*
Tonnerois	4	1751–75	219	*338*
Tamerville	1	1756–92	124	*487*
Pontvourville	1	1756–98	194	*89*
Isigny	1	1761–92	167	*350*
Trévières	1	1761–92	144	*350*
Sennely	1	1770–79	458	*310*
Auneuil	1	1771–90	144	*372*
Beauvais	1	1771–90	209	*372*
Clermont	1	1771–90	142	*372*
Mony	1	1771–90	145	*372*
Marseille	3	1774–94	209	*288*
Paris suburbs	18	1774–94	177	*354*
Weighted mean			213	
1780–1820				
Duravel	1	1770–1800	199	*89*
Tonnerois	4	1776–1800	235	*338*
Vexin	20	1780–92	146	*339*

Table 10 — *Continued*

Place	Number of Parishes	Period	Deaths per 1,000 Live Births	Source
Argenteuil	1	1780–89	275	*365*
Brittany and Anjou	21	1780–99	237	*308*
Boulay	7	1780–1809	186	*400*
Boulay	1	1780–1809	180	*398*
Bilhères d'Ossau	1	1780–1819	151	*89*
Mogneneins	1	1780–1819	208	*299*
St. Trivier	1	1780–1819	288	*300*
Soudeilles	1	1780–1819	124	*89*
Thoissey	1	1780–1819	226	*299*
Sainghin	1	1790–1809	175	*334*
Grenoble	1	1790–1814	219	*297*
Meulan	3	1790–1829	155	*413*
Weighted mean			195	
Germany *Pre-1750*				
Braunsen	1	pre-1750	179	*502*
Grafenhausen	1	pre-1750	90	*502*
Horinghausen	1	pre-1750	133	*502*
Massenhausen (Hesse)	1	pre-1750	102	*502*
Öschelbronn	1	pre-1750	194	*502*
Vasbeck	1	pre-1750	132	*502*
Werdum	1	pre-1750	156	*502*
Anhausen	1	1692–1749	250	*500*
Mean			154	
1740–90				
Massenhausen (Bavaria)	1	1750–89	351	*509*
Anhausen	1	1750–99	425	*500*
Mean			388	
1780–1820				
Braunsen	1	1750–1849	131	*502*
Grafenhausen	1	1750–1849	222	*502*
Horinghausen	1	1750–1849	151	*502*
Kreuth	1	1750–1849	219	*502*
Massenhausen (Hesse)	1	1750–1849	145	*502*
Öschelbronn	1	1750–1849	257	*502*
Vasbeck	1	1750–1849	184	*502*
Werdum	1	1750–1849	110	*502*
Thalhausen	1	1780–1819	447	*509*
Massenhausen (Bavaria)	1	1790–1819	365	*509*
Anhausen	1	1800–1849	365	*500*
Mean			236	

Table 10 — *Continued*

Place	Number of Parishes	Period	Deaths per 1,000 Live Births	Source
Scandinavia				
Pre-1750				
All Denmark		1645–99	206	*580*
Glostrup	1	1677–1740	243	*617*
1740–90				
Glostrup	1	1741–70	284	*617*
Denmark	26 rural	1741–1801	225	*600*
Finland	8 urban	1749–73	290	*622*
Finland	53 rural	1749–73	197	*622*
All Finland		1751–90	225	*623*
North Sweden	(7) manorial	1756–75	223	*583*
North Sweden	(7) peasant	1756–75	200	*583*
South Sweden	(7) manorial	1756–75	283	*583*
South Sweden	(7) peasant	1756–75	195	*583*
1780–1820				
North Sweden	(7) manorial	1780–1810	190	*583*
North Sweden	(7) peasant	1780–1810	170	*583*
South Sweden	(7) manorial	1780–1810	227	*583*
South Sweden	(7) peasant	1780–1810	161	*583*
All Finland		1791–1820	210	*623*
Sweden	(4) urban	1800–1810	186	*583*
Spain				
Pre-1750				
Palamos	1	1705–09	255	*663*
Plencia	1	1740–49	308	*665*
Mean			281	
1740–90				
Palamos	1	1742–76	211	*663*
Granada	1	1768–77	335	*665*
Mean			273	
1780–1820				
Plencia	1	1790–99	152	*665*
Palamos	1	1790–1819	192	*663*
Otero de Herreros	1	1800–1804	317	*665*
Mean			220	

Table 10 — *Continued*

Place	Number of Parishes	Period	Deaths per 1,000 Live Births	Source
Switzerland				
Pre-1750				
Geneva	5	1580–1739	296	*695*
Entlebuch	1	1730–60	217	*674*
Weighted mean			283	
1740–90				
Geneva	5	1740–79	248	*695*
Entlebuch	1	1760–90	182	*674*
Weighted mean			237	
1780–1820				
Silenen	1	1741–1830	290	*668*
Geneva	5	1780–97	264	*695*
Entlebuch	1	1790–1820	178	*674*
Weighted mean			255	

Bibliography

THIS BIBLIOGRAPHY INCLUDES all works used in the preparation of this book. Direct citations in the text or in the right-hand column of the appendix tables are by the number that precedes each entry. Cross-references within the bibliography are also by number. I do not presume that the bibliography is comprehensive: it is limited to what I have been able to get access to and read during the time available for the book's preparation. The addendum includes some late entries.

Abbreviations of Journal Titles

ADH	*Annales de démographie historique*
AESC	*Annales: Economies, sociétés, civilisations*
AHR	*American Historical Review*
CSSH	*Comparative Studies in Society and History*
DH	*Démographie historique: Bulletin de la société de démographie historique*
EHR	*Economic History Review*
FHS	*French Historical Studies*
G	*Genus*
JEEH	*Journal of European Economic History*
JEH	*Journal of Economic History*
JIH	*Journal of Interdisciplinary History*
LPS	*Local Population Studies*
P	*Population*
PP	*Past and Present*
PS	*Population Studies*
RHES	*Revue d'histoire économique et sociale*
RHMC	*Revue d'histoire moderne et contemporaine*
RSH	*Revue suisse d'histoire*

SEHR *Scandinavian Economic History Review*
SH   *Social History*
SHR   *Scottish Historical Review*
TRHS *Transactions of the Royal Historical Society*
VSWG *Vierteljahrschrift für Sozial- und Wirtschaftsgeschichte*

Contents

A. General Symposia

1. Bechhofer, F., ed. *Population Growth and the Brain Drain.* Edinburgh, 1969.
2. Deprez, P., ed. *Problèmes de mortalité.* Liège, 1965.
3. Garden, M., ed. *Démographie urbaine, XVᵉ-XXᵉ siècle.* Lyon, 1977.
4. Glass, D. V., and Eversley, D. E. C., eds. *Population in History.* London, 1965.
5. Glass, D. V., and Revelle, R., eds. *Population and Social Change.* London, 1972.
6. Imhof, A. E., ed. *Biologie des Menschen in der Geschichte.* Stuttgart, 1978.
7. Lee, R. D., ed. *Population Patterns in the Past.* New York, 1977.
8. Lee, W. R., ed. *European Demography and Economic Growth.* London, 1979.
9. Tilly, C., ed. *Historical Studies of Changing Fertility.* Princeton, 1978.

B. Methodology and Sources

10. Dupâquier, J. "Problèmes de representativité dans les études fondées sur la reconstitution de famille." *ADH,* 1972.
11. Fleury, M., and Henry, L. *Des registres paroissiaux à l'histoire de la population. Manuel de dépouillement et d'exploitation de l'état civil ancien.* Paris, 1956. *Nouveau manuel de dépouillement et d'exploitation de l'état civil ancien.* Paris, 1965.
12. Henry, L. *Manuel de démographie historique.* Geneva and Paris, 1967.
13. _____. "The Verification of Data in Historical Demography." *PS* 22 (1968).
14. Hollingsworth, T. H. "The Importance of the Quality of the Data in Historical Demography." *Daedalus* 97 (1968).
15. Imhof, A. E. *Einführung in die Historische Demographie.* Munich, 1977.
16. Schofield, R. S. "Representativeness and Family Reconstitution." *ADH,* 1972.
17. Terrisse, M. "Aux origines de la méthode de reconstitution des familles. Les Suédois d'Estonie de Hannes Hyrenius." *P* 30 (1975).
18. Wrigley, E. A., ed. *Identifying People in the Past.* London, 1973.

C. Europe: General

19. Armengaud, A. "Population in Europe, 1700–1914." In *26,* vol. 4.
20. Bairoch, P. "Population urbaine et taille des villes en Europe de 1600 à 1970." *RHES* 54 (1976). Reprinted in *3.*
21. Bardet, J.-P. "La démographie des villes de la modernité (XVIᵉ-XVIIIᵉ siècles): mythes et réalités." *ADH,* 1974.
22. Berkner, L. K., and Mendels, F. "Inheritance Systems, Family Structure and Demographic Patterns in Western Europe." In *9.*
23. Biraben, J.-N. "Essai sur l'évolution du nombre des hommes." *P* 34 (1979).
24. Chaunu, P. *La Civilisation de l'Europe classique.* Paris, 1970.
25. Cipolla, C. M. *The Economic History of World Population.* London, 1962.
26. _____, ed. *The Fontana Economic History of Europe.* 4 vols. London and Glasgow, 1969–73.
27. Coale, A. J. "The Demographic Transition Reconsidered." *International Population Conference,* vol. 1. Liège, 1973.
28. Dainville, F. de. "Grandeur et population des villes au XVIIIᵉ siècle." *P* 13 (1958).
29. Dupâquier, J. "De l'animal à l'homme: le mécanisme auto-régulateur des populations traditionelles." *Revue de l'Institut de Sociologie,* 1972.
30. _____. "Histoire et démographie." *P* 32 (1977).
31. Fischer, W. "Rural Industrialization and Population Change." *CSSH* 15 (1973).
32. Guillaume, P., and Poussou, J.-P. *Démographie historique.* Paris, 1970.

33. Helleiner, K. F. "The Vital Revolution Reconsidered." *Canadian Journal of Economics and Political Science* 23 (1957). Reprinted in *4*.

34. _____. "The Population of Europe from the Black Death to the Eve of the Vital Revolution." In *Cambridge Economic History of Europe*, vol. 4, ed. E. E. Rich and C. H. Wilson. Cambridge, 1967. This essay was completed in 1955.

35. Imhof, A. E., and Larsen, O. *Sozialgeschichte und Medezin-Probleme der quantifizierenden Quellenarbeit in der Sozial- und Medezingeschichte.* Oslo and Stuttgart, 1975.

36. Ladurie, E. Le Roy. "Pour une histoire de l'environnement: la part du climat." *AESC* 25 (1970).

37. _____. *Times of Feast, Times of Famine: A History of Climate since the Year 1000.* London, 1972.

38. Lamb, H. H. *Climate Present, Past and Future.* 2 vols. London, 1977.

39. Langer, W. L. "Europe's Initial Population Explosion." *AHR* 69 (1963).

40. _____. "American Foods and Europe's Population Growth, 1750–1850." *Journal of Social History* 8 (1975).

41. Laslett, P. *Family Life and Illicit Love in Earlier Generations.* Cambridge, 1977.

42. McKeown, T. *The Modern Rise of Population.* London, 1976.

43. _____. "Fertility, Mortality and Causes of Death." *PS* 32 (1978).

44. _____. Brown, R. G., and Record, R. G. "An Interpretation of the Modern Rise of Population in Europe." *PS* 27 (1972).

45. Medick, H. "The Proto-industrial Family Economy: The Structural Function of Household and Family during the Transition from Peasant Society to Industrial Capitalism." *SH* 3 (1976).

46. Mendels, F. F. "Recent Research in European Historical Demography." *AHR* 75 (1970).

47. _____. "Proto-Industrialization: The First Phase of the Industrialization Process." *JEH* 32 (1972).

48. Mols, R. P. R. *Introduction à la démographie historique des villes d'Europe du XIVe au XVIIIe siècle.* 3 vols. Louvain, 1954–56.

49. _____. "Population in Europe, 1500–1700." In *26*, vol. 2.

50. Parry, M. L. "Secular Climatic Change and Marginal Agriculture." *Transactions of the Institute of British Geographers* 64 (1975).

51. Reinhard, M., Armengaud, A., and Dupâquier, J. *Histoire générale de la population mondiale.* 3d ed. Paris, 1968.

52. Schofield, R. "Historical Demography: Some Possibilities and Some Limitations." *TRHS*, 5th ser. 21 (1971).

53. Sharlin, A. "Natural Decrease in Early Modern Cities: A Reconsideration." *PP* 79 (1978).

54. Smith, D. S. "A Homeostatic Demographic Regime: Patterns in West European Family Reconstitution Studies." In *7*.

55. Teuteberg, H. J. "The General Relationship between Diet and Industrialization." In *European Diet from Pre-industrial to Modern Times,* ed. E. Forster and R. Forster. New York, 1975.

56. Tilly, C. "The Historical Study of Vital Processes." In 9.
57. Wilson, C. H., and Parker, G., eds. *An Introduction to the Sources of European Economic History, 1500-1800*. London, 1978.
58. Wrigley, E. A. *Population and History*. London, 1969.

D. Europe: Mortality

59. Appleby, A. B. "Famine, Mortality and Epidemic Disease: A Comment." *EHR*, 2d ser. 30 (1977).
60. Beveridge, W. I. B. *Influenza: The Last Great Plague*. London, 1977.
61. Biraben, J.-N. "Conséquences économiques des mesures sanitaires contre la peste du moyen age au 18ᵉ siècle." *Annales cisalpines d'histoire sociale*, 1973.
62. _____. *Les Hommes et la peste en France et dans les pays européens et méditerranéens*. 2 vols. Paris and The Hague, 1975-76.
63. Cipolla, C. M., and Zanetti, A. "Peste et mortalité différentielle." *ADH*, 1972.
64. Cohen, J. E. "Childhood Mortality, Family Size and Birth Order in Preindustrial Europe." *Demography* 12 (1975).
65. Curtin, P. D. "Epidemiology and the Slave Trade." *Political Science Quarterly* 83 (1968).
66. Dubos, R., and Dubos, J. *The White Plague*. London, 1953.
67. Flinn, M. W. "The Stabilisation of Mortality in Pre-industrial Western Europe." *JEEH* 3 (1974).
68. _____. "Plague in Europe and the Mediterranean Countries." *JEEH* 8 (1979).
69. Hirst, L. F. *The Conquest of Plague*. Oxford, 1953.
70. Ladurie, E. Le Roy. "Un Concept: l'unification microbienne du monde (XIVᵉ-XVIIᵉ siècles)." *RSH* 23 (1973).
71. McNeill, W. H. *Plagues and Peoples*. London, 1977.
72. Meuvret, J. "Réflexions d'un historien sur les crises démographiques aiguës avant le XVIIIᵉ siècle." In 2.
73. Norris, J. "East or West? The Geographic Origin of the Black Death." *Bulletin of the History of Medicine* 51 (1977).
74. Post, J. D. "Famine, Mortality and Epidemic Disease in the Process of Modernization." *EHR*, 2d ser. 29 (1976).
75. _____. *The Last Great Subsistence Crisis in the Western World*. Baltimore and London, 1977.
76. Prinzing, F. *Epidemics Resulting from Wars*. Oxford, 1916.
77. Ruwet, J. "Crises démographiques. Problèmes économiques ou crises morales." *P* 9 (1954).
78. Vilar, P. "Réflexions sur la 'crise de l'ancien type,' 'inégalité des récoltes,' et 'sous-développement.' " In *Conjoncture économique, structures sociales. Hommage à Ernest Labrousse*. Paris and The Hague, 1974.

E. Europe: Fertility and Marriage

79. Burguière, A. "De Malthus à Max Weber: le mariage tardif et l'esprit d'entreprise." *AESC* 27 (1972). Translated into English in *Family and Society*, ed. R. Forster and O. Ranum. Baltimore, 1976.
80. Charbonneau, H. "Effets du déséquilibre des structures démographiques sur la nuptialité." *ADH*, 1978.
81. Coale, A. J. "The Decline of Fertility in Europe from the French Revolution to World War II." In *Fertility and Family Planning*, ed. S. J. Behrman, Ann Arbor, 1969.
82. Diers, C. J. "Historical Trends in the Age of Menarche and Menopause." *Psychological Reports* 34 (1974).
83. Drake, M. "Age at Marriage in the Pre-industrial West." In *1.*
84. Fairchilds, C. "Female Sexual Attitudes and the Rise of Illegitimacy: A Case Study." *JIH* 8 (1978).
85. Flandrin, J.-L. *L'eglise et le contrôle des naissances.* Paris, 1970.
86. _____. "Mariage tardif et vie sexuelle. Discussions et hypothèses de recherche." *AESC* 27 (1972).
87. _____. "L'Attitude à l'égard du petit enfant et les conduites sexuelles dans la civilisation occidentale: structures anciennes et évolution." *ADH*, 1973.
88. _____. "Contraception, Marriage and Sexual Relations in the Christian West." In *Biology of Man in History*, R. Forster and O. Ranum ed.. Baltimore, 1975.
89. _____. *Familles. Parenté, maison, sexualité dans l'ancienne société.* Paris, 1976.
90. _____. "Repression and Change in the Sexual Life of Young People in Medieval and Early Modern Times." *Journal of Family History* 2 (1977).
91. Frisch, R. E. "Population, Food Intake and Fertility." *Science* 199 (6 January 1978).
92. Hajnal, J. "European Marriage Patterns in Perspective." In *4.*
93. Hélin, E. *La Prévention des naissances dans la famille.* Paris, 1960.
94. Holmberg, I. "Variations in Natural Fertility." In *567.*
95. Jain, A. K., Hsu, T. C., Freedman, R., and Chang, M. C. "Demographic Aspects of Lactation and Postpartum Amenorrhoea." *Demography* 7 (1970).
96. Ladurie, E. Le Roy. "L'Amenorrhée de famine (XVIIe-XXe siècles)." *AESC* 24 (1969). Translated into English in *Biology of Man in History*, ed. R. Forster and O. Ranum. Baltimore, 1975; and into German in *6.*
97. Lestaeghe, R. "Nuptiality and Population Growth." *PS* 25 (1971).
98. Shorter, E. "Illegitimacy, Sexual Revolution and Social Change in Modern Europe." *JIH* 2 (1971).
99. _____. "Female Emancipation, Birth Control and Fertility in European History." *AHR* 78 (1973).
100. _____. *The Making of the Modern Family.* London, 1976.

101. Tilly, L. A., and Scott, J. W. *Women, Work and Family.* New York, 1978.
102. Wrigley, E. A. "Fertility Strategy for the Individual and the Group." In *9.*

F. Belgium

103. Arnould, M.-A. "Mortalité et épidemies sous l'ancien régime dans le Hainaut et quelques régions limitrophes." In *2.*
104. Bruneel, C. *La Mortalité dans les campagnes: le duché de Brabant aux XVIIe et XVIIIe siècles.* 2 vols. Louvain, 1977.
105. Deprez, P. "The Demographic Development of Flanders in the Eighteenth Century." In *4.*
106. _____. "The Low Countries." In *8.*
107. Gutmann, M. P. "Putting Crises in Perspective. The Impact of War on Civilian Populations in the Seventeenth Century." *ADH,* 1977.
108. _____. "Why They Stayed: The Problem of Wartime Population Loss." *Tijdschrift voor Geschiedenis* 91 (1978).
109. Hélin, E. "La Population de l'ancienne paroisse St. Rémy à Liège." *Le Vieux Liège* 101-2 (1953).
110. _____. *La Démographie de Liège aux XVIIe et XVIIIe siècles.* Brussels, 1963.
111. _____. "Le Déroulement de trois crises à Liège au XVIIIe siècle." In *2.*
112. _____. "Les Recherches sur la mortalité dans la région liègeoise (XVe–XIXe siècles)." In *2.*
113. _____. "Une Solicitude ambiguë: l'évacuation des enfants abandonnés." *ADH,* 1973.
114. Houdaille, J. "Nuptialité et fecondité en Flandre et au Brabant du XVIIe au XIXe siècle." *P* 32 (1977).
115. Méens, M. "La Mortalité à Meerhout-en-Campine de 1686 à 1815." *Population et famille* 33 (1974).
116. Mendels, F. F. "Industry and Marriages in Flanders before the Industrial Revolution." In *Population and Economics. Proceedings of Section V of the IV Congress of the International Economic History Association 1968,* ed. P. Deprez. Winnipeg, 1970.
117. Mols, R. P. R. "Die Bevölkerungsgeschichte Belgiens im Lichte der heutigen Forschung." *VSWG* 46 (1959).
118. Morineau, M. "Démographie ancienne: monotonie ou variété des comportements." *AESC* 20 (1965).
119. Ruwet, J. "Crises démographiques: problèmes économiques ou crises morales? Le Pays de Liège sous l'ancien régime." *P* 9 (1954).
120. _____. "Les inégalités devant la mort. Les Pays-Bas et la principauté de Liège du XVIe au XVIIIe siècle." In *2.*
121. Vandenbroeke, C. "Caractéristiques de la nuptialité et de la fecondité en Flandre et au Brabant aux XVIIe–XIXe siècles." *ADH,* 1977.
122. van der Wee, H. "Typologie des crises et changements de structures aux Pays-Bas (XVe–XVIe siècles)." *AESC* 18 (1963).

123. van Werveke, H. "La Mortalité catastrophique en Flandre au XVIIᵉ siècle." In 2.

G. Eastern Europe

124. Andorka, R. "Fertility, Nuptiality and Household Structure of Peasant Communities of Hungary in the 18th–19th Centuries." Mimeographed. Budapest, n.d.
125. _____. "La Prévention des naissances en Hongrie dans la région 'Ormansag' depuis la fin du 18ᵉ siècle." P 26 (1971).
126. _____. "Un Exemple de faible fecondité légitime dans une région de la Hongrie. L'Ormansag à la fin du 18ᵉ siècle et au début du 19ᵉ siècle: contrôle des naissances ou faux-semblants?" ADH, 1972.
127. _____. "Birth Control in the Eighteenth and Nineteenth Centuries in Some Hungarian Villages." LPS 22 (1979).
128. Beskrovny, L. G., Kabouzan, V. M., and Latsounski, V. K. "Bilan démographique de la Russie en 1789–1815." ADH 1965.
129. Danyi, D. "La Migration et les méthodes nominatives: l'exemple hongrois." ADH, 1972.
130. Duka, N. Z. "Epidemics of Smallpox and Its Mortality in Pressbourg at the End of the 18th Century (1776–1800)." Tortenetti statisztikai Tanulmanyok 3 (1977).
131. Farago, T. "Household Structure and Development of Rural Society in Hungary, 1787–1828." Torteneti statisztikai Tanulmanyok 3 (1977).
132. Fugedi, E. "Present Situation of the Hungarian Historical Demography, 1769–1869." Mimeographed. Budapest, n.d.
133. Gieysztor, I. "Introduction à la démographie de l'ancienne Pologne (XVIᵉ–XVIIIᵉ siècles)." ADH, 1977.
134. Helczmanovzki, H. "Austria-Hungary." In 8.
135. Horska, P. "L'Etat actuel des recherches sur l'évolution de la population dans les pays tcheques aux XVIIIᵉ et XIXᵉ siècles." ADH, 1967.
136. Horvath, R. "Quelques données inconnues sur la mortalité de la peste de Debrecen, 1739–40, et celle du cholera en Hongrie, 1831, 1866, 1872–73." Bulletin de l'Institut International de Statistique 33 (1961).
137. Houdaille, J. "La Nuptialité à Poznan au début du XIXᵉ siècle." P 32 (1977).
138. Hunyadi, I. "La Population d'un comitat hongrois (Györ) vers 1550." ADH, 1974.
139. Husa, V. "Notes d'information sur les sources et les recherches de démographie historique en Tschecoslovaquie." In 2.
140. Hyrenius, H. "Fertility and Reproduction in a Swedish Population Group Without Family Limitation." PS 12 (1958–59).
141. Kabusan, V.-M. "La Colonisation paysanne de la côte nord de la Mer Noire (Novo Russie) de 1719 à 1857." ADH, 1970.

142. Kahk, J., Ligi, H., Palli, H., Vahtre, S., and Pullat, A. "Sur l'histoire démographique de l'Estonie." *ADH*, 1972.

143. Kovacsics, J. "An Account of Research Work in Historical Demography in Hungary." In 2.

144. _____. "Situation démographique de la Hongrie à la fin du XVIIIᵉ siècle (1787-1815)." *ADH*, 1965.

145. Kula, W. "La Seigneurie et la famille paysanne dans la Pologne du 18ᵉ siècle." *AESC* 27 (1972). Translated into English in *Family and Society*, ed. R. Forster and O. Ranum. Baltimore, 1976.

146. Lesky, E. "Die Österreichische Pestfront an k.k. Militärgrenze." *Saeculum* 8 (1957).

147. McNeill, W. H. *Europe's Steppe Frontier*. Chicago and London, 1964.

148. Norbert, D. Z. "Epidemics of Smallpox and Its Mortality at Presbourg at the End of the Eighteenth Century." *Torteneti statisztikai Tanulmanyok* 3 (1977). In Hungarian with English summary.

149. Norwood, F. A. "Les Migrations des Hutterites d'Alexanderwohl." *ADH*, 1970.

150. Palli, H. "Historical Demography of Estonia in the 17th-18th Centuries and Computers." In *Studia historica in honorem Hans Kruus*. Tallinn, 1971.

151. _____. "Parish Registers, Revisions of Land and Souls, Family Reconstitution and Household in Seventeenth- and Eighteenth-Century Estonia." In *567*.

152. Pascu, S. "Les Sources et les recherches démographiques en Roumanie (période pré-statistique)." In 2.

153. Rothenburg, G. E. "The Austrian Sanitary Cordon and the Control of Bubonic Plague: 1710-1871." *Journal of the History of Medicine and Allied Sciences* 28 (1973).

154. Rubner, H. "En forêt de Bohème: immigration et émigration (1500-1960)." *ADH*, 1970.

155. Tinta, A. "Contributii la canoasteres agriculturii si populatiei din Banat al XVIII-lea." *Populatie si societate* 2 (1977).

156. Vodarsky, Y.-E. "Le Mouvement migratoire de la population russe durant la deuxième moitié du XVIIᵉ siècle et le début du XVIIIᵉ siècle." *ADH*, 1970.

H. England

157. Appleby, A. B. "Disease or Famine? Mortality in Cumberland and Westmorland, 1580-1640." *EHR*, 2d ser. 26 (1973).

158. _____. "Nutrition and Disease: The case of London, 1550-1750." *JIH* 6 (1975).

159. _____. *Famine in Tudor and Stuart England*. Stanford, 1978.

160. Baker, D. *The Inhabitants of Cardington in 1782*. Bedfordshire Historical Record Society, vol. 52. Bedford, 1973.

161. Blanchard, I. "Population Change, Enclosure and the Early Tudor Economy." *EHR* 2d ser. 23 (1970).

162. Bradley, L. "The Most Famous of All English Plagues: A Detailed Analysis of the Plague at Eyam, 1665-66." In *225*.

163. Brent, C. "Devastating Epidemic in the Countryside of Eastern Sussex between Harvest Years 1558 and 1640." *LPS* 14 (1975).

164. Buckatzsch, E. J. "Places of Origin of a Group of Immigrants into Sheffield, 1624-1799." *EHR*, 2d ser. 2 (1950).

165. _____. "The Constancy of Local Populations and Immigration in England before 1800." *PS* 5 (1951-52).

166. Butcher, A. F. "The Origins of Romney Freemen, 1433-1523." *EHR*, 2d ser. 27 (1974).

167. Chambers, J. D. "The Vale of Trent, 1670-1800." *EHR*, supp. 3 (1957).

168. _____. "Population Change in a Provincial Town, Nottingham, 1700-1800." In *Studies in the Industrial Revolution*, ed. L. S. Pressnell. London, 1960. Reprinted in *187*.

169. _____. *Population, Economy and Society in Pre-industrial England.* London, 1972.

170. Cherry, S. "The Role of a Provincial Hospital: The Norfolk and Norwich Hospital, 1771-1880." *PS* 26 (1972).

171. Clark, P. "The Migrant in Kentish Towns, 1580-1640." In *Crisis and Order in English Towns, 1500-1700*, ed. P. Clark and P. Slack. London, 1972.

172. _____. "Migration in England during the Late Seventeenth and Early Eighteenth Centuries." *PP* 83 (1979).

173. Clarkson, L. *Death, Disease and Famine in Pre-industrial England.* Dublin, 1975.

174. Cornwall, J. "Evidence of Population Mobility in the Seventeenth Century." *Bulletin of the Institute of Historical Research* 40 (1967).

175. _____. "English Population in the Early Sixteenth Century." *EHR*, 2d ser. 23 (1970).

176. Cowgill, U. M. "Historical Study of the Season of Birth in the City of York." *Nature* 209 (1966).

177. _____. "Life and Death in the 16th Century in the City of York." *PS* 21 (1967).

178. Crafts, N. F. R. "Eighteenth-Century Local Population Studies in the Context of Aggregate Estimates for England and Wales." *LPS* 13 (1974).

179. _____, and Ireland, N. J. "The Role of Simulation Techniques in the Theory and Observation of Family Formation." *PS* 29 (1975).

180. _____. "A Simulation of the Impact of Changes in Age at Marriage before and during the Advent of Industrialization in England." *PS* 30 (1976).

181. _____. "Family Limitation and the English Demographic Revolution: A simulation Approach." *JEH* 36 (1976).

182. Creasey, D. "Occupations, Migration and Literacy in East London, 1580-1640." *LPS* 5 (1970).

183. Creighton, C. *A History of Epidemics in Britain.* 2 vols. 2d ed. London, 1965.

184. Cunningham, C. "Christ's Hospital: Infant and Child Mortality in the Sixteenth Century." *LPS* 18 (1977).

185. Doolittle, I. G. "The Effects of the Plague on a Provincial Town in the Sixteenth and Seventeenth Centuries (Colchester)." *Medical History* 19 (1975).
186. Drake, M. "An Elementary Exercise in Parish Register Demography." *EHR*, 2d ser. 14 (1962).
187. _____, ed. *Population in Industrialization*. London, 1969.
188. Dyer, A. D. *The City of Worcester in the Sixteenth Century*. Leicester, 1973.
189. Edwards, J. K. "Norwich Bills of Mortality, 1707–1830." *Yorkshire Bulletin of Economic and Social Research* 21 (1969).
190. Edwards, W. J. "Marriage Seasonality, 1761–1810: An assessment of Patterns in Seventeen Shropshire Parishes." *LPS* 19 (1977).
191. Eversley, D. E. C. "A Survey of Population in an Area of Worcestershire from 1660 to 1850 on the Basis of Parish Registers." *PS* 10 (1957). Reprinted in *4*.
192. Finlay, R. A. P. "Gateways to Death? London Child Mortality Experience, 1570–1653." *ADH*, 1978.
193. Fisher, F. J. "Influenza and Inflation in Tudor England." *EHR*, 2d ser. 18 (1965).
194. Flinn, M. W. *British Population Growth, 1700–1850*. London, 1970.
195. Glass, D. V. "Notes on the Demography of London at the End of the Seventeenth Century." *Daedalus* 97 (1968). Reprinted in *5*.
196. Gooder, A. *Plague and Enclosure. A Warwickshire Village in the Seventeenth Century*. Coventry and North Warwickshire History Pamphlets, no. 2. 1965.
197. _____. "The Population Crisis of 1727–30 in Warwickshire." *Midland History* 1 (1972).
198. Habakkuk, H. J. *Population Growth and Economic Development since 1750*. Leicester, 1971.
199. Hair, P. E. H. "Bridal Pregnancy in Earlier Centuries." *PS* 20 (1966).
200. _____. "Bridal Pregnancy in Rural England Further Examined." *PS* 24 (1970).
201. _____. "Deaths from Violence in Britain: A Tentative Secular Survey." *PS* 25 (1971).
202. Hammer, C. I. "The Mobility of Skilled Labour in Late Medieval England: Some Oxford Evidence." *VSWG* 63 (1976).
203. Hanley, H. "Population Mobility in Buckinghamshire, 1578–1583." *LPS* 15 (1975).
204. Harrison, G. A., Horns, R. W., and Küchemann, C. F. "Social Class and Marriage Patterns in Some Oxfordshire Parishes." *Journal of Biosocial Science* 3 (1971).
205. Hatcher, J. *Plague, Population and the English Economy, 1348–1530*. London, 1977.
206. Holderness, R. A. "Personal Mobility in Some Rural Parishes of Yorkshire, 1777–1812." *Yorkshire Archaeological Journal* 42 (1971).
207. Hollingsworth, M. F., and Hollingsworth, T. H. "Plague Mortality Rates by Age and Sex in the Parish of St. Botolphs Without, Bishopsgate, London, 1603." *PS* 25 (1971).

208. Hollingsworth, T. H. "A Demographic Study of the British Ducal Families." *PS* 11 (1957). Reprinted in *4* and *187*.
209. _____. "Demography of the British Peerage." *PS* 18 (1965), supp.
210. Hoskins, W. G. "The Population of an English Village, 1086–1801: A Study of Wigston Magna." *Transactions of the Leicestershire Archaeological and Historical Society* 33 (1957).
211. Howson, W. G. "Plague, Poverty and Population in Parts of North-west England, 1580–1720." *Transactions of the Historic Society of Lancashire and Cheshire* 112 (1960).
212. Johnston, J. A. "The Impact of the Epidemics of 1727–1730 in South-west Worcestershire." *Medical History* 15 (1971).
213. Jones, R. E. "Population and Agrarian Change in Eighteenth-Century Shropshire parish." *LPS* 1 (1968).
214. _____. "Infant Mortality in Rural North Shropshire, 1561–1810." *PS* 30 (1976).
215. Krier, D. F., and Loschky, D. J. "Income and Family Size in Three Eighteenth-Century Lancashire Parishes." *JEH* 29 (1969).
216. Küchemann, C. F., Boyce, A. J., and Harrison, G. A. "A Demographic and Genetic Study of a Group of Oxfordshire Villages." *Human Biology* 39 (1967). Reprinted in *Applied Historical Studies*, ed. M. Drake. London, 1973.
217. Laslett, P. *The World We Have Lost.* London, 1965.
218. _____, and Harrison, J. "Clayworth and Cogenhoe." In *Historical Essays*, ed. H. E. Bell and R. L. Ollard. London, 1963.
219. _____, and Oosterveen, K. "Long-Term Trends in Bastardy." *PS* 27 (1973).
220. Lee, R. "Probleme der Bevölkerungsgeschichte in England, 1750–1850: Fragestellungen und vorläufige Ergebnisse." *VSWG* 40 (1973).
221. _____. "Population in Pre-industrial England: An econometric Analysis." *Quarterly Journal of Economics* 87 (1973).
222. _____. "Estimating Series of Vital Rates and Age Structures from Baptisms and Burials: A New Technique with Applications to Pre-industrial England." *PS* 28 (1974).
223. Levine, D. "The Demographic Implications of Rural Industrialization: A Family Reconstitution Study of Shepshed, Leicestershire, 1600–1851." *SH* 1 (1976).
224. _____. *Family Formation in an Age of Nascent Capitalism.* New York, 1977.
225. Local Population Studies. *The Plague Reconsidered.* Matlock, 1977.
226. Loschky, D. J. "Urbanisation and England's Eighteenth-Century Crude Death Rate." *JEEH* 1 (1972).
227. _____, and Krier, D. F. "Income and Family Size in Three Eighteenth-Century Lancashire Parishes: A Reconstitution Study." *JEH* 29 (1969).
228. McKeown, T., and Brown, R. G. "Medical Evidence Related to English Population Changes in the Eighteenth Century." *PS* 9 (1955). Reprinted in *4* and *187*.
229. Maltby, B. "Easingwold Marriage Horizons." *LPS* 2 (1969).

230. _____. "Parish Registers and the Problem of Mobility." *LPS* 6 (1971).
231. Martin, J. M. *The Rise of Population in Eighteenth-Century Warwickshire.* Dugdale Society Occasional Papers, no. 23, Oxford, 1976.
232. _____. "Marriage and Economic Stress in the Felden of Warwickshire during the Eighteenth Century." *PS* 31 (1977).
233. _____. "The Rich, the Poor and the Migrant in Eighteenth-Century Stratford-on-Avon." *LPS* 20 (1978).
234. Morris, C. "The Plague in Britain." *Historical Journal* 14 (1971).
235. Morrow, R. B. "Family Limitation in Pre-industrial England: A Reappraisal." *EHR* 2d ser. 31 (1978).
236. Mullett, C. F. "A Century of English Quarantine." *Bulletin of the History of Medicine* 23 (1949).
237. Outhwaite, R. B. "Age at Marriage in England from the Late Seventeenth to the Nineteenth Century." *TRHS*, 5th ser. 23 (1973).
238. _____. "Food Crises in Early Modern England: Patterns of Public Response." In *Proceedings of the Seventh International Economic History Congress*, ed. M. W. Flinn. Edinburgh, 1978.
239. _____. "Population Change, Family Structure and the Good of Counting." *Historical Journal* 22 (1979).
240. Palliser, D. M. "Epidemics in Tudor York." *Northern History* 8 (1973).
241. _____. "Dearth and Disease in Staffordshire, 1540–1670." In *Rural Change and Urban Growth, 1500–1800*, ed. C. W. Chalklin and M. A. Havinden. London, 1974.
242. Patten, J. *Rural-Urban Migration in Pre-industrial England.* School of Geography, Oxford University, Research Paper 6. Oxford, 1973.
243. _____. "Patterns of Migration and Movement of Labour to Three Pre-industrial East Anglian Towns." *Journal of Historical Geography* 2 (1976).
244. Pickard, R. *The Population and Epidemics of Exeter in Pre-Census Times.* Exeter, 1947.
245. Pickles, M. F. "Mid-Wharfedale, 1721–1812: Economic and Demographic Change in a Pennine dale." *LPS* 16 (1976).
246. Razzell, P. E. "Population Change in Eighteenth-Century England: A Reinterpretation." *EHR*, 2d ser. 18 (1965). Reprinted in *187*.
247. _____. "Population Growth and Economic Change in Eighteenth- and early Nineteenth-Century England and Ireland." In *Land, Labour and Population in the Industrial Revolution*, ed. E. L. Jones and G. E. Mingay. London, 1967.
248. _____. *The Conquest of Smallpox.* Firle, Sussex, 1977.
249. _____. *Edward Jenner's Cowpox Vaccine: The History of a Medical Myth.* Firle, Sussex, 1977.
250. Reynolds, G. "Infant Mortality and Sex Ratios at Baptism As Shown by Reconstruction of Willingham, a Parish at the Edge of the Fens in Cambridgeshire." *LPS* 22 (1979).
251. Rich, E. E. "The Population of Elizabethan England." *EHR*, 2d ser. 2 (1950).

252. Rogers, C. D. *The Lancashire Population Crisis of 1623*. Manchester, 1975.
253. Ryerson, A. J. "Medical Advice on Child-rearing, 1550–1900." *Harvard Educational Review* 41 (1961).
254. Schofield, R. S. "Age-specific Mobility in an Eighteenth-Century Rural English Parish." *ADH*, 1970.
255. _____. "Perinatal Mortality in Hawkshead, Lancashire." *LPS* 4 (1970).
256. _____. " 'Crisis' mortality." *LPS* 9 (1972).
257. _____. "An Anatomy of an Epidemic: Colyton, November 1645 to November 1646." In *225*.
258. _____, and Berry, B. M. "Age at Baptism in Pre-industrial England." *PS* 25 (1971).
259. _____, and Wrigley, E. A. "Infant and Child Mortality in Late Tudor and Early Stuart England." In *Health, Medicine and Mortality in the Sixteenth Century*, ed. C. Webster. Cambridge, 1979.
260. Shrewsbury, J. F. D. *A History of Bubonic Plague in Britain*. Cambridge, 1970.
261. Sigsworth, E. "A Provincial Hospital in the Eighteenth and Early Nineteenth Centuries." *College of General Practitioners, Yorkshire Faculty Journal*, 1966.
262. Skipp, V. *Crisis and Development. An Ecological Case-Study of the Forest of Arden, 1570–1674*. Cambridge, 1978.
263. Slack, P. "The Local Incidence of Epidemic Disease: The Case of Bristol, 1540–1650." In *225*.
264. Smith, R. M. "Population and Its Geography in England, 1500–1730." In *An Historical Geography of England and Wales*, ed. R. Dodgshon and R. Butlin. New York, 1978.
265. Sogner, S. "Aspects of the Demographic Situation in 17 Parishes in Shropshire, 1711–1760: An Exercise Based on Parish Registers." *PS* 17 (1963).
266. Spufford, M. *Contrasting Communities: English Villagers in the Sixteenth and Seventeenth Centuries*. Cambridge, 1974.
267. Spufford, P. "Population Movements in Seventeenth-Century England." *LPS* 4 (1970).
268. Sutherland, I. "When Was the Great Plague? Mortality in London, 1563 to 1665." In *5*.
269. Tranter, N. L. "Population and Social Structure in a Bedfordshire Parish: The Cardington Listing of Inhabitants, 1782." *PS* 21 (1967).
270. _____. *Population since the Industrial Revolution: The Case of England and Wales*. London, 1973.
271. Turner, D. "A Lost Seventeenth-Century Demographic Crisis? The Evidence of Two Counties." *LPS* 21 (1978).
272. West, F. "Infant Mortality in the East Fen Parishes of Leake and Wrangle." *LPS* 13 (1974).
273. Wrightson, K. "Infanticide in Earlier Seventeenth-Century England." *LPS* 15 (1975).
274. Wrigley, E. A. "Family Limitation in Pre-industrial England." *EHR*, 2d ser. 19 (1966). Reprinted in *187*.

275. _____, ed. *An Introduction to English Historical Demography*. London, 1966.

276. _____, "A Simple Model of London's Importance in Changing English Society and Economy, 1650-1750." *PP* 37 (1967).

277. _____. "Mortality in Pre-industrial England: The Example of Colyton, Devon, over Three Centuries." *Daedalus* 97 (1968). Reprinted in *5*.

278. _____. "The Process of Modernization and the Industrial Revolution in England." *JIH* 3 (1972).

279. _____. "Clandestine Marriage in Tetbury in the Late 17th Century." *LPS* 10 (1973).

280. _____. "Births and Baptisms: The Use of Anglican Baptism Registers as a Source of Information About the Number of Births in England before the Beginning of Civil Registration." *PS* 31 (1977).

281. _____. "A Note on the Life-time Mobility of Women in a Parish Population in the Later Eighteenth Century." *LPS* 18 (1977).

282. Yasumoto, M. "Urbanization and Population in an English Town: Leeds during the Industrial Revolution." *Keio Economic Studies* (Tokyo), October 1973.

I. France

283. Ackermann, E. "The Commune of Bonnières-sur-Seine in the Eighteenth and Nineteenth Centuries." *ADH*, 1977.

284. Ariès, P. "Sur les origines de la contraception en France." *P* 8 (1953).

285. Armengaud, A. "Agriculture et démographie au XVIIIᵉ siècle. Réflexions sur un livre récent." *RHES* 49 (1971).

286. _____. *La Famille et l'enfant en France et en Angleterre au XVIᵉ au XVIIIᵉ siècle. Aspects démographiques*. Paris, 1975.

287. Baehrel, R. *Une Croissance: la Basse-Provence rurale (fin du XVIᵉ siècle − 1789)*. 2 vols. Paris, 1961.

288. Bardet, J.-P. "Enfants abandonnés et enfants assistés à Rouen dans la seconde moitié du XVIIIᵉ siècle." In *340*.

289. _____. "La Démographie des villes de la modernité (XVIᵉ–XVIIIᵉ siècles): mythes et réalités." *ADH*, 1974.

290. Baulant, M. "La Famille en miettes. Sur un aspect de la démographie au XVIIᵉ siècle." *AESC* 27 (1972). Translated into English in *Family and Society*, ed. R. Forster and O. Ranum. Baltimore, 1976.

291. Beaudry, R. "Alimentation et population rurale en Périgord au XVIIIᵉ siècle." *ADH*, 1976.

292. Bécart, F. "Saint André d'Hébertot au XVIIᵉ et au XVIIIᵉ siècles: étude démographique." *Annales de Normandie* 27 (1977).

293. Benedict, P. "Catholics and Huguenots in Sixteenth-Century Rouen: The Demographic Effects of the Religious Wars." *FHS* 9 (1975-76).

294. Bernard, R.-J. "L'Alimentation paysanne en Gévaudan au XVIIIᵉ siècle." *AESC* 24 (1969). Translated into English in *European Diet from Pre-industrial to Modern Times*, ed. E. Forster and R. Forster. New York, 1975.

295. Berthet, P. "Villes et campagnes en Savoie au XVIᵉ siècle." In *3*.
296. Berthieu, R. "Les Nourrissons à Cormeilles-en-Parisis (1640–1789)." *ADH*, 1975.
297. Bideau, A. "La Population de Thoissey aux XVIIIᵉ et XIXᵉ siècles. Etude de démographie historique." *Bulletin du Centre d'Histoire Economique et Sociale de la Région Lyonnaise* 2 (1972).
298. _____. "L'Envoi des jeunes enfants en nourrice. L'exemple d'une petite ville: Thoissey-en-Dombes (1740–1840)." In *340*.
299. _____. "La Mortalité des enfants dans la chatellenie de Thoissey-en-Dombes. Essai de pathologie historique (1670–1840)." In *3*.
300. _____; Brunet, G.; and Desbos, R. "Variations de mortalité des enfants: l'exemple de la chatellenie de Saint-Trivier-en-Dombes (1730–1869)." *ADH*, 1978.
301. Billot, C. "Les Enfants abandonnés à Chartres à la fin du moyen age." *ADH*, 1975.
302. Biraben, J.-N. "Certain Demographic Characteristics of the Plague Epidemic in France, 1720–22." *Daedalus* 97 (1968). Reprinted in *5*.
303. Blacker, J. G. C. "Social Ambitions of the Bourgeoisie in 18th-Century France, and Their Relation to Family Limitation." *PS* 11 (1957–58).
304. Blayo, Y. "Trois paroisses d'Ille-et-Vilaine." *ADH*, 1969.
305. _____. "Mouvement naturel de la population française de 1740 à 1829." *P* 30 (1975).
306. _____. "La Mortalité en France de 1740 à 1829." *P* 30 (1975).
307. _____. "La Proportion de naissances illégitimes en France de 1740 à 1860." *P* 30 (1975).
308. _____, and Henry, L. "Données démographiques sur la Bretagne et l'Anjou de 1740 à 1829." *ADH*, 1967.
309. Bornarel, M. "Quelques aspects de l'évolution démographique et de la formation de la population grenobloise de 1680 à 1880." In *3*.
310. Bouchard, G. *Le Village immobile. Senneley-en-Sologne au XVIIIᵉ siècle.* Paris, 1972.
311. Bourdelais, P., and Raulot, J.-Y. "Des risques de la petite enfance à la fin du XVIIᵉ siècle. Gestation, allaitement et mortalité." *ADH*, 1976.
312. Bourdelais, P., and Raulot, J.-Y. "La Reprise de fecondité après décès: indicateur des conditions d'accouchement." *ADH*, 1977.
313. Bouvet, M., and Bourdin, P. M. *A travers la Normandie des XVIIᵉ et XVIIIᵉ siècles.* Caen, 1968.
314. Bricourt, M.; Lachiver, M.; and Queruel, J. "La Crise de subsistance des années 1740 dans le ressort du parlement de Paris." *ADH*, 1974.
315. Cabourdin, G. Review of S. Dreyer-Roos, *La Population de Strasbourg sous l'Ancien Régime (1681–1789).* In *ADH*, 1967.
316. _____. "Mariages et origine des époux dans un bourg Lorrain. Vézelise (1578–1633)." *ADH*, 1970.
317. Chamoux, A. "Marital Fertility Rates in Châtillon-sur-Seine (Burgundy), France, 1772 to 1789." Mimeographed. 1969.
318. _____. "La Reconstitution des familles: espoirs et réalité." *AESC* 27 (1972).

319. _____. "Démographie historique et ordinateur: l'exemple de Reims." *DH* 10 (1973).

320. _____. "L'Enfance abandonnée à Reims à la fin du XVIIIe siècle." *ADH*, 1973.

321. _____. "Town and Child in Eighteenth-Century Rheims." *LPS* 13 (1974).

322. _____, and Dauphin C. "La Contraception avant la Révolution Française: l'exemple de Châtillon-sur-Seine." *AESC* 24 (1969).

323. Chance, A., *et al.* "Honfleur de 1680 à 1780." *DH* 15 (1975).

324. Charbonneau, H. *Tourouvre-au-Perche aux XVIIe et XVIIIe siècles.* Paris, 1970.

325. Chaunu, P. Review of A. Plaisse, *La Baronnie du Neubourg. Essai d'histoire agraire, économique et sociale. AESC* 17 (1962).

326. _____. "Malthusianisme démographique et Malthusianisme économique. Réflexions sur l'échec industriel de la Normandie à l'époque du demarrage." *AESC* 27 (1972).

327. _____. "Réflexions sur la démographique normande." In *340.*

328. Coppolani, J. "Bilan démographique de Toulouse de 1789 à 1815." In *Contributions à l'histoire démographique de la Révolution Française.* Commission d'Histoire Economique et Sociale de la Révolution Française: mémoires et documents, 18. Paris, 1965.

329. Corvisier, A. "Service militaire et mobilité géographique au XVIIIe siècle." *ADH*, 1970.

330. Croix, A. "La Démographie du pays Nantais au XVIe siècle." *ADH*, 1967.

331. _____. "Deux notes sur Nantes." *ADH*, 1970.

332. _____. *Nantes et le pays nantais au XVIe siècle.* Paris, 1974.

333. Delasselle, C. "Les Enfants abandonnées à Paris au XVIIIe siècle." *AESC* 30 1975.

334. Deniel, R., and Henry, L. "La Population d'un village du Nord de la France, Sainghin-en-Mélantois de 1665 à 1851." *P* 20 (1965).

335. Depauw, J. "Amours illégitimes et société à Nantes au XVIIIe siècle." *AESC* 27 (1972). Translated into English in *Family and Society*, ed. R. Forster and O. Ranum. Baltimore, 1976.

336. Desaive, J.-P.; Goubert, J.-P.; Ladurie, E. Le Roy; Meyer, J.; Muller, O.; and Peter, J.-P. *Médecins, climat et épidemies à la fin du XVIIIe siècle.* Paris, 1972.

337. Desjardins, F. "Etude démographique du pays d'Arthes aux XVIIe et XVIIIe siècles (1668–1819)." *DH* 3 (1971).

338. Dinet, D. "Quatre paroisses du Tonnerois." *ADH*, 1969.

339. Dupâquier, J. "Sur la population française au XVIIe et au XVIIIe siècle." *Revue historique* 239 (1968). Translated into English in *Essays in French Economic History*, ed. R. E. Cameron. Homewood, Ill., 1970.

340. _____, ed. *Hommage à Marcel Reinhard. Sur la population française au XVIIIe et au XIXe siècles.* Paris, 1973.

341. _____, "Croissance démographique régionale dans le bassin parisien au XVIIIe siècle." In *340.*

342. _____. "La France de Louis XIV, était-elle surpeuplée? Réflexions d'un historien sur la répartition géographique du peuplement." *ADH*, 1974.

343. _____. "Caractères originaux de l'histoire démographique française au XVIIIe siècle." *RHMC* 23 (1976).

344. _____. *Statistiques démographiques du bassin parisien, 1636-1720.* Paris, 1977.

345. _____. "Etude comparative des données concernant la fecondité dans 25 monographies concernant le bassin parisien à la fin du XVIIe siècle et au début du XVIIIe siècle." *Seminaire sur la fecondité naturelle.* Paris, 1977.

346. _____. "Réflexions sur la mortalité du passé: mesure de la mortalité des adultes d'après les fiches de familles." *ADH*, 1978.

347. _____. *La Population rurale du bassin parisien à l'époque de Louis XIV.* Lille, 1979.

348. _____, and Lachiver, M. "Sur les débuts de la contraception en France ou les deux malthusianismes." *AESC* 24 (1969).

349. Dureau, J., and Salome, F. "Flins-sur-Seine aux XVIIIe–XIXe siècles." *DH* 7 (1972).

350. El Kordi, M. *Bayeux au XVIIe et XVIIIe siècles.* Paris and The Hague, 1970.

351. Engelmann, G. "Etude démographique d'un village de la commune de Toulouse: Pouvourville, 1756-1798." *Annales du Midi* 77 (1965).

352. Fine-Souriac, A. "La Limitation des naissances dans le sud-ouest de la France: fecondité, allaitement et contraception au Pays de Sault du milieu du XVIIIe siècle à 1914." *Annales du Midi* 90 (1978).

353. Frêche, G. "La Population de Languedoc et des intendances d'Auch, de Montaubon, et du Roussillon aux XVIIe et XVIIIe siècles." *P* 26 (1971).

354. Galliano, P. "La Mortalité infantile (indigènes et nourrissons) dans la banlieue sud de Paris à la fin du XVIIIe siècle (1774-1794)." *ADH*, 1966.

355. Ganiage, J. *Trois villages d'Ile de France au XVIIIe siècle.* Paris, 1963.

356. _____. "Nourrissons parisiens en Beauvaisis." In *340.*

357. Garden, M. *Lyon et les lyonnais au XVIIIe siècle.* Paris, 1970.

358. _____. "L'Attraction de Lyon à la fin d l'ancien régime." *ADH*, 1970.

359. _____. "Les verriers de Givors au XVIIIe siècle." In *340.*

360. _____. "Quelques remarques sur l'habitat urbain. L'exemple de Lyon au XVIIIe siècle." *ADH*, 1975.

361. _____. "L'Émigration du Massif Central vers Lyon dans la seconde moitié du XVIIIe siècle." In *464.*

362. _____. "La Démographie des villes françaises du XVIIIe siècle: quelques approches." In *3.*

363. Gascon, R. "Immigration et croissance au XVIe siècle: l'exemple de Lyon (1529-1563)." *AESC* 25 (1970).

364. Gautier, E., and Henry, L. *La Population de Crulai, paroisse Normande.* Paris, 1958.

365. Giachetti, J. C., and Tyvaert, M. "Argenteuil, 1740-1790." *ADH*, 1969.

366. Girard, P. "Aperçus de la démographie de Sotteville-lès-Rouen vers la fin du XVIIIe siècle." *P* 14 (1959).

367. Godechot, J., and Moncassin, S. "Démographie et subsistances en Languedoc du XVIIIe siècle au début du XIXe." *Bulletin d'histoire économique et sociale de la Révolution Française*, 1965.

368. Goubert, J.-P. "The Extent of Medical Practice in France around 1780." *Journal of Social History* 10 (1977).

369. _____, and Lebrun, F. "Médecins et chirurgiens dans la société française du XVIIIᵉ siècle." *Annales cisalpines d'histoire sociale* 4 (1973).

370. Goubert, P. "En Beauvaisis: problèmes démographiques du XVIIᵉ siècle." *AESC* 7 (1952). Reprinted in *385*.

371. _____. "Une Richesse historique en cours d'exploitation: les registres paroissiaux." *AESC* 9 (1954).

372. _____. *Beauvais et le Beauvaisis de 1600 à 1730*. Paris, 1960.

373. _____. "Registres paroissiaux et démographie dans la France du XVIIᵉ siècle." *ADH*, 1965.

374. _____. "La Mortalité en France sous l'ancien régime. Problèmes et hypothèses." In *2*. Reprinted in *385*.

375. _____. "Recent Theories and Research in French Population History between 1500 and 1700." In *4*. Translated into French in *385*.

376. _____. "The French Peasantry of the Seventeenth Century: A Regional Example." In *Crisis in Europe, 1560-1660*, ed. T. Aston. London, 1965.

377. _____. "Legitimate Fecundity and Infant Mortality in France during the 18th Century: A Comparison." *Daedalus* 97 (1968). Reprinted in *5*. Translated into French in *385*.

378. _____. *Cent mille provinciaux au XVIIᵉ siècle*. Paris, 1968.

379. _____. "La Famille française au XVIIIᵉ siècle." In *Saggi di demografia storica*, ed. M. Livi Bacci. University of Florence, Serie Ricerche Empiriche, no. 2. Florence, 1969.

380. _____. *L'Ancien Régime*. Paris, 1969. Translated into English as *The Ancien Régime*. London, 1973.

381. _____. "Les Fondements démographiques." In *Histoire économique et sociale de la France*, vol. 2, ed. F. Braudel and E. Labrousse. Paris, 1970.

382. _____. "Historical Demography and the Reinterpretation of Early Modern French History." *JIH* 1 (1970-71). Reprinted in *The Family in History*, ed. T. K. Rabb and R. I. Rotberg. New York and London, 1973.

383. _____. "Vingt-cinq ans de démographie historique: bilan et réflexions." In *340*. Reprinted in *385*.

384. _____. "Disparités de l'ancienne France rurale." In *385*.

385. _____. *Clio parmi les hommes*. Paris and The Hague, 1976.

386. _____. "Family and Province: A Contribution to the Knowledge of Family Structure in Early Modern France." *Journal of Family History* 2 (1977).

387. Gouesse, J.-M. "Migrations féminines et mariages. Quelques exemples bas-normands (XVIIᵉ et XVIIIᵉ siècles)." *ADH*, 1976.

388. Henry, L. "Une Richesse démographique en friche: les registres paroissiaux." *P* 8 (1952).

389. _____. "The Population of France in the Eighteenth Century." In *4*.

390. _____. "La Fécondité des mariages dans le quart sud-ouest de la France de 1720 à 1829." *AESC* 27 (1972).

391. _____. "Mobilité et fécondité d'après les fiches de famille." *ADH*, 1976.

392. _____. "Fécondité des mariages dans le quart sud-est de la France de 1670 à 1829." *P* 33 (1978).

393. _____, and Blayo, Y. "La Population de la France de 1740 à 1860." *P* 30 (1975).

394. _____, and Houdaille, J. "Fécondité des mariages dans le quart nord-ouest de la France de 1670 à 1829." *P* 28 (1973).

395. _____, and Levy, C. "Quelques données sur la région autour de Paris au XVIIIᵉ siècle." *P* 17 (1962).

396. Hohenberg, P. "Maize in French Agriculture." *JEEH* 6 (1977).

397. Houdaille, J. "Un Village du Morvan: Saint-Agnan." *P* 16 (1961).

398. _____. "La Population de Boulay (Moselle) avant 1850." *P* 22 (1967).

399. _____. "La Population de Remmesweiler en Sarre aux XVIIIᵉ et XIXᵉ siècles." *P* 25 (1970).

400. _____. "La Population de sept villages des environs de Boulay (Moselle) aux XVIIIᵉ et XIXᵉ siècles." *P* 26 (1971).

401. _____. "La Fécondité des mariages de 1670 à 1829 dans le quart nord-est de la France." *ADH*, 1976.

402. _____. "Fécondité des familles souveraines du XVIᵉ au XVIIIᵉ siècles. Influence de l'âge du père sur la fécondité." *P* 31 (1976).

403. Hufton, O. "Begging, Vagrancy, Vagabondage and the Law: One Aspect of the Problem of Poverty in Eighteenth-Century France." *European Studies Review* 2 (1972).

404. _____. *The Poor in Eighteenth-Century France, 1750–1789.* Oxford, 1974.

405. _____. "Women and the Family Economy in Eighteenth-Century France." *FHS* 9 (1975–76).

406. Jacquart, J. "La Fronde des princes dans la région parisienne et ses conséquences matérielles." *RHMC* 7 (1960).

407. _____. "La Population de la chatellenie de la Ferte-Alais du XVIᵉ au XVIIIᵉ siècle." In *340.*

408. _____. *La Crise rurale en Ile-de-France, 1550–1670.* Paris, 1974.

409. Jouan, M.-H. "Les Originalités démographiques d'un bourg artisanal normand au XVIIIᵉ siècle: Villedieu-les-Poëles, 1711–1790." *ADH*, 1969.

410. Kintz, J.-P. Etudes alsaciennes." *ADH*, 1969.

411. _____. "La Mobilité humaine en Alsace. Essai de présentation statistique, XIVᵉ–XVIIIᵉ siècles." *ADH*, 1970.

412. _____. "Démographie en pays lorrains au XVIᵉ siècle." *ADH*, 1975.

413. Lachiver, M. *La Population de Meulan du XVIIᵉ au XIXᵉ siècle.* Paris, 1969.

414. _____. "Une Etude et quelques esquisses." *ADH*, 1969.

415. _____. "Fécondité légitime et contraception dans la région parisienne." In *340.*

416. _____. "Une Source méconnue pour l'étude de la mobilité géographique en France au XVIIIᵉ siècle. Les congés et translations de domicile." *P* 32 (1977).

417. Ladurie, E. Le Roy. "Démographie et funestes secrets: le Languedoc, fin XVIIIᵉ, début XIXᵉ siècles." *Annales de l'histoire de la Révolution Française,* 1965.

418. _____. *Les Paysans de Languedoc*. Paris, 1966. Translated into English (abbreviated version) as *The Peasants of Languedoc*. Urbana, Ill., 1974.

419. _____. "Révolution Française et contraception: dossiers languedociens." *ADH*, 1966.

420. _____. "L'Histoire immobile." *AESC* 29 (1974).

421. Lebrun, F. "Registres paroissiaux et démographie en Anjou au XVIᵉ siècle." *ADH*, 1965.

422. _____. "Mobilité de la population en Anjou au XVIIIᵉ siècle." *ADH*, 1970.

423. _____. *Les Hommes et la mort en Anjou aux 17ᵉ et 18ᵉ siècles*. Paris, 1971.

424. _____. "Naissances illégitimes et abandons d'enfants en Anjou au XVIIIᵉ siècle." *AESC* 27 (1972).

425. _____. "Une Grande Épidemie en France au XVIIIᵉ siècle: la dysentérie de 1779." In *340*.

426. _____. "Démographie et mentalités: le mouvement des conceptions sous l'ancien régime." *ADH*, 1974.

427. _____. *La Vie conjugale sous l'ancien régime*. Paris, 1975.

428. _____. "Les Épidémies en Haute-Bretagne à la fin de l'ancien régime (1770-1789). Présentation d'une enquête collective." *ADH*, 1977.

429. _____. "Les Crises démographiques en France aux XVIIᵉ et XVIIIᵉ siècles." Mimeographed. Rennes, 1979.

430. Lefebvre-Teillard, A. *La Population de Dôle au XVIIIᵉ siècle*. Paris, 1969.

431. Le Goff, A. "Bilan d'une étude de démographie historique: Auray au XVIIIᵉ siècle." *ADH*, 1974.

432. Lelong, J. "Saint-Pierre-Eglise." *ADH*, 1969.

433. Lepetit, B. "Démographie d'une ville en gestation: Versailles sous Louis XIV." *ADH*, 1977.

434. Leroux, J. "Trois-Monts, 1603-1792." *DH* 20 (1977).

435. Lesgold, E., and Richard, M. "Saint-Denis aux XVIIᵉ et XVIIIᵉ siècles." *DH* 1 (1970).

436. Lettin, A. "Naissances illégitimes et fille-mères à Lille au XVIIIᵉ siècle." *RHMC* 17 (1970).

437. Levi, G. "Migrazione e popolazione nelle Francia del XVII e XVIII secolo." *Rivista storica italiana* 33 (1971).

438. Lévy, C., and Henry, L. "Ducs et pairs sous l'ancien régime: caractéristique démographique d'une caste." *P* 15 (1960).

439. Leymond, D. "La Communauté de Duravel au XVIIIᵉ siècle." *Annales du Midi* 79 (1967).

440. McLaren, A. "Some Secular Attitudes Toward Sexual Behaviour in France: 1760-1860." *FHS* 8 (1973-74).

441. Marion, M. "Une Famine en Guyenne (1747-48)." *Revue historique* 46 (1891).

442. Meuvret, J. "Les Crises de subsistances et la démographie de la France d'ancien régime." *P* 1 (1946). Reprinted in *445*.

443. _____. "Demographic Crisis in France from the Sixteenth to the Eighteenth Century." In *4*.

444. _____. "Prices, Population and Economic Activities in Europe, 1688–1715: A note." In *New Cambridge Modern History*, vol. 6, ed. J. S. Bromley. Cambridge, 1970.

445. _____. *Etudes d'histoire économique*. Paris, 1971.

446. _____. *Le problème des subsistances à l'époque Louis XIV*. 2 vols. Paris, 1977.

447. Miller, G. *The Adoption of Inoculation for Smallpox in England and France*. Philadelphia, 1957.

448. Mogensen, N.-W. "Structures et changements démographiques dans vingt paroisses normandes sous l'ancien régime. Une analyse sociale." *ADH*, 1975.

449. Molinier, A. "Enfants trouvés, enfants abandonnés, et enfants illégitimes en Languedoc aux XVIIᵉ et XVIIIᵉ siècles." In *340*.

450. Morel, M.-F. "Théories et pratiques de l'allaitement en France au XVIIIᵉ siècle." *ADH*, 1976.

451. Morineau, M. "La Pomme de terre au XVIIIᵉ siècle." *AESC* 25 (1970). Translated into French in *Food and Drink in History*, ed. R. Forster and O. Ranum. Baltimore, 1979.

452. _____. *Les Faux-semblants d'un démarrage économique: agriculture et démographie en France au XVIIIᵉ siècle*. Paris, 1971.

453. _____. "Révolution agricole, révolution alimentaire, révolution démographique." *ADH*, 1974.

454. Neveux, H. "L'Expansion démographique dans un village du Cambrésis. Saint-Hilaire (1450–1575)." *ADH*, 1971.

455. Noël, R. "La Population de la paroisse de Laguiole d'après un recensement de 1691." *ADH*, 1967.

456. Perronin, C. "Limons, paroisse batelière de Basse-Auverne au XVIIIᵉ siècle." In *464*.

457. Perrot, J.-C. *Genèse d'une ville moderne. Caen au XVIIᵉ siècle*. Paris and The Hague, 1975.

458. Peter, J.-P. "Une Enquête de la société royale de médecine (1774–1794). Malades et maladies à la fin du XVIIIᵉ siècle." *AESC* 22 (1967).

459. _____. "Les Mots et les objets de la maladie. Remarque sur les épidémies et la médecine dans la société française de la fin du XVIIIᵉ siècle." *Revue historique* 1971.

460. _____. "Disease and the Sick at the End of the Eighteenth Century." In *Biology of Man in History*, ed. R. Forster and O. Ranum. Baltimore, 1975.

461. Peyronnet, J.-C. "Les Enfants abandonnés et leurs nourrices à Limoges au XVIIIᵉ siècle." *RHMC* 23 (1976).

462. Poitou, C. "Ergotisme, ergot de seigle et épidémies en Sologne au XVIIIᵉ siècle." *RHMC* 23 (1976).

463. _____. "La Mortalité en Sologne orléanaise de 1670 à 1870." *ADH*, 1978.

464. Poitrineau, A., ed. *Entre faim et loup. . . .Les problèmes de la vie et de l'émigration sur les hautes terres françaises au XVIIIᵉ siècle*. Clermont-Ferrand, 1976.

465. Polton, J.-C. "Coulommiers et Chailly-en-Brie." *ADH*, 1969.

466. Ponsot, P. "Douvres-la-Délivrance (1650–1792): une inversion démographique?" *Annales de Normandie* 14 (1964).

467. Pontet, J. "La Démographie d'un port sous la révolution: l'agglomération bayonnaise (1789–1799)." In *3*.

468. Poussou, J.-P. "Les Mouvements migratoires en France et à partir de la France de la fin du XVe siècle au début du XIXe siècle: approche pour une synthèse." *ADH*, 1970.

469. _____. "Note sur la mobilité urbaine dans la deuxième moitié du XVIIIe siècle vue à travers les registres de sépultures de l'hôpital Saint-Andre de Bordeaux." In *340*.

470. _____. "Les Relations villes-campagnes en Aquitaine dans la deuxième moitié du XVIIIe siècle: quelques réflexions méthodologiques sur les attractions urbaines et les échanges migratoires." In *3*.

471. Regnier, C. "Pont-à-Mousson. Le mariage au XVIIIe siècle." *DH* 23 (1978).

472. Revel, J. "Autour d'une épidémie ancienne: la peste de 1666–1670." *RHMC* 17 (1970).

473. Rivier, P., and Allegret, S. "Trois paroisses de l'est Parisien." *DH* 4 (1971).

474. Robert, P. "Rumont, 1720–1790." *ADH*, 1969.

475. Rostan, M. "Un Comportement démographique en pays d'émigration: l'exemple du haut Livradois au XVIIIe siècle." In *464*.

476. Rozet, M. "Les Échanges de population entre villages voisins. Le cas d'Anthony et sa couronne." *ADH*, 1977.

477. Saunier, D. "Peut-on parler de comportements démographiques spécifiques chez les vignerons de la Basse-Auvergne au XVIIIe siècle?" In *464*.

478. Sheppard, T. F. *Lourmarin in the Eighteenth Century: A Study of a French Village*. Baltimore and London, 1971.

479. Sudre, M. "Aspects démographiques de la paroisse Saint-Michel de Bordeaux (1660–1680)." *ADH*, 1974.

480. Sussman, G. D. "The Wet-Nursing Business in Nineteenth-Century France." *FHS* 9 (1975).

481. _____. "Parisian Infants and Norman Wet Nurses in the Early Nineteenth Century: A Statistical Study." *JIH* 7 (1977).

482. Terrisse, M. "Un Faubourg du Havre: Ingouville." *P* 16 (1961).

483. _____. "Le Rattrapage de nuptialité d'après peste à Marseille (1720–1721)." In *340*.

484. Todd, E. "Mobilité géographique et cycle de vie en Artois et en Toscane au XVIIIe siècle." *AESC* 30 (1975).

485. Valmary, P. *Familles paysannes au XVIIIe siècle en Bas-Quercy*. Paris, 1965.

486. van de Walle, E. "France." In *8*.

487. Wiel, P. "Une Grosse Paroisse du Cotentin aux XVIIe et XVIIIe siècles: Tamerville." *ADH*, 1969.

488. Zens, N., and Delange, J.-Y. "Lisieux aux XVIIe et XVIIIe sieclès." *DH* 12 (1974).

489. Zink, A. *Azereix: la vie d'une communauté rurale à la fin du XVIIIe siècle*. Paris, 1969.

J. Germany

490. Berkner, L. K. "Inheritance, Land Tenure and Peasant Family Structure: A German Regional Comparison." In *Family and Inheritance in Rural Western Europe, 1200–1700,* ed. J. Goody, J. Thirsk, and E. P. Thompson. Cambridge, 1976.

491. _____. "Peasant Household Organisation and Demographic Change in Lower Saxony (1689–1766)." In *7.*

492. François, E. "La Population de Coblence au XVIIIe siècle. Déficit démographique et immigration dans une ville de résidence." *ADH,* 1975.

493. _____. "La Mortalité urbaine en Allemagne au XVIIIe siècle." *ADH,* 1978.

494. Franz, G. *Der Dreissigjährige Krieg und das deutsche Volk: Untersuchungen zur Bevölkerungs- und Agrargeschichte.* Stuttgart, 1961.

495. Houdaille, J. "Quelques résultats sur la démographie de trois villages d'Allemagne de 1750 à 1879." *P* 25 (1970).

496. _____. "Evolution de la fécondité en Hesse au XVIIIe et XIXe siècle." *P* 32 (1977).

497. Imhof, A. E., ed. *Historische Demographie als Sozialgeschichte. Giessen und Umgebung vom 17. bis 19. Jahrhundert.* 2 vols. Marburg, 1975.

498. _____, "Structure of Reproduction in a West-German Village, 1690–1900." In *567.*

499. Knodel, J. "Infant Mortality and Fertility in Three Bavarian Villages: An Analysis of Family Histories from the 19th century." *PS* 22 (1968).

500. _____. "Two and a Half Centuries of Demographic History in a Bavarian Village." *PS* 24 (1970).

501. _____. "Ortssippenbücher als Quelle fur die historische Demographie." *Gesellschaft und Geschichte* 1 (1975).

502. _____. "Natural Fertility in Pre-industrial Germany." *PS* 32 (1978).

503. _____, and Shorter, E. "The Reliability of Family Reconstitution Data in German Village Genealogies." *ADH,* 1976.

504. _____, and Walle, E. van de. "Breast-Feeding, Fertility and Infant Mortality: An Analysis of Some Early German Data." *PS* 21 (1967).

505. Kuhn, W. *Geschichte der Deutschen Ostsiedlung in der Neuzeit.* 2 vols. Cologne and Graz, 1955–57.

506. Lee, W. R. "Zur Bevölkerungsgeschichte Bayerns 1750–1850: Britische Forschungsergebnisse." *VSWG* 62 (1975).

507. _____. "Bastardy and the Socio-economic Structure of South Germany." *JIH* 7 (1977). And "Reply." *ibid.,* 8 (1978).

508. _____. "Primary Sector Output and Mortality Changes in Early XIXth Century Bavaria." *JEEH* 6 (1977).

509. _____. *Population Growth, Economic Development and Social Change in Bavaria, 1750–1850.* New York, 1977.

510. _____. "Germany." In *8.*

511. Ruwet, J. "Crises de mortalité et mortalité de crise à Aix-la-Chapelle (XVIIe-début du XVIIIe siècle)." In *2.*

512. Sabean, D. "Household Formation and Geographical Mobility: A Family Register Study for a Wurttemberg Village, 1760–1900." *ADH*, 1970.

K. Holland

513. Dalle, D. *De Bevolkning van Veurne-Ambacht in de 17de en de 18de Eevw.* Brussels, 1963.
514. Faber, J. A. "Het probleem van de dalende graanaanvoer uit de Oostzeelanden in de tweede helft van de zeventiende eevw." *A. A. G. Bijdragen* 9 (1963).
515. _____, *et al.* "Population Changes and Economic Developments in the Netherlands: A Historical Survey." *A. A. G. Bijdragen* 12 (1965). Summarized in French by J. Dupâquier in *ADH*, 1965.
516. Houdaille, J. "Une Étude par reconstitution des familles à Maasland, village de Hollande." *P* 31 (1976).
517. Mentink, G. J., and van der Woude, A. M. *De demografische ontvikkeling te Rotterdam en Cool in de 17ᵉ en 18ᵉ eevw.* Rotterdam, 1965.
518. Parker, G. "The Economic Costs of the Dutch Revolt." In *War and Economic Development*, ed. J. M. Winter. Cambridge, 1975.
519. Petersen, W. "The Demographic Transition in the Netherlands." *American Sociological Review* 25 (1960).
520. Schuurman, A. J. "De bevolking van Duiven, 1665–1795. Een historisch-demografische studie." *A. A. G. Bijdragen* 22 (1979).
521. Slicher van Bath, B. H. "Report on the Study of Historical Demography in the Netherlands." *A. A. G. Bijdragen* 11 (1964).
522. _____. "Historical Demography and the Social and Economic Development of the Netherlands." *Daedalus* 97 (1968). Reprinted in *5*.
523. _____. "Contrasting Demographic Development in Some Parts of the Netherlands during the Depression Period of the Seventeenth and Eighteenth Centuries." In *1*.
524. van der Woude, A. M. "Het Noorderkwartier. Deel III." *A. A. G. Bijdragen* 16 (1972).
525. _____, and Mentink, G. J. "La Population de Rotterdam au XVIIᵉ et au XVIIIᵉ siècle." *P* 21 (1966).

L. Ireland

526. Connell, K. H. *The Population of Ireland, 1750–1845.* Oxford, 1950.
527. Cullen, L. M. "Irish History Without the Potato." *PP* 40 (1968).
528. _____. "Population Trends in Seventeenth-Century Ireland." *Economic and Social Review* 6 (1975).
529. Dickson, R. J. *Ulster Emigration to Colonial America, 1718–1775.* London, 1966.
530. Drake, M. "Marriage and Population Growth in Ireland, 1750–1845." *EHR*, 2d ser. 16 (1963–64).

531. _____. "The Irish Demographic Crisis of 1740–41." *Historical Studies* 6 (1968).
532. Kennedy, R. E. *The Irish. Emigration, Marriage and Fertility.* Berkeley, Los Angeles, and London, 1973.
533. Lee, J. "Marriage and Population in Pre-Famine Ireland." *EHR*, 2d ser. 21 (1968).

M. Italy

534. Aymard, M. "Epidémies et médecins en Sicile à l'époque moderne." *Annales cisalpines d'histoire sociale* 4 (1973).
535. _____, and Delille, G. "La Démographie historique en Italie: une discipline en limitation." *ADH*, 1977.
536. Bellettini, A., and Tassinari, F. *Fonti per la studio della popolazione del suburbio di Bologna dal secolo XVI alla fine dell'ottocento.* Bologna, 1977.
537. Beloch, K. J. *Bevölkerungsgeschichte Italiens.* 2 vols. Berlin and Leipzig, 1937–40.
538. Cananzi, D. I., and Davico, R. "Démographie et histoire sociale: trends démographiques siciliens entre le XVIe et le XIXe siècles." *DH* 7 (1972).
539. Cipolla, C. M. "Four Centuries of Italian Demographic Development." In *4.*
540. _____. *Cristofano and the Plague: A Study in the History of Public Health in the Age of Galileo.* London, 1973.
541. _____. *Public Health and the Medical Profession in the Renaissance.* Cambridge, 1976.
542. _____. "The 'Bills of Mortality' of Florence." *PS* 32 (1978).
543. Corsini, C. A. "Problemi delle ricerche di demografia storica." In *XXVI Riunione Scientifica Societa Italiana di Statistica.* Florence, 1969.
544. _____. "La Fécondité naturelle de la femme mariée. Le cas des nourrices." *G* 30 (1974).
545. _____, ed. *Pour connaître la population de la Toscane aux XVIIe, XVIIIe et XIXe siècles.* Florence, 1974.
546. _____, "Lignes d'un programme pour l'étude de la population de la Toscane aux XVIIe et XIXe siècles." In *545.*
547. _____. "Materiali per lo studio della famiglia in Toscana nei secoli XVII–XIX: gli esposti." *Quaderni storici* 33 (1976).
548. _____. "Self-regulating Mechanisms of Traditional Populations before the Demographic Revolution: European Civilizations." *International Population Conference Mexico, 1977,* vol. 3. Liège, 1977.
549. _____. "Is the Fertility Reducing Effect of Lactation Really Substantial?" *International Union for the Scientific Study of Population, Seminar on Natural Fertility.* Paris, 1977.
550. Felloni, G. "Per la storia della popolazione di Genova nei secoli XVI e XVII." *Archivio storico italiano* 110 (1952).
551. Herlihy, D., and Klapisch-Zuber, C. *Les Toscans et leurs familles. Une étude du Catasto florentin de 1427.* Paris, 1978.

552. Litchfield, R. B. "Demographic Characteristics of Florentine Patrician Families, Sixteenth to Nineteenth Centuries." *JEH* 29 (1969). Translated into Italian in *Saggi di demografia storica. Serie Ricerche Empiriche*, vol. 2. Florence, 1969.

553. Livi Bacci, M. *A History of Italian Fertility during the Last Two Centuries.* Princeton, 1977.

554. ————. *La société italienne devant les crises de mortalité.* Florence, 1978.

555. ————. "Les Répercussions d'une crise de mortalité sur la fécondité: une vérification empirique." *ADH*, 1978.

556. Panta, L. del. "Italy." In *8*.

557. ————, and Livi Bacci, M. "Chronologie, intensité et diffusion des crises de mortalité en Italie: 1600–1850." *P* 32 (1977).

558. Pullan, B. "The Famine in Venice and the New Poor Law (1527–29)." *Bolletino dell'Instituto di Storia della Societa e della Stato* 5–6 (1963–64).

559. Rossi, F. "Storia della popolazione di Adrie del 16 al 19 secolo." *G* 26 (1970).

560. Schifini, S. "Exploitation des listes nominatives de population à Fiesole." *P* 26 (1971).

561. Weiner, G. M. "The Demographic Effects of the Venetian Plagues of 1575–1577 and 1630–31." *G* 26 (1970).

562. Zanetti, D. E. "La Morte a Milano nei secoli XVI–XVIII. Appunti per une ricerca." *Revista storica italiana* 88 (1976).

563. ————. "The Patriziato of Milan from the Domination of Spain to the Unification of Italy: An Outline of the Social and Demographic History." *SH* 6 (1977).

N. Scandinavia

564. Ågren, K.; Gaunt, D.; Eriksson, I.; Rogers, J.; Norberg, A.; and Åkerman, S. *Aristocrats, Farmers, Proletarians: Essays in Swedish Demographic History.* Uppsala, 1973.

565. Åkerman, S. "An Evaluation of the Family Reconstitution Technique." *SEHR* 25 (1977).

566. ————. "A Demographic Study of a Pre-transitional Society." In *567*.

567. ————; Johansen, H. C.; and Gaunt, D., eds. *Chance and Change. Social and Economic Studies in Historical Demography in the Baltic Area.* Odense, 1978.

568. Andersen, O. *The Population of Denmark.* Copenhagen, 1977.

569. ————. "Denmark." In *8*.

570. Backer, J. E. "Population Statistics and Population Registration in Norway. Part 1. The Vital Statistics of Norway, an Historical Review." *PS* 2 (1947–49).

571. Berg, J., and Lagercrantz, B. *Scots in Sweden.* Stockholm, 1962.

572. Drake, M. "The Growth of Population in Norway, 1735–1855." *SEHR* 13 (1965).

573. ————. *Population and Society in Norway, 1735–1865.* Cambridge, 1969.

574. _____. "Fertility Controls in Pre-industrial Norway." In 5.

575. _____. "Norway." In 8.

576. Dyrvik, S. "Historical Demography in Norway, 1660-1801: A Short Survey." *SEHR* 20 (1972).

577. _____. Mykland, K., and Oldervoll, J. *The Demographic Crisis in Norway in the 17th and 18th Centuries.* Bergen, Oslo, and Tromsö, 1976.

578. Eklit, J. "Household Structure in Denmark, 1769-1890." In 567.

579. Engleson, H. *Dysenteriestudien.* Lund, 1937.

580. Frederiksen, K. *Familierekonstitution: en Modelstudie over Bevolkningsforholdene i Sejrø sogn 1663-1813.* Copenhagen, 1976.

581. Friberg, N. *Dalarnas Bevolkning på 1600-talet.* Stockholm, 1953.

582. _____. "Sources and Methods of Investigations on the Population in Sweden." In *Colloque de démographie Historique, Budapest 1965*, ed. Kovacsics, J. Budapest, 1968.

583. Fridlizius, G. "Some New Aspects on Swedish Population Growth." *Economy and Society* 18 (1975).

584. _____. "Sweden." In 8.

585. Gaunt, D. "Family Planning and the Pre-industrial Society: Some Swedish Evidence." In 564.

586. _____. Historisk demografi eller demografisk historia? En oversikt och ett debatinlagg om ett tvärvetenskapligt dilemma." *Historisk Tidskrift*, 1973.

587. _____. "Familj, hushåll och arbetsintensitet. En tolkning av demografiska variationer i 1600- och 1700-talens Sverige." *Scandia* 42 (1976). Translated into German in 6.

588. _____. "Early Swedish Parish Records and Their Background." Mimeographed. Uppsala, 1977.

589. _____. "Pre-industrial Economy and Population Structure. The Elements of Variance in Early Modern Sweden." *Scandinavian Journal of History* 2 (1977).

590. _____. "Natural Resources – Population – Local Society: The Case of Pre-industrial Sweden." *Peasant Studies* 6 (1977).

591. _____. "I slottets skugga." *Ale* 2 (1977).

592. _____. "Household Typology: Problems – Methods – Results." In 567.

593. Gille, H. "Demographic History of the Northern European Countries in the 18th Century." *PS* 3 (1949).

594. *Historisk Statistik för Sverige: Befolkning, 1720-1950.* Stockholm, 1955.

595. Hofsten, E., and Lundström, H. *Swedish Population History. Main Trends from 1750 to 1970.* Stockholm, 1976.

596. Imhof, A. E. *Aspekte der Bevölkerungsentwicklung in den nordischen Ländern, 1720-1750.* 2 vols. Berne, 1976.

597. _____, and Lindskog, B. J. "Les Causes de la mortalité en Suède et en Finlande entre 1749 et 1773." *AESC* 29 (1974). Translated into German in 6.

598. Johansen, H. C. "Some Aspects of Danish Rural Population Structure in 1787." *SEHR* 20 (1972).

599. _____. *Bevolkningsudvickling og Familiestruktur i de 18. Århundrede.* Odense, 1975.

600. _____. "The Position of the Old in the Rural Household in a Traditional Society." *SEHR* 24 (1976).

601. Juhasz, L. "Les Crises démographiques en Norvège (XVIIᵉ-XVIIIᵉ siècles)." *DH* (1972).

602. Jutikkala, E. "The Great Finnish Famine in 1696-97." *SEHR* 3 (1955).

603. _____. "Finland's Population Movement in the Eighteenth Century." In *4*.

604. _____, and Kauppinen, M. "The Structure of Mortality during Catastrophic Years in a Pre-industrial Society." *PS* 25 (1971).

605. Lassen, A. "The Population of Denmark in 1660." *SEHR* 13 (1965).

606. Makela, A. "Deserted Lands and Tenements in Hattula and Porvo to 1607." *SEHR* 25 (1977).

607. Moe, T. "Some Economic Aspects of Norwegian Population Movements 1740-1940: An Econometric Study." *JEH* 30 (1970).

608. _____. *Demographic Developments and Economic Growth in Norway, 1740-1940.* New York, 1977.

609. Nerdrum, M. "Household Structure in Finström Parish, Åland, 1760-62 and 1840-42." In *567*.

610. Ofstad, K. "Population Statistics and Population Registration in Norway: Part 3, Population Censuses." *PS* 3 (1949-50).

611. Pitkänen, K. "The Reliability of the Registration of Births and Deaths in Finland in the Eighteenth and Nineteenth Centuries: Some Examples." *SEHR* 25 (1977).

612. Saugstad, L. F., and Ødegård, Ø. "Marriage Pattern and Kinship in Preindustrial and Present-day Norway." In *567*.

613. Sogner, S. "La Population norvégienne (1789-1815)." *ADH*, 1965.

614. _____. A Demographic Crisis Averted?" *SEHR* 24 (1976).

615. _____. "Illegitimacy in Old Rural Society." In *567*.

616. Sundbärg, G. *Bevölkerungsstatistik Schwedens, 1750-1900.* Stockholm, 1907.

617. Thestrup, P. "Methodological Problems of a Family Reconstitution Study in a Danish Rural Parish before 1800." *SEHR* 20 (1972).

618. _____. "Household Structure on the Island of Tåsinge, 1678." In *567*.

619. Thomas, D. S. *Social and Economic Aspects of Swedish Population Movements, 1750-1933.* New York, 1941.

620. Tomasson, R. F. "Premarital Sexual Permissiveness and Illegitimacy in the Nordic Countries." *CSSH* 18 (1976).

621. Turpeinen, O. "Infectious Diseases and Regional Differences in Finnish Death Rates." *PS* 32 (1978).

622. _____. "Regional Differences in Fertility Rate and Family Planning in Pre-industrial Finland." In *567*.

623. _____. "Infant Mortality in Finland, 1749-1865." *SEHR* 27 (1979).

624. Utterström, G. "Some Population Problems in Pre-industrial Sweden." *SEHR* 2 (1954).

625. _____. "Climatic Fluctuations and Population Problems in Early Modern History." *SEHR* 3 (1955).
626. _____. "Migratory Labour and the Herring Fisheries of Western Sweden in the Eighteenth Century." *SEHR* 7 (1959).
627. _____. "Population and Agriculture in Sweden, circa 1700–1830." *SEHR* 9 (1961).
628. _____. "Two Essays on Population in Eighteenth-century Scandinavia." In *4*.
629. Widén, L. "Mortality and Causes of Death in Sweden during the Eighteenth Century." *Statistik Tidskrift*, 1975.
630. Winberg, C. *Folkökning och proletarisering. (Kring den sociala strukturomvandlingen på Sveriges landsbygd under den agrara revolutionen).* Gothenburg, 1975.
631. _____. "Population Growth and Proletarianization." In *567*.

O. Scotland

632. Adam, M. I. "The Highland Emigration of 1770." *SHR* 16 (1919).
633. Flinn, M. W., ed. *Scottish Population History from the Seventeenth Century to the 1930s.* Cambridge, 1977.
634. _____. "Malthus, Emigration and Potatoes in the Scottish North-west, 1770–1870." In *Comparative Aspects of Scottish and Irish Economic and Social History, 1600–1900*, ed. L. M. Cullen and T. C. Smout. Edinburgh, 1977.
635. Mitchison, R. M. "Local and Central Agencies in the Control of Famine in Pre-industrial Scotland." In *Proceedings of the Seventh International Economic History Congress*, ed. M. W. Flinn. Edinburgh, 1978.
636. Mullett, C. J. "Plague Policy in Scotland, 16th–17th Centuries." *Osiris* 9 (1950).
637. Perceval-Maxwell, M. *The Scottish Migration to Ulster in the Reign of James I.* London, 1973.
638. Smout, T. C. "Famine and Famine Relief in Scotland." In *Comparative Aspects of Scottish and Irish Economic and Social History, 1600–1900*, ed. L. M. Cullen and T. C. Smout. Edinburgh, 1977.
639. _____. "Coping with Plague in Sixteenth- and Seventeenth-century Scotland." *Scotia* 2 (1978).

P. Spain

640. Añes, G. *Las crisis agrarias en la España moderna.* Madrid, 1970.
641. Bennassar, B. *Valladolid au siècle d'or. Une ville de Castille et sa compagne au XVIe siècle.* Paris and The Hague, 1967.
642. _____. *Recherches sur les grandes épidémies dans le nord de l'Espagne à la fin du XVIe siècle.* Paris, 1969.

643. Casey, J. "Moriscos and the Depopulation of Valencia." *PP* 50 (1971).
644. Castillo, A. "Population et "richesse" en Castille durant la seconde moitié du XVIᵉ siècle." *AESC* 20 (1965).
645. Chaunu, P. *L'Espagne de Charles Quint.* 2 vols. Paris, 1973.
646. Garcia del Real, F. "Algunas reflexiones sobre la población española de principios del siglo XVIII." *Annales de economía* 15 (1972).
647. _____. "La población española en la segunda mitad del siglo XVIII." *Moneda y credito* 123 (1972).
648. _____. "Economía y población en las sociedades preindustriales. El siglo XVIII europeo." *Estudios geograficos* 134 (1974).
649. Houdaille, J. "Evolution démographique de quelques villages du nord-ouest de l'Espagne du XVIᵉ au XIXᵉ siècle." *P* 31 (1976).
650. Larquié, C. "Quartiers et paroisses urbaines: L'exemple de Madrid au XVIIᵉ siècle." *ADH*, 1974.
651. Livi Bacci, M. "Fertility and Nuptiality Changes in Spain from the Late 18th to the Early 20th Century." *PS* 22 (1968).
652. _____. "Fertility and Population Growth in Spain in the Eighteenth and Nineteenth Centuries." *Daedalus* 97 (1968). Reprinted in *5.*
653. Morgado, N. A. "Portugal." In *8.*
654. Muñoz, M. del C. G. *La población de Talavera de la Reina.* Toledo, 1974.
655. Nadal, J. *La población española, siglos XVI a XX.* Barcelona, 1966.
656. Nadal-Oller, J. "Les Grandes Mortalités des années 1793 à 1812: effets à long terme sur la démographie catalane." In *2.*
657. Nadal, J., and Giralt, E. *La Population Catalane de 1553 à 1717.* Paris, 1961.
658. Nadal, J., and Saez, A. "La Fécondité à Saint Joan de Palamos (Catalogne) de 1700 à 1859." *ADH*, 1972.
659. Nieto, J. I. Gutierrez. "Evolución demográfica de la cuenca del Segura en el siglo XVI." *Hispania* 3 (1969).
660. Ringrose, D. "Immigración, estructuros demográficas y tendencias económicas en Madrid a comenzos de la epoca moderna." *Moneda y credito* 138 (1976).
661. Smith, R. S. "Barcelona 'Bills of Mortality' and Population, 1457–1590." *Journal of Political Economy* 44 (1936).
662. Vilar, P. "Essai d'un bilan démographique de la période 1787–1814 en Catalogne." *ADH*, 1965.
663. _____. "Quelques problèmes de démographie historique en Catalogne et en Espagne." *ADH*, 1965.
664. Vincent, B. "Les Morisques d'Estremadure au XVIᵉ siècle." *ADH*, 1974.
665. _____. "Récents travaux de démographie historique en Espagne (XIVᵉ–XVIIIᵉ siècles)." *ADH*, 1977.
666. Vives, J. Vicens. *An Economic History of Spain.* Princeton, 1969.
667. Weisser, M. "The Decline of Castile Revisited: The Case of Toledo." *JEEH* 2 (1973).

Q. Switzerland

668. Bielmann, J. *Die Lebensverhältnisse im Urnerland während des 18. und zu Beginn des 19. Jahrhundert.* Basel and Stuttgart, 1972.

669. _____. "La Population du pays d'Uri au XVIIIᵉ siècle." *ADH*, 1976.

670. Braun, R. *Industrialisierung und Volksleben: die Veränderungen der Lebensformen in einem ländlichen Industriegebiet vor 1800 (Zürcher Oberland).* Erlenbach-Zurich, 1960.

671. _____. "The Impact of Cottage Industry on an Agricultural Population." In *The Rise of Capitalism*, ed. D. S. Landes. New York, 1966.

672. _____. "Early Industrialization and Demographic Change in the Canton of Zurich." In *9*.

673. Bucher, S. *Bevölkerung und Wirtschaft des Amtes Entlebuch im 18. Jahrhundert.* Lucerne, 1974.

674. _____. "La Population de la vallée d'Entlebuch au XVIIIᵉ siècle." *ADH*, 1976.

675. Burckhardt, A. *Demographie und Epidemiologie der Stadt Basel während der letzten drei Jahrhunderte, 1601-1900.* Basel, 1908.

676. Burri, H. R. *Die Bevölkerung Luzerns im 18. und frühen 19. Jahrhundert.* Lucerne, 1975.

677. _____. "La Population de Lucerne au XVIIIᵉ siècle et au début du XIXᵉ siècle." *ADH*, 1976.

678. _____, and Mattmüller, M. "Demographie, epidemiologie, oekologie in der Schweiz. Bericht zuhanden des Internationalen Historikerkongress von Bukarest, 1980." Mimeographed. Basel, 1979.

679. Caspard, P. "Conceptions prénuptiales et développement du capitalisme dans la principauté de Neuchâtel (1678-1828)." *AESC* 29 (1974).

680. Eckert, E.-A. "Boundary Formation and Diffusion of Plague: Swiss Epidemics from 1562 to 1669." *ADH*, 1978.

681. Head, A.-L. "La Mortalité à Glaris dans les villages agricoles et dans les villages industrialisés (milieu du 18ᵉ siecle–début du 19ᵉ siècle)." *Bulletin du Département d'Histoire Economique (Université de Genève)* 7 (1976-77).

682. _____. "Quelques remarques sur l'émigration des régions préalpines." *RSH* 29 (1979).

683. Henry, L. *Anciennes familles genevoises. Etude démographique: XVIᵉ-XXᵉ siècle.* Paris, 1956.

684. Mattmüller, M. "Einfürhung in die Bevölkerungsgeschichte an Hand von Problemen aus dem Schweizerischen 18. Jahrhundert." Mimeographed. Basel, 1973.

685. _____. "Das Einsetzen der Bevölkerungswelle in der Schweiz: Versuch eines Überblicks über den Stand der Forschung." *VSGW* 63 (1976).

686. _____. "Les Études de démographie historique à l'université de Bâle." *ADH*, 1976.

687. Perrenoud, A. "Les Migrations en Suisse sous l'Ancien Régime: quelques problèmes." *ADH*, 1970.

688. _____. "Malthusianisme et protestantisme: 'un modèle démographique Weberien.' " *AESC* 29 (1974).

689. _____. "L'Inégalité sociale devant la mort à Genève au XVIIᵉ siècle." *P* 30 (1975).

690. _____. "La Mortalité genevoise entre 1625 et 1825." *Bulletin du Département d'Histoire Economique (Université de Genève)* 7 (1976–77).

691. _____. "Variables sociales en démographie urbaine. L'exemple de Genève au XVIIIᵉ siècle." In *3*.

692. _____. "Contribution à l'histoire cyclique des maladies. Deux siècles de variole à Genève (1580–1810)." Mimeographed. Berlin, 1978.

693. _____. "Les Mécanismes de récuperation d'une population frappée par la peste." *RSH* 26 (1978).

694. _____. "La Mortalité à Genève de 1625 à 1825." *ADH*, 1978.

695. _____. *La Population de Genève du seizième au début du dix-neuvième siècle. Etude démographique.* Vol. 1. Geneva, 1979.

696. Piuz, A.-M. "La Disette de 1693–1694 à Genève et ses conséquences démographiques." In *Mélanges publiés par la Faculté des Sciences économiques et sociales de l'Université de Genève.* Geneva, 1965.

697. _____. "Alimentation populaire et sous-alimentation au XVIIᵉ siècle. Le cas de Genève." *RSH* 18 (1968).

698. _____. "Climat, récoltes et vie des hommes à Genèva, XVIᵉ–XVIIIᵉ siècle." *AESC* 29 (1974).

699. Ruesch, H. "Die Demographie der Alpen zwischen 1650 und 1850." *RSH* 29 (1979).

700. Schuermann, M. *Bevölkerung, Wirtschaft und Gesellschaft in Appenzell-Innerhoden im 18. und frühen 19. Jahrhundert.* Basel, 1974.

R. Addendum

701. Almquist, E. L. "Pre-Famine Ireland and the Theory of European Proto-Industrialization: Evidence from the 1841 Census." *JEH* 39 (1979).

702. Tilly, L. A. "The Family and Change." *Theory and Society* 5 (1978).

703. Wrightson, K., and Levine, D. *Poverty and Piety in an English Village. Terling, 1525–1700.* New York, San Francisco, and London, 1979.

Index